Plantation Life

Plantation Life

Corporate Occupation in Indonesia's Oil Palm Zone

———

**TANIA MURRAY LI
AND PUJO SEMEDI**

DUKE UNIVERSITY PRESS *Durham and London* 2021

© 2021 DUKE UNIVERSITY PRESS
All rights reserved
Printed and bound by CPI Group (UK) Ltd, Croydon, CR0 4YY
acid-free paper ∞
Cover design by Drew Sisk
Text design by Aimee C. Harrison
Typeset in Portrait Text and
Helvetica Neue by Westchester Publishing Services

Library of Congress Cataloging-in-Publication Data
Names: Li, Tania, [date] author. | Semedi, Pujo, author.
Title: Plantation life : corporate occupation in Indonesia's oil palm
zone / Tania Murray Li and Pujo Semedi.
Description: Durham : Duke University Press, 2021. | Includes biblio-
graphical references and index.
Identifiers: LCCN 2021003038 (print)
LCCN 2021003039 (ebook)
ISBN 9781478013990 (hardcover)
ISBN 9781478014959 (paperback)
ISBN 9781478022237 (ebook)
Subjects: LCSH: Palm oil industry—Social aspects—Indonesia. |
Palm oil industry—Environmental aspects—Indonesia. | Plantation
workers—Indonesia—Social conditions. | Farms, Small—Government
policy—Indonesia. | Sustainable development—Indonesia. | Rural
development—Indonesia. | BISAC: SOCIAL SCIENCE / Anthropology /
Cultural & Social | HISTORY / Asia / Southeast Asia
Classification: LCC HD9490.5.P343 15573 2021 (print) |
LCC HD9490.5.P343 (ebook) | DDC 338.1/7385109598—dc23
LC record available at https://lccn.loc.gov/2021003038
LC ebook record available at https://lccn.loc.gov/2021003039

Cover art: Dead palms, "Natco" fields, Indonesia, 2010.
Photo by Pujo Semedi.

Contents

Preface

PUJO: A plantation is a giant, an inefficient and lazy giant, but still a giant. It takes up a huge amount of space. It is greedy and careless, destroying everything around. It is alien, strange, and unpredictable. It is human, but you cannot form a normal human relationship with it. It can trample you, eat you, or drain your strength then spit you out. It guards its treasure. You cannot tame it or make it go away. You have to live with it. But it is a bit stupid, so if you are clever you can steal from it.

TANIA: A plantation is a machine that assembles land, labor, and capital in huge quantities to produce monocrops for a world market. It is intrinsically colonial, based on the assumption that the people on the spot are incapable of efficient production. It takes life under control: space, time, flora, fauna, water, chemicals, people. It is owned by a corporation and run by managers along bureaucratic lines.

At some point in our collaboration when we asked each other, "What is a plantation?" we came up with these two different answers. Like most of our exchanges, when we talked through the two definitions, we concluded that both were useful for our analysis as they pushed us to reflect. Why the giant? Why the machine? Can it be both? Our definitions were different because they were the products of situated knowledge: our prior experiences, the books we read, the paths we traveled, and the affective hold "plantation life" had on us. Tania spent her teenage years in Singapore. Her family used to drive to Malaysia on weekends, taking the old road that passed through rubber smallholdings interspersed with villages. It was a peopled landscape in which productive activities and village life were entwined. Around 1990 the new highway passed through monocrop oil palm plantations: mile after mile of monotonous palm, with no villages or people in sight. Every time she drove along it Tania experienced this landscape as machinic, threatening, and desolate. It also made her curious. How did these plantations come to be there? What happened to the villages that were there before? Someone must be doing the work, but where were the workers and how did they live? Tania also conducted undergraduate research upriver in Sarawak where Dayak farmers were concerned that the arrival of oil palm plantations occupying their land would turn them into wage workers, subject to someone else's command. How to read and navigate plantation landscapes became a theme of our Kalimantan research (figure P.1).

FIGURE P.1 Dayak Village on the Tangkos River

For our first trip together up the Tangkos River, a tributary of Kalimantan's mighty Kapuas, Pujo organized a boat. The huge trees and small hamlets along the riverbank reminded Tania of the interior of Sarawak circa 1980, but the gentle view from the boat was deceptive. Fifty meters (55 yards) back from the river, just out of sight, were thousands of hectares of monocrop palm. Had we taken the plantation-built road instead of the river, we would have seen no forest and no hamlets, just oil palm all the way. Malay and Dayak hamlets like this one are tiny enclaves excised from the plantation concession where the original landholders continue to live in their riverside homes but have no access to farmland and no guarantee of plantation jobs. PHOTO: PUJO SEMEDI.

Pujo's definition was inspired by the giant metaphors used by Indonesian intellectuals Rendra and Mangunwijaya to characterize the rapacious crony capitalism of General Suharto's New Order rule.[1] It also came from his knowledge of how plantation corporations appear to villagers and low-level workers (as persons writ large, with intention and force), and his intimate knowledge of how plantations work.[2] He grew up on a tea plantation in Java where his father was the head of transport, and his mother taught at the plantation primary school. For him the vast fields of monocrops that Tania found alienating were both normal and good. He noticed that the children of tea pickers came to school in torn clothes, without shoes, and were malnourished; the children of managers lived in better houses and wore better clothes than he did. He felt pity for the one, and a desire to emulate the other.

When Pujo returned to the tea plantation to conduct post-doctoral research, he discovered another order behind the one he had experienced as a child. This was the order of the giant and the thieves. Plantation archives showed the locations of villages that had been displaced when the plantation occupied their land, and he talked to former workers who had retired without pensions, thrown out like old rags. He found out that the plantation had seldom made a profit during a century of operation. This made him curious. What kind of business can routinely lose money yet still survive? A buried clay pipe (figure P.2), together with a hint from a retired foreman— "the plantation was robbed night and day for decades"—set Pujo's inquiry on a new path.[3]

This history from Java opened up for us the question of how a plantation corporation could be an occupying force (like a giant) and enroll differently situated actors (villages, workers, managers) who both support and steal from it. It was a pattern that emerged strongly when we began our joint research in Kalimantan. Pujo recognized it from our first day, when we witnessed plantation workers sitting in the popular riverside coffee stalls from 9:00 AM in the morning: "these people are all stealing." What surprised Pujo was not that workers stole time but their brazenness: the workers were wearing their official uniforms, publicly performing their disregard for plantation discipline.

In the Javanese plantation Pujo studied, theft was routine but somewhat disguised; it was also euphemized and embedded in moral evaluations. Dutch managers paid themselves a lavish salary and bonuses, blaming losses on coffee leaf rust disease. Native foremen marked up the price of low-quality manure, a practice that continued after the plantation was nationalized in 1958. Foreman manipulated labor by sending company workers to their

FIGURE P.2 The Pipe

On a visit to the tea plantation with Tania, Pujo stopped his ancient jeep on a steep planta-tion road and pointed out a broken clay pipe in a ditch. The pipe was laid in 1882 to flush coffee berries from the top fields down to a processing mill 8 kilometers (5 miles) below. The reason was theft: plantation workers, cart haulers, and surrounding villagers colluded to steal the plantation's coffee berries. Sealed in a clay pipe, the berries would be safe during the entire journey from the top of the plantation to the bottom. Theft continued, however, because thieves broke the clay pipe, and an even more expensive steel pipe did not stop them. The problem of theft was partially solved when the owners converted the plantation from coffee to tea, for which there was no local market. PHOTO: PUJO SEMEDI.

own fields, by adding ghost workers to their work gang (*nggundul*, Javanese for bald heads), or by inflating the number of working days in their section (*ngerol*, acting). They cheated workers by falsifying the weight of the bas-kets used by tea pickers; pickers also cheated, putting freshly plucked leaves under the rain to increase their weight. Stealing from the corporation was backed by a general sense that the corporation was both rich and wasteful. Workers did not call this practice stealing (*nyolong*) but *ngutil*—Javanese for paring a wart, i.e., removing something that is of no use to its owner but po-tentially useful to someone else. Managers called theft by workers theft and attempted to police it, but workers only laughed: "Thieves always outsmart police."

Theft from subordinates was understood by both parties as a natural con-sequence of hierarchy: a foreman had a right to some extra food, called *pangan mandor*. A foreman's cut caused resentment when it exceeded the "normal" amount. When workers talked about stealing by managers, they said *angkut-angkut*, Indonesian for "carrying something away." They called a very corrupt manager *wong rosa*, Javanese for a strong person, someone capable of carrying a heavy load. Among themselves managers did not say corruption but "gathering vitamins and nutritious supplements," suggesting that their rank entitled them to a diet of high quality. When a colleague was called by the plantation's internal audit office, they said he had a problem (in Indonesian, *kena masalah*). This meant he had taken too much, causing intense gossip that made the internal auditors look stupid if they did nothing. Most of the time the outcome was light disciplinary action such as a temporary transfer to a nonjob or "dry position" without a flow of cash, or early retirement. Among day laborers with only outright stealing as a way to earn personal benefit, the rule was simply not to get caught red-handed.

Pujo's ethnographic and historical research on the tea plantation left him feeling very sad, rather embarrassed, and slightly amused. The amusement

FIGURE P.3 Arrivals

Arrival narratives figured prominently in the students' field notes, enabling us to see the plantation zone through their eyes. Most of them imagined Kalimantan as a land of exotic tribes and rich tropical forests, but they were disappointed. The eighteen-hour trip on a slow boat up the busy Kapuas River led them into an industrial zone with bauxite mines left and right, cut timber floating downriver in huge log rafts, bustling trading towns, and endless plantations. When the students arrived at our research site, Javanese plantation workers warned them that the native Dayaks could be dangerous, a racialized caricature they had to navigate alongside the unfamiliar terrain. PHOTO: PUJO SEMEDI.

came from the richly ironic language people used to describe their world. The embarrassment came from seeing his friends and informants do improper things. The sadness came from a sense of wasted opportunity: his research forced him to recognize that for more than a century Indonesia's natural wealth had been looted not only by foreigners but also by its own people, a pattern he saw repeated in Kalimantan. But Pujo combined sadness with anger: anger directed toward the giants that occupy people's land, destroy livelihoods, and accumulate wealth while turning everyone who interacts with them into thieves.

Our book explores the forms of life produced by corporate occupation of Indonesia's oil palm plantation zone. We conducted the research in the period 2010–15, together with more than a hundred students from our two universities who each spent one to twelve months in the research site (figure P.3). We describe our collaborative fieldwork methods in the appendix. For now, we invite readers to travel with us into the plantation zone as we attempt to make sense of the forms of life that emerge there.

Introduction

A plantation is a machine for assembling land, labor, and capital under centralized management for the purpose of making a profit; it is also a political technology that orders territories and populations, produces new subjects, and makes new worlds. The enslavement of Africans to work on plantations in the Americas produced novel social formations throughout the Black Atlantic.[1] Slave plantations organized production and processing on an industrial scale and pioneered the "high modern" management of space, time, and task long before northern manufacturing.[2] Sugar, coffee, and tea produced in tropical "factories in the fields" furnished cheap pleasures to working classes in Europe, energizing the Industrial Revolution.[3] Plantations were also the cornerstone of European colonial expansion in Asia and Africa in the period 1870–1940 as monopoly capital went global in search of mega profits.[4]

Contemporary plantation expansion is no less world-making and its scale is unprecedented. Since 2000 plantation-based production of sugar has expanded massively in Brazil; and in Indonesia and Malaysia millions of hectares of forest and mixed farmlands have been cleared by plantation corporations to grow oil palm. Crude palm oil, the commodity these plantations produce, is a key ingredient in mass-produced junk food, detergents, cosmetics, and cooking oil as well as biofuels.[5] Half of the products in Euro-American supermarkets contain palm oil, and it makes these products cheaper.[6] Indonesia, the focus of our research, produces 50 percent of the world's supply of palm oil, and much of it—around 60 percent—is exported to India, where it is popular as an affordable cooking oil.[7] Palm oil produces extraordinary profits for plantation corporations and involves around fifteen million people in the "plantation life" that our book explores.[8]

Viewed from afar, plantations serve as icons of modernity and orderly development, sometimes tinged with patriotic pride. Their neatly aligned rows of crops and deployment of land and labor on a vast scale are claims to productive efficiency and technical mastery. In Indonesia, managers who attend the College of Plantation Training (LPP) read works by Max Weber on the virtues of modern bureaucracy and rational planning. As it turns out, the evidence on plantation efficiency is mixed: in much of the world crops that were once grown on plantations are now grown on small farms that are often highly efficient in relation to both land and labor, and much easier to manage.[9] Yet arguments for the superior efficiency of large farms and plantations are endlessly repeated and periodically renewed both nationally and on a global scale. In 2011, for example, a World Bank report argued that half the world's potentially arable land was unused and much of the rest was underutilized. It backed up this claim with maps and graphs that characterized parts of the world in terms of their "yield gap," framed as the difference between the dollar value per hectare of the crops small-scale farmers currently produce and the potential dollar value under efficient monocropping. The report argued that inefficient land use was not just wasteful; it was environmentally suspect: concentrating production on efficient farms would create jobs, help feed a burgeoning global population, and protect forest and grassland to mitigate climate change.[10]

Supporters of Indonesia's oil palm corporations defend their expansion in terms of the globally circulating efficiency narrative: palm oil feeds the world and should be produced on massive, modern plantations.[11] Based on such claims, plantation corporations have been permitted to occupy around 40 percent of Indonesia's farmland and squeeze out small mixed farms.[12] Yet, we argue, it is not agronomy or productive efficiency that dictate plantation dominance, it is politics: political economy, political technology, and the order of impunity that characterizes Indonesia's political milieu.

Starting from political economy, critical research on the so-called land-grab sparked by the food and financial crisis of 2007–9 brought attention to the renewed interest of transnational corporations in extracting profits from rural spaces. Studies showed that national corporations are also involved, and both foreign and national corporations receive ample state support.[13] These studies paid particular attention to the losses that corporations impose on rural spaces: loss of customary lands, flexible rural livelihoods, diverse ecosystems, and healthy forests to mitigate climate change. Complementing inquiries focused on profits extracted and losses imposed, *Plantation Life* offers a grounded ethnographic account of the social, economic, and political relations that plantation corporations set in place when they transform vast rural spaces into plantation zones, and of the forms of life they generate.

Our field-based research conducted from 2010 to 2015 focused on two plantations in Tanjung, an oil palm–saturated subdistrict of Sanggau, West Kalimantan.[14] One was Natco, a 5,000-hectare unit of the state-owned plantation corporation PTPN. It operated as a semi-enclosed world in which managers exercised tight control over resident workers. To the tasks of production and the generation of profit, Natco added an expansive social mandate of a utopic kind rather like twentieth-century company towns in the United States, Fordlandia in Brazil, and mines of the Zambian copper belt where workers and their families were provided with facilities to lead exemplary modern lives.[15] Space, time, and mentality were taken under a paternalistic form of corporate guidance.[16] The second plantation was Priva, owned by a private Indonesian corporation with a concession of 39,000 hectares. It had more porous boundaries and fewer social goals. Some workers lived in Priva housing while others were recruited from surrounding villages and commuted daily to work. Much of the production was undertaken by local and migrant out-growers who were bound to Priva until they paid off the debt they assumed for preparation of their 2 hectare (5 acre) oil palm plots. Wedged within and between these two plantations were the hamlets of former landholders who eked out a living from tiny residual patches of land and casual plantation work, people whose struggles were central to the plantation zone as we came to understand it.

The site we studied was specific and we embrace its specificity for the insights it offers on the situated workings of corporate capitalism today. While the elements that comprise plantations are generic (land, labor, capital, seeds, chemicals, technology, markets, management, legal standing), their configuration at particular conjunctures is always unique. Globally circulating capital might seem to be the most generic element, but money only becomes capital when it is brought into relation with land and labor in their concrete forms. As Mezzadra and Neilson argue, every expression of contemporary capitalism is specific, making ethnographic approaches well suited to explore the "spatial, social, legal and political formations with which capital must grapple as it becomes enmeshed in dense constellations of flesh and earth."[17] The dense constellations that both enable corporate profits and generate novel forms of life—plantation life—are the focus of our account.

Our inquiry weaves together two threads of analysis that are often kept apart. One thread drawn from Marx is political economy where the guiding questions concern the modes in which capital, land, and labor are assembled to generate profit for some and impoverishment for others.[18] We build on the work of scholars who examine the global circulation of capital, land appropriation, agrarian class formation, and labor regimes.[19] The second thread drawn from Foucault is political technology where the focus is on the production of subjects and the government of territories and populations. Political technologies, Foucault argues, are not cut from whole cloth. They comprise "discourses, institutions, architectural forms, regulatory decisions, laws, administrative measures, scientific statements, moral and philanthropic propositions."[20] They are pulled together to meet not one overriding purpose (e.g., corporate profit) but a number of purposes (production, revenue, development, order, prestige, well-being) that do not always align.[21] We draw especially on scholarly work that combines these approaches to study political ecologies and power-laden landscapes where the value of different land uses is under dispute, colonial and contemporary technologies of racial rule, and the making of resource frontiers as spaces full of potential for productivity and profit.[22]

Iterative research, reading, and analysis led us to theorize the constitutive role of corporate occupation, imperial debris, and extractive regimes in the formation of plantation life. In the following sections we introduce these theorizations and outline the traction they offer for our account.

Corporate Occupation

Corporate occupation, we suggest, is the principal political technology that sets the conditions for life in Indonesia's plantation zone. Here we parse its components, examining first the plantation corporation and its mandates, then the insights afforded by a focus on corporate occupation.

Corporate Mandates

Economic geographer Joshua Barkan draws attention to the sovereign powers that governments since the Middle Ages have delegated to corporations to enable them to meet a dual mandate: to generate profits *and* serve a public purpose.[23] Corporations have built and run railways and water systems, cities and universities; they have organized imperial trade and the settlement of colonies; and for hundreds of years they have owned and managed plantations. To meet their dual mandate, corporations are delegated the sovereign's right to privatize public wealth (land, water, forest) and to cause harms to people and species that stand in their way. Assessing corporate harms, Barkan reframes Foucault's crucial question about biopower, "Given that this power's objective is essentially to make live, how can it let die?" to ask, "How [is it that] a global order of corporate capitalism, created and repeatedly justified for its abilities 'to improve life . . . ,' results in a system that routinely denies housing, clothes, food, work, and essential medicines; that exposes populations to unsafe living conditions and environmental hazards?"[24] We make the tension between state-enabled corporate profit, purported public benefit, and licensed harm a cornerstone of our analysis.

Indonesia's laws make the public purpose of delegating sovereign powers to plantation corporations explicit. The 2007 Investment Law begins "in consideration of the need to promote a society which is just and prosperous as stipulated by . . . the Constitution there must be continuous national economic development." Hence the law facilitates foreign and domestic investment to meet national development goals. The 2014 Plantation Law number 39) states that "the earth, water and natural resources contained in the territory of the Republic of Indonesia [are] a gift from God Almighty to be exploited and used for the greatest prosperity and welfare of the people." It notes the capacity of plantations to develop the national economy and bring about people's prosperity and welfare in a fair and equitable way (*secara berkeadilan*).

Indonesia's focus on corporate-led growth as the centerpiece of the national development strategy ramped up in 2020 with an Omnibus Bill to Create Jobs which drastically overhauled land, labor, and environmental laws to ease foreign investment. The bill was met with public protests, and many Indonesians read words about corporate-led development and its contribution to the "people's prosperity and wellbeing" with suspicion. Yet there is no sustained national debate on what constitutes the people's well-being or how best to accomplish it. The current maldistribution of wealth in Indonesia is catastrophic: Indonesia is the third most unequal country in the world (after Russia and Thailand), where four men own more wealth than 100 million people.[25] Yet the position of the oligarchy is hardly challenged, and the neoliberal narrative, according to which corporations generate wealth that trickles down to secure "the people's prosperity," generally prevails. Plantation corporations thrive in this milieu.

In the name of public benefit, Indonesia's plantation corporations are granted many privileges. Laws favor corporations and grant them access to subsidized land, credit, bailouts, and other forms of "corporate welfare" that absolve them from the capitalist imperative to operate efficiently or be competitive in market terms.[26] Their privileges and monopolies are embedded in what anthropologist Hannah Appel calls the "licit life of capitalism," the one backed by laws, contracts, and corporate reports.[27] As we will show, corporations are also supported by officials and politicians at every level of the state apparatus who are officially tasked (and privately compensated) to smooth their path. Government agencies are supposed to regulate corporations, but their activities are ultimately an internal matter—a sovereign supervising its own instrument, a head directing its hand.[28] Crucially, the production of harm is a licensed part of the corporate mandate. Indonesia's plantation corporations monopolize land and water; they destroy forests and exude chemicals; they burden out-growers (contract farmers) with debt; and they cast aside people and species for which they have no use. These harms are well known but they are normalized as the anticipated but uncounted cost that must be paid to bring prosperity to remote regions.

Building on the work of philosopher Giorgio Agamben, Barkan explores "the paradox of the sovereign ban, in which legal exceptions and the abandonment of populations are justified as vital to the security of political communities."[29] We examine the workings of this paradox in Tanjung's plantation zone, where corporations ejected former landholders and abandoned old and injured workers without means of livelihood. For Barkan abandoned people meet Agamben's criteria for *homo sacer:* they can be killed or left to die, but their death is not recognized as a sacrifice because their lives have no economic or moral value.

In Tanjung, plantation managers selected which people and species to nurture or abandon. To push back, unwanted people used theft and extortion to extract paltry shares of plantation wealth; they also attempted to rework the boundary of the corporations' moral responsibility and insisted that the sacrifice corporations imposed on them be recognized and compensated. Sacrificing oneself for the common good has value in Indonesia—fighters who sacrificed their lives to achieve independence from the Dutch are one example. But a wasted sacrifice, called in Indonesian *mati konyol* (pointless death), betrays the sacrificiant and leaves a bad feeling. We explore this betrayal as a material, embodied, and affectively charged situation.

Occupation

At the heart of the betrayal we encountered in Tanjung's plantation zone was the overwhelming power of corporations that had been installed as an occupying force. The Indonesian term for occupation of land is *pendudukan*; for control of a territory and its population by a powerful alien force without consent it is *penjajahan,* the term used for Dutch colonial rule. When we heard villagers say, "We are colonized by the corporation" (*kami dijajah perusahaan*), they were flagging illegitimacy: rule without consent that injured them in various ways. They were also noting the reliance of both colonial powers and corporations on an extreme social division that ascribes differential value to people and the places they inhabit. Villagers whose land was targeted for corporate occupation had little or no say in the matter. They were not deemed capable of participating in a dialogue with the officials who issued corporate land concessions, or with plantation managers. As in colonial times the extreme social divide that separated officials and managers from villagers rendered the concept of such a dialogue absurd.

The term "occupation" usually refers to foreign military seizure of a territory and the subjugation of its resident population. We stretch the term to theorize corporate presence in the plantation zone because it enables us to explore three key relationships. First, it draws attention to novel spatial and political arrangements: the forceful seizure and occupation of territory by a corporation, the presence of armed police and guards tasked with protecting corporate property, and the reorganization of rule over people and territory. As scholars examining occupied Palestine have noted, the spatial and political formats of occupation are plural.[30] In Tanjung plantation cores comprise a continuous space with a single boundary and a resident population governed by corporate management intensely and directly. Out-grower areas where farming households produce oil palm fruit to feed corporate mills are governed indirectly through a political and material infrastructure imposed by the corporations (block layout, roads, co-ops, credit schemes, harvest schedules, and so forth). Interstitial areas and remnant hamlets (called enclaves) look superficially like ordinary villages and have had no formal change in their legal status, but they too are occupied in quite specific ways.

The patchwork spatial arrangements of the plantation zone make occupation by corporations quite different from occupation by haciendas, a difference recognized in a comparative study by anthropologists Sydney Mintz and Eric Wolf. The hacienda format grants landlords formal control over huge areas of land and state-like powers over the entire resident population.[31] Production is secondary. With plantations the priority is reversed. In Indonesia it is *only* the state's production mandate that is formally delegated to plantation corporations. Other public purposes such as the extension of territorial control, the management of populations, and the development of remote regions are treated as by-products.[32]

The novel political arrangements set in place by corporate occupation are undeclared. Plantation corporations have no legal responsibility or jurisdiction outside their concession borders. Nevertheless, they curtail villagers' access to land, water, and livelihood and remake their political institutions to conform to corporate requirements. Like villagers in occupied Palestine described by Saree Makdisi, villagers in a plantation zone are subjected to a ban without a ban—an exclusion from "normal citizenship" that is not legally inscribed. Corporations and their state allies engage in what Makdisi calls the "denial of denial"—denial that an occupation occurred or that an occupied population is present or that anyone has suffered a loss.[33]

The implications of denial are especially profound in Indonesia because of the way citizenship works. Villagers living outside plantation boundaries are classified as ordinary citizens (*rakyat biasa*) who enjoy "normal" legal rights under the constitution including "human rights" upheld by a national commission (Komnas HAM). Yet ethnographic research has shown that effective citizenship in Indonesia is not primarily a matter of law.[34] The term *rakyat* flags both legal rights *and* a relationship of acute hierarchy (sometimes called feudal) in which ordinary people must rely on the mediation of people in power (*orang besar, orang kuasa*) to advance their projects or provide protection when their survival is under threat. People in power are expected to help "small people" (*rakyat biasa, orang kecil*) to solve problems. No ordinary Indonesian, rural or urban, would approach a site of higher authority (a government or corporate office, a court) without being accompanied by, or bearing a letter of recommendation from, an official or person of power who can vouch for them.

The language of Indonesia's constitution confirms hierarchy. It does not focus on the rights and entitlements of citizens but on the duty of the state (politicians and officials) to furnish benefits such as peace, prosperity, and development. It is a state modeled on the family in which parents have duties but children have few rights.[35] It is intrinsically infantilizing and it leaves "small people," who are shorn of protection, radically exposed. Under corporate occupation, government officials, politicians, and local leaders back the corporations and "small people" are on their own.

Second, theorizing corporate presence as occupation helps to account for the novel social positions, subjectivities, and moral evaluations that emerge when people are conscripted to a form of life—a plantation life—the conditions of which they cannot control. It is well known that in zones of military occupation government officials and village leaders collaborate with the occupying force; ordinary residents become complicit; people who are initially intent on removing the occupier settle into modes of coexistence; and uprisings have limited goals. Moral evaluations morph as stealing from the occupier becomes routine. Theft may take the multiple forms James Scott identified as the "weapons of the weak," but predatory practices that target neighbors are also defended on the grounds that everyone needs to hustle. Wealth, and the practices people use to acquire it, become a domain of contention in which the boundary between the licit and the illicit is prized open and allegiances fracture and realign.[36] Our research in Tanjung indicates that military occupation and corporate occupation operate in a similar way. Workers and villagers in the plantation zone did not mobilize to remove corporations; local elites both collaborated and stole from them and ordinary people took what they could. Corporate giants were firmly installed yet beset by thieves from all sides.

Third, conceptualizing corporations as an occupying force resonates with the dual mandate of both colonial and military rule. Occupying powers often present themselves as a benevolent force intent on improving the lives of the subject population and treat the seizure of assets and profit-making as secondary. As an occupying force, plantation corporations are supposed to bring prosperity and introduce the subject population to new and improved ways of living. Like the colonial technologies examined by David Scott, corporate occupation is "concerned above all with disabling old forms of life by systematically breaking down their conditions and with constructing in their place new conditions so as to enable—indeed, to oblige—new forms of life to come into being."[37] In the idiom of Talal Asad and David Scott, residents in Tanjung's plantation zone were "conscripts of modernity": their previous ways of organizing their landscapes and livelihoods, their families and communities, were thoroughly disabled and they were obliged to develop new ones under conditions the occupiers imposed.[38]

To trace the contours of subject formation under corporate occupation we pay attention to the emergence of novel desires, dispositions, and institutions. We attend to the futures that workers and villagers in the plantation zone imagined for coming generations, and the pathways they saw as open or closed. We ask what they considered to be a "rightful share" of plantation wealth—the share due to them as original landholders, workers, or neighbors of a plantation.[39] Unsurprisingly, we found that the benefits of the promised modernity were unevenly distributed, as some people enjoyed a full package of modern facilities while others were deprived of access to even basic means of livelihood. People who were excluded from benefits did not accept their relegation to a permanent waiting room, or to the peculiar temporality identified by Elizabeth Povinelli as "the future anterior tense," in which problems will have been dealt with "from the perspective of the last man."[40] But their non-acceptance of relegation was not heroic. As Povinelli observes, for people who have been seriously harmed survival is an accomplishment. They may disappear from public discourse but they persist in living, they endure; hence the form taken by their "plantation life" is a crucial part of our analysis.

Imperial Debris

Imperial debris is the second pillar of our theorization of plantation life. *Imperial debris* is Ann Stoler's label for "the rot that remains" from the political technologies of colonial rule.[41] Behind the dual mandate extended to plantation corporations past and present is a racialized proposition that has been embedded in Indonesian law and political discourse since colonial times: corporations must make land productive because Indonesian farmers are not capable of doing this on their own. Racialism, defined by Cedric Robinson as "the legitimation and corroboration of social organization as natural by reference to the 'racial' components of its elements," was not eradicated with the removal of Indonesia's white colonial masters.[42] Rather, it looped around remnants of Indonesia's version of feudalism, was entrenched in law, and continues to be enacted in the everyday comportment of "big people" toward people they regard as social inferiors.

Robinson theorized "racial capitalism" as a format that both builds on and produces race-like divides as it marshals land and labor to generate profit. He noted the "immense expenditures of psychic and intellectual energies" that were required to create the figure of "the Slav," "the Irishman," and "the Negro" as persons naturally suited for brute labor, and to produce "Ireland" and "Africa" as wild spaces available for appropriation.[43] His insights continue to have global traction. In colonial Southeast Asia the production of empty spaces ripe for corporate occupation and the selection of bodies suited to manual labor centered on the "myth of the lazy native" famously explored by Syed Hussein Alatas.[44] According to this myth, whichever natives were present on the spot were sure to be incompetent farmers and unsuitable workers. Colonial officials used these racialized assessments to justify the installation of plantations and the importation of migrants to do plantation work.

The myth of the lazy native continues to embed an extreme social divide at the core of Indonesia's plantation life today. Government officials, plantation managers, and many ordinary plantation workers whom we met in

Tanjung were convinced that they were utterly different from and superior to local villagers. Education and concepts of ethnocultural pluralism may modify the social divide to some degree, but a rot remains.[45] Indonesians do not usually call this deeply hierarchical social divide racial; they call it feudal or colonial, terms that recognize the divide as a social fact but hint that in modern Indonesia where the constitution declares all citizens to be equal, such a divide is not quite legitimate. Beyond everyday comportment, it is in the fields of land law and assessments of productivity that the imperial debris of racial rule is most deeply entrenched.

Land Law

As Brenna Bhandar has shown, racial (or race-like) divisions are constitutive of colonial and contemporary land regimes in which the association between a kind of person, a kind of land use, and the inferiority of customary property rights is circular.[46] In Indonesia the chain of reasoning goes like this: the national land agency grants concessions to plantation corporations on the grounds that they can utilize the land efficiently; implicitly, customary landholders cannot use land efficiently; hence their customary land rights do not qualify as full property rights; their low productivity and incomplete property rights confirm that they are people of low value; as people of low value they cannot be expected to use land efficiently, and they can legitimately be displaced by corporations.[47]

Drawing directly on the colonial land law of 1870, Indonesia's 1960 land law (which is still in force) treats much of the nation's land mass as state land that can be granted on concession to plantation, mining, and timber corporations. The law offers very weak protection for customary land rights that may be recognized only if they do not interfere with national economic development. Vigorous campaigning by activists has pressured the Ministries of Forestry and Land Affairs to create procedures for the formal recognition of customary land rights, but the conditions are difficult to meet and require decades of NGO facilitation and significant funds. By 2020 such rights had only been recognized for a tiny portion of the 40 million hectares of state-claimed forest land that activists argue should be returned to the jurisdiction of indigenous or customary communities (*masyarakat adat*).[48]

Villagers who do not claim membership in customary communities are also exposed to land seizure. Circa 2015 formal individual land titles issued by the national land agency covered only 20 percent of rural farmland parcels; for the rest, tenure continues to be based on custom.[49] Villagers have a clear sense of what is theirs; they have customary processes to resolve disputes that arise among themselves; and their land rights may receive vague and partial forms of state recognition in formats like tax receipts, but their rights are not strong enough to prevent a corporation bearing a government-issued concession from occupying their land.[50] Officials acknowledge that corporate land acquisition is often handled incorrectly: consent is falsified or coerced, compensation is inadequate, prices are manipulated, and corporations make promises they fail to keep. But they do not recognize the colonial basis of the land law that discounts customary land rights and turns all corporations into vehicles of occupation. As Christian Lund points out, corporations complete the "primitive accumulation" that was already accomplished in law in 1870; they make the legal seizure real as their bulldozers clear homes and farms from land to which the state laid claim long ago. "Theft," Lund writes, "was laundered in advance."[51]

Productivity

In Indonesia official assessments of who is or is not a productive farmer continue to be replete with imperial debris. Colonial officials acknowledged that farmers in Java and Bali were skilled at producing rice in their intricately terraced fields, but they had no respect for farmers who grew rice by the extensive forest-fallow or swidden method that they saw as wasteful. Their assessment was entrenched in transmigration, a program of internal colonization initiated in the 1920s when the colonial government sent land-short farmers from crowded islands to settle on the so-called outer islands where land was said to be underutilized. After independence, state-sponsored transmigration continued and new policies supplemented the goal of population distribution with an explicit mandate of social and economic development.[52] Contemporary transmigrants sent to remote areas are supposed to model modern farming techniques for emulation by local farmers who are still defined as backward. Unsurprisingly, when transmigrants arrived in Tanjung, local Malay and Dayak villagers regarded them as elements of the occupation: they occupied villagers' customary land and their presence, together with their presumed superior farming skills, embodied an insulting claim that villagers native to Kalimantan are social inferiors.

When it came to global market crops, colonial authorities readily dismissed native production as inefficient. Yet scholars have shown that Indonesia's small-scale farmers have been adept and enthusiastic producers of global market crops for three centuries. As Clifford Geertz and many others have recognized, colonial agrarian policies were not designed to pull reluctant villagers into the market economy; their purpose was to confine villagers to subsistence pursuits and protect state-backed corporations from local competition.[53] Circa 1700, farmers in Java eagerly planted coffee to take advantage of a new export market. They were successful until their production was suppressed by the Netherlands East Indies Corporation (VOC, 1602–1799) that imposed a monopoly on trade in coffee and set prices so low that farmers burned their coffee bushes in disgust. From then on they had to be coerced to meet quotas for coffee and, later, for sugar, but wherever they were paid a fair market price their productivity doubled.[54]

In the 1870s when the colonial government started to grant plantation concessions to foreign investors, the rationale was again productivity, but planters were nervous. In Sumatra planters lobbied colonial authorities to forbid local villagers and former plantation workers from producing tobacco for fear they would outcompete plantations. In Java planters insisted that local farmers be discouraged from planting tea. In the 1920s farmers in Sumatra and Kalimantan adopted rubber cultivation so eagerly they put the less efficient rubber plantation corporations into decline. During the 1930s Depression smallholder rubber production was deliberately suppressed, this time to sustain the market price for struggling corporations.[55] As Michael Dove has long insisted, the privileges and monopolies granted to contemporary oil palm corporations at the expense of willing and productive smallholders continue this colonial motif.[56] Plantation corporations are not especially efficient producers nor do they bring development to remote regions, but they are very effective technologies for generating and extracting streams of revenue and profit, the topic to which we now turn.

Extractive Regimes

Our theorization of extractive regimes as constitutive elements of plantation life hinges on the recognition that extractive regimes are plural. One purpose of plantations is to extract a global market product from natural elements such as soil, seeds, water, and human labor. Another is to extract profit for corporations, their shareholders, and the banks that finance them. A third is to extract revenue to fill state coffers and generate foreign exchange. A fourth, of particular relevance in contemporary Indonesia, is the extraction of unearned income (rent), which is funneled to diverse parties both within and far beyond the plantation zone. These four elements work together in different configurations. Here we outline the contours of the extractive regimes that were set in place through Indonesia's plantation history and the violence of 1965–66, contemporary practices of illicit extraction and the order of impunity in which they thrive, and the impressive profits that draw transnational and national corporations into oil palm production.

Plantation Histories

In Indonesia's so-called liberal period that began in 1870, the colonial government granted concessions to plantation corporations so they could generate revenues to pay for colonial administration and yield profits for shareholders in the mother country. Yet as the colonial historian Furnivall observed the revenues collected were outstripped by planters' demands for infrastructure to support their enterprise. Hence shareholders profited handsomely, but state coffers remained bare, and there were never sufficient funds for native development, a problem that still continues.[57] Java's late colonial plantations were dedicated to sugar, coffee, and tea. They covered 1.3 million hectares by the 1920s and recruited workers from surrounding areas on a "free" (untied) basis.[58] In Sumatra by 1930 the plantation belt covered almost a million contiguous hectares. The primary crop was tobacco, followed by rubber, which was introduced around 1910.

Labor law in the form of Coolie Ordinances bound workers to corporations through contracts backed by a system of debt and coercive enforcement. Workers were recruited initially from China and later from Java. Managers were licensed to mete out physical punishment, backed by penal codes that classified worker actions such as insufficient effort or attempting to abscond as criminal. Colonial laws permitted plantation corporations to make their own rules and protected them from interference in their "internal affairs." Colonial officials, Dutch politicians, and other critics who were concerned about the fate of contract workers or land-squeezed native farmers struggled to make headway against corporations that held sovereign powers as the designated production machines of colonial rule.[59]

State support for plantation corporations wavered for a period. During the Japanese occupation in 1942–45, foreign planters were interned, and workers started to plant food crops and build dwellings on concession land. Planters who attempted to return during or after the independence war (1946–49) faced stiff opposition from these workers-turned-farmers. Sukarno, president of the new republic, saw foreign-owned plantations as vehicles for continued (neo)colonial extraction. Under his rule the struggle over plantation land and plantation workers' demands for better pay and conditions grew in strength, organized in part by the Communist-linked plantation workers' union Sarbupri and the Peasant Front (Barisan Tani Indonesia).[60] The situation changed radically in 1957 when Sukarno nationalized foreign-owned plantations. His goal was to reassert national sovereignty and stop the outflow of Indonesia's wealth. He envisaged a state-owned plantation corporation supervised by the Ministry of Agriculture that would harness the productive powers of corporate agriculture for public purposes. But due to the urgency of restoring plantation production to generate foreign exchange, and as a tactic to satisfy the economic demands of the army, he placed the nationalized plantations under temporary military management. He was outmaneuvered by the army, which turned these plantations into a source of funds for military operations and private enrichment and established the order of impunity that supplies both a precondition and incentive for expanding corporate presence today.[61]

From 1957 onward, army officers allied with bureaucrats, politicians, and entrepreneurs to entrench their control over nationalized plantations, take what they wanted, and attack or intimidate their opponents. The military-crony-corporate cabals that formed at this time consolidated their hold in 1965–66 when the army and its allies ousted Sukarno and massacred an estimated half-million Communists and union members, eliminating the most significant counterforce in the plantation sector and in society at large. Intellectuals were jailed or silenced and from then on, writes historian Geoffrey Robinson, "an entire tradition of leftist thinking, writing, and political action" that had been formative of Indonesian culture and public debate since the 1920s was "decimated and rendered illegitimate."[62]

Since 1966 there has been no labor movement, farmers' organization, or political party capable of checking the power of the military-crony-corporate cabals that continue to operate both within and outside the law.[63] These cabals work closely with transnational corporations that seek access to Indonesia's resources. Within a year of the massacres and the commencement of General Suharto's New Order rule, the government restored relations with foreign corporations by compensating them for nationalized plantations and declared the country open for fresh foreign investment (figure I.1). The World Bank and IMF promptly offered the government financial support to build the infrastructure that corporations require, a policy they justified in terms of an expanded corporate mandate that included the provision of jobs and national economic development.[64]

In the 1980s the Indonesian government adopted increasingly "neoliberal" policies to encourage foreign and domestic investment in plantations. It was pushed further in this direction during the Asian financial crisis of

FIGURE I.1 Rubber Plantation Workers, 1967

In stunning archival footage from 1967, an NBC reporter speaks to a Balinese academic who offers candid justification for killing communists, then cuts directly to footage of the Goodyear rubber corporation that is back in business with former union members now prisoners, working its fields at gunpoint. In the reporter's words, "Bad as things are, one positive fact is known: Indonesia has fabulous wealth in natural resources, and the New Order wants it exploited." Source: "Indonesia 1967: American reporter for NBC speaks to a genocidaire in Bali." https://www.youtube.com/watch?v=DI42TlCZcik.

1997–98 when the conditions of the IMF bailout required Suharto and his successors to open more sectors to foreign investment.[65] Laws governing mining, plantations, and labor were revised to favor corporations. The IMF and donors also pressed the government to decentralize powers to district level where elected politicians were supposed to be more accountable to the people.[66] The result was an intensified grab for land and timber and "the replication ad infinitum of the predatory pattern of state–business relations" at every spatial scale.[67]

The Political Milieu

A constitutive feature of the extractive regimes that have been entrenched in Indonesia since 1966 is the capacity of government officials, politicians, and their corporate allies to take what they want because they can. Their impunity is "ordered" in the sense that is pervasive, institutionalized, and hierarchically arranged: people of high status are expected to take the most. The order of impunity is similar to the one Achille Mbembe describes in postcolonial Africa, which is grounded in privilege, petty tyranny, predation, the "privatization of public prerogatives," and the "socialization of arbitrariness."[68] For Southeast Asia scholars Jacqui Baker and Sarah Milne, Indonesia falls into a category they dub "dirty money states" in which officials and politicians harvest revenue from corporations, cronies, and ordinary people through rents, tolls, and extortion, and distribute a portion of the spoils to neutralize opponents and cultivate clients.[69] These are not "failed states" but states that run along particular lines. They thrive on obscurity, on laws that contradict one another, on spatial plans that overlap, on interdepartmental secrecy and competition, and on minimal public accountability. Their massive compendia of state-sanctioned statistics do not produce legibility; they produce "domains of incalculability" because no one quite knows what the numbers represent.[70] Unsurprisingly, there is little public trust in bureaucrats and politicians.[71]

Rent seeking—the attempt to capture unearned wealth through the exercise of power—is a practice so pervasive in Indonesia's public sector that neither businesses nor individuals can avoid it. Studies by political scientists, anthropologists, and investigative journalists have exposed the tight links between politicians and corporations in all branches of government and industry, and the widespread privatization of public office. Officials and politicians rate ministries according to their capacity to generate private revenue streams: public works, forestry, and the judiciary are notoriously wet or lucrative. Officials and politicians pay to obtain lucrative positions, with the cost adjusted to the revenue the position is expected to generate.[72] State-owned enterprises—a category that includes state-owned plantations—are veritable money trees, both for the directors and managers who run them and for the many politicians and cronies who tap into their wealth.[73]

In daily discourse rent-seeking is referred to with euphemisms such as cutting, circumcision, pruning, collection, contribution, or donation. A common term for such transfers is *tahu sama tahu*, which roughly translates as "Let's keep it simple because we both know how the system works." A popular term for everyday extraction is the "mafia system," which in the Indonesian context does not denote the activity of a criminal family or violent gang but rather the use of choke points in bureaucratic structures to install toll booths and collect rent. Enforcement by thugs is a possibility, but violence is not the principal modus operandi; extraction is built into the system since toll booths prevent movement until payment is made. A toll booth is a position of monopoly, however petty; hence there is a school mafia that operates to extract tolls from parents before children can sit for their exams, a land mafia that extracts tolls whenever a signature is needed for a land transaction, and so on.[74] Mafia practices are not usually referred to as corruption, a word Indonesians reserve for officials who "misuse public funds" (*penyalahgunaan uang negara*). Corruption, when exposed, provides an opportunity for the judicial mafia (police, court officials, judges) to squeeze the accused into paying tolls to have the case handled in a "family way" (*secara kekeluargaan*) or in a "peaceful way" (*jalan damai*), which minimizes the public shame, the cost, and the lengthy process of formal prosecution.[75]

Mafia practices were rampant within Tanjung's plantation zone, as our ethnographic analysis will show; but they were also integral to the processes by which the two corporations we studied came to occupy village land. To operationalize their state-granted mandate and the privileges bestowed on them, all plantation corporations need the support of particular politicians and bureaucrats who supply signatures, issue business licenses, and solve problems. The cost of obtaining this support escalated after 2000 when responsibility for issuing business and location permits shifted from the national to the district level. Circa 2015 the tolls corporations paid to obtain these two permits for a 10,000 hectare oil palm plantation were around IDR3 billion (USD300,000), with an additional IDR3 billion if a forest release permit was required.[76] Securing the release of the designated land by dislodging its occupants and obtaining an environmental assessment report require additional payments. Only after these steps are complete can corporations obtain a formal plantation concession license (HGU) issued by the Land Bureau in Jakarta. In turn, a concession license furnishes corporations with two essential elements: a legal right to land to put into production and a document they can use as collateral for bank loans to finance their operations. Viewed sequentially, the capital corporations invest is primarily used to pay tolls; clearing land and planting palms is paid for by loans subsidized by the concession license.

Extractive practices that route through concession licenses were strikingly revealed by investigative journalists in a 2017 series called "Indonesia for Sale." The focus was district election financing: district heads in Kalimantan had issued location permits for thousands of hectares to shell corporations that were set up overnight in the names of their friends and family members. The owners of these shell corporations quickly sold them to national and transnational plantation corporations for millions of dollars and channeled the funds back to the candidates to finance their reelection. Issuing and selling location permits in this way falls outside the definition of corruption according to Indonesian law. Plantation corporations bought "clean" permits to which they would not have had access without the district head's need for funds.[77] The enabling context for these murky corporate-crony transactions has two parts. One is the corporate mandate: politicians are entitled to issue location permits on the grounds that plantations bring prosperity to their regions; the second is the absence of counterforces to hold corporations or politicians to account. As we noted earlier, since the genocidal massacres of 1965–66 and the suppression of critical debate there has been no effective labor movement, political party, or other organization capable of checking the power of these entrenched crony-corporate cabals.

Indonesia's order of impunity does not make law irrelevant, but as we will show, the role of law in a plantation zone is deeply ambiguous. Managers in Tanjung referred to law when attempting to defend corporations against crony predation and villagers' protests. Local officials, villagers, and workers referred to law when attempting to hold corporations to account. But the role of law was weakened by the degradation of citizenship under corporate occupation. Our analysis pays attention to how law works both to favor corporations and to limit them; to mixed mandates that require officials to protect corporations on one side and protect "small people" on the other; and to mafia practices that channel wealth, together with the sense of unease these practices generate.

Corporate Profit

Corporate profit is a key element of the political economy of Indonesia's plantation zone since it is profit that attracts corporations. It is also crucial to the political technology of corporate occupation and the order of impunity that enables it: without money to pay diverse claimants, corporations could not secure the necessary political support. According to industry analysts Indonesia's oil palm corporations are fantastically profitable. When the price of crude palm oil (CPO) is above USD770 per ton (CIF Rotterdam), production is profitable for efficient producers, while "at higher prices, palm oil production businesses are quite literally 'money pumps.'"[78] For the period 2010–20 the average price was USD809, well above the money pump threshold.[79] Even in 2015 when the price for crude palm oil dropped to USD600 the average gross margin for eleven publicly listed plantation corporations with operations that were upstream only (i.e., a plantation with its onsite mill) was 27 percent.[80] Put differently, in 2015 an investor who purchased high quality ready-to-harvest oil palm for USD9,000 per hectare could expect to make an immediate return of 16.5 percent per hectare per annum; no global bonds paid anything close.[81]

Significantly, it is the upstream end of the palm oil business that is the most profitable. A few vertically integrated global corporations handle much of the "downstream" refining of crude palm oil and its marketing, but these processes are not especially lucrative. In 2015 the Wilmar Corporation refined 35 percent of the CPO produced in the ASEAN region, owned fifty-four bulk carriers, and conducted specialized processing, but its margins downstream were low; hence its gross margin across the supply chain was only 8.3 percent compared with an average margin of 27 percent for corporations with only upstream activities.[82] Upstream profits give corporations a huge financial incentive to occupy land and engage directly in growing oil palm, and the banks that finance them together with the cronies who support them share in that incentive.[83] It would be much less lucrative for corporations to focus on downstream refining and leave oil palm growing to smallholders.

As in colonial times plantation corporations and their allies have an incentive to suppress smallholders' autonomous production because it challenges their monopoly over land and labor, and threatens the narrative that only corporations can produce efficiently. Contra this narrative, multiple studies confirm that smallholders can produce as much palm oil per hectare as plantations, and "no agronomic specificity of oil palm justifies the necessity to resort to an estate [plantation] dominated development regime."[84] Cultivating the palms is not complicated, and even on plantations there is no mechanization and hence no technical economy of scale. Workers weed, fertilize, and harvest palms manually. Independent farmers with access to high quality seedlings and fertilizer who tend their fields assiduously not only match or exceed plantation productivity per hectare; they produce at a much lower cost per ton because they do not need to pay for administrators, supervisors, and guards.[85]

The main technical challenges with oil palm are milling and transportation. The palms yield fresh fruit bunches that must be harvested every two weeks and processed at a mill within forty-eight hours before the oil quality drops. Good roads and sufficient mill capacity are essential. Although small mills suited to five hundred hectares of palms can do the job, the model favored by corporations is to build large mills and link them to plantations of between ten thousand and twenty thousand hectares to keep the mills supplied with fruit.[86] Giant mills conjure the need for giant plantations and serve to legitimate giant profits, while alternative ways of growing palms and milling palm fruit receive no political or corporate support.

According to official statistics, circa 2015 the total land area planted with oil palm was at least 12 million hectares; around 8 million more hectares were held in unlicensed plantations, unrecorded smallholdings, and corporate "land banks."[87] Nationally, the industry has five components. (1) The state-owned plantation corporation (PTPN) controls around 9 percent of the planted area. (2) Publicly listed national and transnational corporations control around 23 percent.[88] (3) Private unlisted corporations (mainly Indonesian owned) control around 23 percent. Smallholders control around 44 percent, with significant variation by province.[89] Smallholdings are divided between (4) out-growers bound to corporations that are legally obliged to provide out-grower plots to compensate villagers for their loss of land, and (5) independent smallholders.[90] The latter include migrants who buy land from customary land holders or encroach on primary forest with corporate-crony backing; government officials, plantation managers, urban professionals, and entrepreneurs who buy land and hire managers to run unlicensed plantations; and customary landholders who plant oil palm on their own land as a lucrative part of their livelihood portfolios.[91] A diversity of corporate and smallholder enterprises was present in Tanjung, and we explore the stakes of different models more fully in that context.

Inside Plantation Worlds

Extractive regimes are constitutive of plantation worlds, but they are not the only elements in play. Our interest is not limited to what can be extracted from plantations (palm oil, profits, revenues, rent) or what corporate occupation impairs (customary land rights, mixed farms, diverse ecologies, "normal" village citizenship). We are interested in the forms of life that plantation corporations install, a topic that is already the subject of a rich body of scholarship. Here we draw out some key insights from this prior work while being alert to the risk that the use of a single label—plantation—may suggest a false equivalence. Like the key word "proletarian" examined by anthropologist James Ferguson, the word "plantation" comes with "residues of prior uses [which] create analogical associations through which prior historical instances or paradigmatic sociological cases can set the terms (quite literally) with which we describe and compare other cases."[92] Hence we do not attempt to compare plantations as variations on an ideal type but focus on a few key elements and their resonance across different conjunctures.[93]

Slave plantations in the Americas shared some organizational features with Indonesia's contemporary oil palm plantations (monocrop production, task-based division of labor, orderly layout, tight surveillance), but the cradle-to-grave social provisions enjoyed by workers at the state plantation Natco had more in common with twentieth-century company towns. The shared political milieu gave Tanjung's plantation zone much in common with the site of Newmont's Batu Hijau gold mine in eastern Indonesia, skillfully examined by anthropologist Marina Welker, although the spatial arrangements were very different: the Batu Hijau mine occupied a consolidated, well-guarded site of 400 hectares, while in Tanjung subdistrict five adjacent plantations covered 65,000 hectares in an almost-continuous block.[94]

Oil palm plantations in Indonesia and Malaysia are technically similar, but the surrounding context is distinct. In Malaysia rural youth have good prospects for education and urban jobs, hence the occupation of their parents' land does not necessarily rob them of desirable farming futures. Indonesian migrant workers do most of the work on Malaysia's plantations. In Indonesia young people struggle to find paid work of any kind, so holding on to family or community land coveted by corporations may be their best option.[95] As geographer Michael Watts stresses the commodity does not determine other arrangements, and the political and ecological dynamics of the site of insertion shape the forms that technical systems take on the ground.[96]

The relationship between plantations and surrounding social, economic, and political formations is a classic theme of plantation research. Economist George Beckford highlighted the "persistent poverty" and regional under-development that plantation corporations generated over the centuries in the Caribbean as they funneled products and profits quickly overseas.[97] His finding has a much broader resonance that continues to be overlooked by plantation supporters who repeat a globally traveling mantra that equates the arrival of plantations with prosperity and rural development. At a finer grain, research by anthropologists Michel-Rolph Trouillot, Julian Steward, Eric Wolf, and Sydney Mintz exposed diverse connections between planta-tions and surrounding populations variously engaged in seasonal plantation work or farming, an insight we build on with our concept of the plantation zone as a variegated space.[98]

Highlighting the co-constitution of plantations and their social milieu, sociologist Edgar Thompson argued that slave plantations of the US South did not survive alone but as elements in a constellation of institutions such as church, state, and school that were laced through with concepts of race.[99] Sydney Mintz built on Thompson's work as he traced a trajectory from sugar plantations through patterns of consumption and on to the history of global capitalism.[100] Contemporary scholars attentive to black geographies such as Katherine McKittrick, Deborah Thomas, and Michaeline Crichlow argue that the effects of racialized plantation systems continue to resonate in the United States and in Caribbean social orders centuries after the end of slavery, albeit in diverse and uneven ways.[101] As these scholars show, the new worlds that plantations make stretch not only into surrounding areas, our main focus in this book, but far beyond their spatial and temporal boundaries.

The machinic quality of plantations, their species reduction, replicability, and scalability are the world-making effects emphasized by Donna Haraway, Anna Tsing, and interlocutors who suggest that the past five hundred years could be named the "plantationocene." In "their sixteenth- and seventeenth-century sugarcane plantations in Brazil," writes Tsing, "Portuguese planters stumbled on a formula for smooth expansion. They crafted self-contained, interchangeable project elements, as follows: exterminate local people and plants; prepare now-empty, unclaimed land; and bring in exotic and isolated labor and crops for production. This landscape model of scalability became an inspiration for later industrialization and modernization."[102] Tsing's description captures a core feature of plantation formats but as Tsing recognizes, and as our research in Tanjung confirms, the operations needed to establish and run plantations are more complex than the model suggests. People and plants are not quite exterminated; land is not quite emptied; labor is not quite isolated; and plantations are welcomed and opposed by different social forces and nonhuman associates that render them fragile on multiple fronts.

Our ethnographic analysis attends to the material fixity of plantations and the formidable powers that support them, and to their fragility and the ongoing challenge of holding apparent settlements in place. We take inspiration from Alexei Yurchak's account of Soviet people's experience of socialism before it collapsed, a mood captured in the title of his book: *Everything Was Forever, Until It Was No More.* Yurchak argues that the collapse was

> completely unexpected by most Soviet people and yet, as soon as people realized that something unexpected was taking place, most of them also immediately realized that they had actually been prepared for that unexpected change. . . . For years that system managed to inhabit

incommensurable positions: it was everlasting and steadily declining, full of vigor and bleakness, dedicated to high ideals and devoid of them. None of these positions was a mask. They were each real and . . . mutually constitutive.[103]

The incommensurability identified by Yurchak is manifest in the contradictory spaces, practices, and affective states that are readily encountered in a plantation zone. From one perspective Indonesia's plantations are exemplary sites of modernity. They begin with the production of a tabula rasa and the use of bulldozers to remove trees, carve terraces into hillsides, and obliterate signs of former cultivation. The replacement of diverse species with uniform rows of crops, together with landscaped and guarded offices, housing complexes, and massive mills, make plantation professionals proud. From other perspectives, a plantation landscape is a site of ruination and vehicle of loss. There is no single spatiality dictated by state and corporate plans.

Following Donald Moore, we attend to the "consequential materiality of milieu" while recognizing that plantations are "entangled landscapes" in which "multiple spatialities" mingle and diverge across axes of inequality, identity, and power.[104] We draw further insight from Yael Navaro-Yashin, who shows how architectural forms, objects, and administrative practices come to have affective force. She examines "the eeriness discharged" by abandoned or looted objects; fear or anxiety due to "what might happen to you if you step outside your proper polity"; and melancholy experienced as "a loss of a sense of moral integrity."[105] In this spirit we dwell on photos to explore the affects generated by spaces, objects, and practices based on our own experiences and those recounted by interlocutors (figure I.2).

Attending to the "materiality of milieu" leads us to consider how plantations' spatial boundaries and corporate boundary-making practices (e.g., the recruitment and retirement of workers, the distinction between residents and visitors, and the difference between the physical layout of a plantation and surrounding farms and villages) produce a differentiated sense of belonging. We identify practices that alternately bind workers and managers to their employer and drive them away. We ask which engagements with humans, nonhuman species, and technology become sources of pride and which generate alienation or revulsion. We track how bureaucrats, managers, workers, and villagers become complicit in the production of harms and the unease their complicity generates. In the contexts examined by Navaro-Yashin (a "make-believe space" of unrecognized nationhood) and Yurchak

FIGURE I.2 Dead Palms

Multiple spatialities with different affective resonance are well illustrated in this photo of dead oil palms. Oil palms dominate plantation landscapes but do not eliminate other life forms: there are insects and fungi, ferns and lichens, grasses and shrubs that compete with palms for light, water, and nutrition; rats that eat palm fruit; snakes that eat rats and disturb plantation workers; and cattle that workers raise to supplement their incomes. The palms in this picture were injected with herbicide to kill them because they were too tall to be harvested by men using a scythe attached to a long pole, the industry's preferred low-cost technology. To Pujo the dead palms looked like zombie soldiers, tragic figures awaiting new marching orders that would never come. For workers nearing retirement the dead palms were a scary reminder of their own disposability. To former landholders the killings signaled disrespect for mother nature; more alarmingly, the new palm seedlings that workers had planted underneath the dying palms indicated that the corporation planned to renew its concession. For managers the dead palms were as they should be, but the seedlings were an embarrassment: they were overgrown with weeds and the "horseshoe" terraces on which they were planted were undersized. A young man hired by a contractor to dig the terraces told us that the contractor had colluded with the manager to bill Natco IDR60,000 (USD6) per terrace, yet he only received IDR17,000 (USD1.70) for backbreaking work in the heat with a hoe. Offended by what he saw as managers' excessive greed, the young man made his terraces smaller than required but just big enough to keep his job. PHOTO: STÉPHANE BERNARD.

(late Soviet rule), people who did not necessarily articulate explicit critiques nevertheless experienced the discomfort of living a life in which nothing was quite (or only) what it claimed to be. These were worlds of hypocrisy, betrayal, theater, public secrets, and living lies as well as hope and high ideals. The plantation life we encountered in Tanjung had the same doubled character: the rational bureaucratic machine was also a marauding giant; managers were both technicians and thieves; promises of prosperity were both true and false; the environment was both clean and crawling with parasites; everyone sensed that something was quite wrong with plantation life, but it was a form they knew how to navigate.

Jamaican novelist and scholar Sylvia Wynter offers critical insights on the doubled character of plantation life and its profoundly ambivalent affects. She locates a fulcrum of ambivalence in the dyad of "the plantation and the plot." While the plantation furnished the official narrative of slave plantation life, Wynter argues that it was the plot—the patch of ground allocated to slaves for self-provisioning—that furnished its "secretive histories." Crucially, she recognizes the life-affirming character of the plot without evading its contradictions. Farm plots that enabled slave survival, creativity, and sociality also increased plantation profits by reducing the cost of food slave owners needed to supply. Building on Wynter's work, Katherine McKittrick suggests that the plot "illustrates a social order that is developed within the context of a dehumanizing system," an order that is both dissident and complicit.[106] Workers in Tanjung were not allocated subsistence plots, but they did engage in theft and predation as modes of survival and protest. Theft bound workers to plantations but left them with a bad taste; becoming a thief had elements of victory, but it was hardly a cause for celebration.

....

We approached our research and writing with a sense of urgency. City dwellers in Malaysia, Indonesia, and Singapore know plantations mainly by the smog that can torment them for months on end: thick acrid air from forest fires, usually attributed to plantation land clearing. Indonesian media seldom cover rural areas that seem peripheral to the country's economic and political dynamics. Land conflicts, corruption, protests, and blockades are familiar newsfare in cities close to plantation zones, but only the most egregious cases involving injury or death cause a stir.[107] Decades of critique by differently positioned observers have challenged but not dislodged the claim that plantation corporations bring prosperity to rural areas. The debate over oil palm is especially polarized. On one side are politicians, officials, and corporate supporters who stress the oil palm industry's contribution to national prosperity. On the other side are critics who highlight the ecological risks of monocrop production, forest and species loss, and violations of human and labor rights.[108] Many observers are unsure how to weigh benefits and harms.

In 2012 the district head of Sanggau opened a seminar we organized to present our research findings with an upbeat message: Sanggau was booming because of oil palm. Pak Jaelani, a prominent Dayak elder who attended the seminar, was skeptical. He proposed a program of ground-checking. "Three times I have proposed to the provincial parliament that we need a team of politicians, officials, intellectuals, companies, farmers and NGOs to go to the field together, after we prepare a questionnaire, to find out for sure: can oil palm provide for our wellbeing into the future? If so, then we can all agree but if not, why do we continue?" The massive presence of oil palm in Sanggau District makes the question Pak Jaelani posed fundamental: Can oil palm provide for people's wellbeing into the future or not? He accurately noted that there is very little data with which to answer the question.

In Kalimantan most of the oil palm is grown by plantation corporations whose presence continues to expand on the basis of promised benefits that have not been confirmed, while many reported harms are not addressed. Our book delves deeply into the processes and practices that produce both benefits and harms in the plantation zone and distribute them unevenly. Its primary purpose, however, is to explore how plantation corporations remake landscapes and livelihoods, produce new subjects, and generate novel forms of life.

Our examination proceeds by posing a series of questions.

In chapter 1 we ask: *How did Natco and Priva become established in Tanjung, and what novel sets of relations did their presence generate?* We examine the premises embedded in land acquisition, the tactics used to acquire and hold on to land, and the fragilities that resulted for both the occupiers and the occupied Malay and Dayak population.

In chapter 2 we ask: *Who worked in these two plantations and why?* Contemporary plantation workers are not bonded, hence workers' presence is an indicator of how they assess bodily, financial, and moral risks and rewards. We examine how Natco and Priva hired and expelled workers, the political technologies that secured a fragile compliance, and the predatory relations that emerged.

In chapter 3 we ask: *What did it mean for farmers to be bound to a corporation?* We develop our analysis by contrasting the extreme fragility of oil palm outgrowers whose livelihoods depended on Priva with the relative robustness of independent Malay and Dayak farmers who controlled their own land, labor, and investments.

In chapter 4 we ask: *What were the forms of life that emerged in the plantation zone?* We examine the everyday operation of law as it both enabled and constrained corporate operations, the hierarchies and tensions engendered by the modernity-project at Natco, and the daily struggles of former landholders living in tiny enclaves that were both occupied and abandoned.

In chapter 5 we ask: *Why are corporate oil palm plantations still expanding across Indonesia?* Twenty years of critical scrutiny have failed to dislodge the argument that plantation corporations bring prosperity to remote areas, and reforms to make plantations more "sustainable" are giving corporate occupation new life. We explore the limits of reform agendas and the powers deployed to support corporations at smallholders' expense.

Our conclusion highlights the role of corporate occupation in extending the reach of global capital and conscripting millions of rural Indonesians to a plantation life the terms of which they cannot control.

1

Establishing Plantations

Plantations that originate in corporate mandates, investor dreams, and the schemes of bureaucrats and politicians have to be established somewhere, on specific patches of ground that have their own history, geography, and population. In this chapter we ask: How did Natco and Priva become established in the subdistrict of Tanjung and what novel sets of relations did their presence generate? The two corporations arrived bearing different assumptions about the land rights of the in situ population, and they had different tactics for land acquisition. Natco made a unilateral grab backed by force that set up a single line of fracture between the corporation and customary landholders who continued to live nearby. Priva's process created multiple fractures as it turned village leaders into collaborators, set neighbors and kin against one another, and made many people complicit with the occupation.

The story began in 1980 when Sanggau District was selected by the state-owned plantation corporation PTPN as the site to expand operations from its base in Sumatra's colonial-era plantation zone. In the subdistrict of Tanjung,

PTPN blazed a trail that four private corporations soon followed. The extent of the occupation was revealed to us on our first visit to the subdistrict office when an official turned to the cabinet behind his desk to pull out a rolled map. "This subdistrict is a plantation zone," he said, pointing to the five shaded blocks that together took up around half the subdistrict land area (map 1.1). The map was made by the Sanggau District Plantation Department around 1996 and showed the borders of concessions that had already been approved. Its precondition was a well-worn colonial assumption: even if there happened to be some natives on the spot, their presence was not significant enough to interrupt the grand vision of corporate-led development. But to proceed from the map to actual plantations, the corporations had to take hold of their assigned blocks and deal with customary landholders, a process we track for the two blocks that became the site of our research (map 1.2).

Holding the Line at Natco

PTPN had a mandate to bring modernity and prosperity to Kalimantan's supposedly backward and neglected regions: "We called it Project Sanggau," a manager recalled. The project was to install 18,000 hectares of oil palm plantation divided into four units, one of which was Natco, with an area around 5,000 hectares. Natco's managers were mainly Bataks who had risen through the ranks in Sumatra's dense plantation zone, which dated from colonial times. Alongside technical and managerial skills, they had absorbed a colonial attitude. They saw themselves as pioneers tasked with taming the wilderness and putting order in its place. "The Dayaks had not built anything here, they didn't even wear clothes," one manager remarked. His characterization portrayed villagers as static, primitive, unproductive, and socially distinct from the pioneering "we" of Project Sanggau.[1]

The manager's way of valuing people and landscapes demanded quite specific intellectual work. It ignored the transformations of the preceding centuries during which eight different Dayak groups speaking distinct languages as well as Malays and Banjars had moved into the area to grow rice and harvest forest products destined for world markets. It overlooked their history of adaptation: they had lived for seven decades as neighbors of a colonial rubber plantation that preceded Natco at the same site; they had adopted rubber as their own principal cash crop and forged relations with Chinese rubber traders; and they had absorbed two generations of Javanese ex-plantation workers who married into the local population. The manager's failure to note that

MAP 1.1 Tanjung Subdistrict Plantation Zone

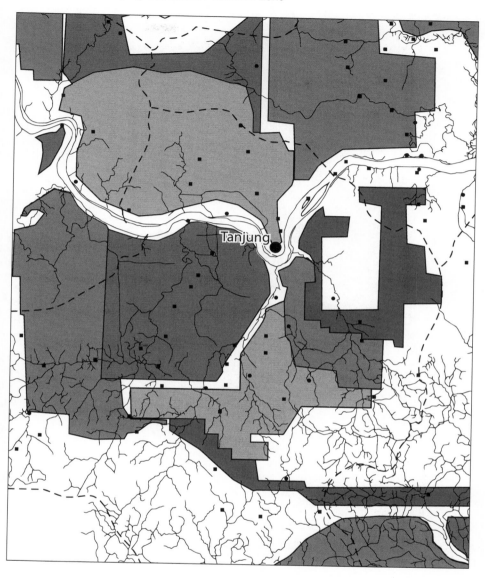

The shaded blocks shown on the map are plantation concessions; white areas are strips of residual village land along rivers and state-claimed forestland that might yet be released for plantation development. The tiny dark squares dotted inside and around the shaded blocks tell a big story. They mark the original hamlets of Dayak and Malay villagers who were not evicted when the corporations arrived. Instead, their hamlets were "enclaved"—excised from the corporate concessions but shorn of farmland—hence the tiny size of the squares. Formally, corporations have no responsibility for the enclaves, although life there is profoundly shaped by their presence. MAP: DINAS PERKEBUNAN SANGGAU/D. L. GUMELAR.

MAP 1.2 Field Research Site

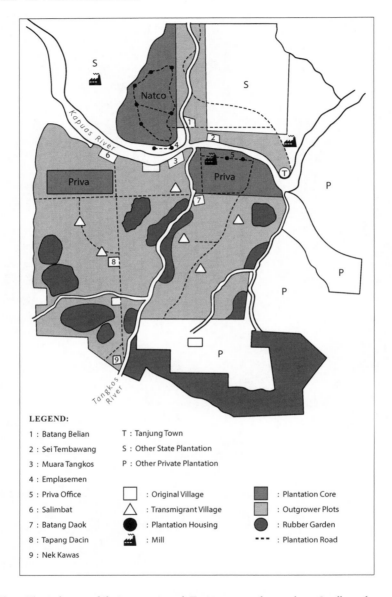

LEGEND:

1 : Batang Belian
2 : Sei Tembawang
3 : Muara Tangkos
4 : Emplasemen
5 : Priva Office
6 : Salimbat
7 : Batang Daok
8 : Tapang Dacin
9 : Nek Kawas

T : Tanjung Town
S : Other State Plantation
P : Other Private Plantation

☐ : Original Village
△ : Transmigrant Village
● : Plantation Housing
🏭 : Mill

▨ : Plantation Core
▨ : Outgrower Plots
● : Rubber Garden
--- : Plantation Road

From Natco the motorbike journey to reach Tanjung town takes one hour. Small wooden boats ferry people and motorbikes across the river from Natco to Muara Tangkos. From Muara Tangkos to Nek Kawas takes around three hours by motorbike, a distance of 22 kilometers (13½ miles) made onerous by the poor quality of the roads that Priva built to connect its out-grower plots to the mill. Alongside the plantation roads are several patches of rubber that were reserved by their owners when Priva arrived, making corporate occupation of the concession area incomplete. MAP: F. D. PRATAMA/D. L. GUMELAR.

the local population was productive, multilingual, and heterogenous was no accident. Attending to local history would undermine the colonial premise of corporate occupation and the sharp social boundary that separated the occupiers from the people whose land and livelihoods they displaced.

Origin Stories

Project Sanggau's official inaugural document emphasizes the local population's backwardness. After noting that some villagers were unwilling to release their land, causing delays, it continues, "The index of people's motivation is low due to their low demand for necessities. In addition to that, their skill and knowledge are not adequate. All this results in low working capacity. Yet with the opening of big and modern estates in the remote area of West Kalimantan there seemed to be an improvement of the people's way of thinking and living."[2] A table that lists construction projects completed by PTPN from 1979 to 1984 has the title, "The First Oil Palm Estate and Palm Oil Mill Built by the Dayak People of West Kalimantan." The title is inaccurate: Dayak people did not build the mills or the plantations; they were designed by Batak plantation managers and built by Javanese migrant workers. Dayaks were largely excluded. Perhaps the authors hoped that the reference to Dayak agency would assuage Dayak political leaders who had vigorously opposed PTPN's plans. The leaders were especially alarmed by the plan to allocate out-grower plots to thousands of transmigrants from other islands. They accurately foretold that future generations of Dayak farmers would be squeezed for land and, collectively, Dayaks would lose territorial control: they would live under occupation. Dayak leaders were successful in rolling back the proposed transmigration scheme from 3,000 to 350 families, but the rest of Project Sanggau went ahead.[3]

The area eventually taken over by Natco had changed hands several times. In 1899 the British-owned Kapuas Rubber Corporation had obtained a seventy-five-year concession for 12,000 hectares. The concession was taken over by a Dutch corporation NV Kapoewas Rubber Maatschappij in 1910, then nationalized in 1958 and placed under the control of an army-owned corporation NV Agris, which went bankrupt in the 1970s.[4] Throughout the seventy-five-year concession only 600 hectares was ever planted with rubber. Local Malay and Dayak farmers continued to cultivate rice on the remaining 11,400 hectares. A Dayak elder Pak Jamin from the hamlet of Salimbat recalled people taking huge baskets with 100 kilograms (220 pounds) of rice to the company's representative each harvest to acknowledge that they were farming on company land. The concession was so huge, however, that some villagers may not have been aware that the land they farmed had a paper claimant. Villagers did not work for the Dutch corporation that hired workers directly from Java on three-year contracts. As neighbors of the plantation, their relations with managers and workers were generally cordial. Pak Jamin's parents told him that a Dutch manager had spoken to them directly, saying, "You should plant some of this rubber, it will be good for your family." Villagers did indeed plant rubber and sold their rubber sheets to Chinese traders who married into local Dayak communities, a pattern that continued in 2015 in upriver areas beyond the reach of oil palm.

Cordial relations and peaceful coexistence continued after the rubber plantation was taken over by NV Agris. Born in 1942, Dayak elder Pak Doan of Batang Belian used to play soccer with NV Agris workers. His hamlet had about a dozen houses and plenty of land to grow swidden rice. "It was like being in the middle of the sea," he recalled. "We had as much land as we wanted. . . . In a good year we harvested enough rice to last for three years. We had vegetables and wild pigs, and cash from the rubber trees we planted." All this changed in 1980 when Natco took over part of the 12,000 hectare expired concession and started to plant oil palm. There were no negotiations. From Natco's perspective there was no need to seek permission from villagers because their customary land rights, if any, had been abrogated in 1899 with the initial concession. Pak Doan remembered that a team of officials including the district head's deputy, the subdistrict head, and a surveyor came to ask his father to sign a document he couldn't read: "He just believed what they told him, that the land would be returned to them after twenty-five years, and the company would give them jobs."

Villagers had no copies of the documents they signed, which probably related to the compensation Natco agreed to pay for their rubber and fruit trees (not for the land). "Natco cleared all the land at once," Pak Doan recalled. "Some people tried to plant rice between the young palms, but the company stopped them." From Pak Doan's perspective this was an absurd restriction: Why not use good, clear land to grow food for a few years while the palms were still small? He countered plantation managers' insistence on monoculture with his own knowledge of how different plants can co-exist and offered grounds for renewed relations of mutual accommodation between villagers and the corporation, but to no avail. Not only did Natco occupy a huge area; it arrived with overwhelming force, wielding bulldozers to tear down rubber trees and move soil, accompanied by soldiers and armed police. The use of force and the failure to negotiate were clear signs that managers and officials did not view villagers as potential interlocutors or as subjects with rights. They saw them as social inferiors and as a threat to orderly development (figure 1.1). "Now we are braver," Pak Doan said, "we fight back."

Pak Jamin argued that Natco's decision back in 1980 to compensate farmers only for their fruit and rubber trees was unfair. "They should have paid us for the axe head," he said, "because it was our hard work that cleared the land. Natco saved a lot of money because we made our rice fields there." He was applying an indigenous principle common across Southeast Asia in

FIGURE 1.1 Guarding against Arson

On our first morning at Natco a manager took us on a tour of the plantation. The housing blocks looked like a military camp because of the orderly layout, checkpoints, and guards. This was not a place someone could enter without permission. Signposts made this clear: "Visitors must report." As we drove around the plantation, we found the uniform rows of palms that spread out endlessly on all sides unsettling, and the absence of a human presence to enliven the landscape made it inhospitable. The plantation roads had no names, just numbers written in code. We did not see any workers until we stopped at a guard hut built on a small hill. There were four guards, all Dayak. Their task was to look out for fires. Villagers set fire to the dying palms to catch palm tree rats and squirrels that dropped out half-dead. They speared them to eat or to sell—IDR15,000 (USD1.50) for a squirrel and IDR10,000 (USD1) for a fat rat. Fire could spread and destroy the young palm seedlings. Whether accident or arson, such fires reminded managers that signposts were not enough to seal the plantation from its neighbors, hence the need for guards. PHOTO: TANIA LI.

which labor is the source of property: if you create something through your own sweat, it is yours.[5] He did not dispute the idea of a government-issued concession as one basis for property, but he wanted the indigenous property system to be recognized as well. His argument emphasized individual property rights, not communal territory, probably because so many different Dayak groups had moved into the area over the preceding century that no group asserted customary jurisdiction over the entire concession area.

Individual compensation for villagers' trees was better than nothing, but even that was not paid as promised. A cabal of officials stole much of the compensation money, a theft big enough to cause a scandal that was reported in the newspapers and discussed in the district parliament.[6] Five years later a formal investigation found that thirty-one government officials had been involved, including six from the land office, seven from the district office, four from the office of education and culture, three village heads, four staff from the district court, two from religious affairs, four from the subdistrict office, and one from the district attorney's office. Officials from the PTPN head office and the district military office were also suspected. Yet impunity ruled: the district attorney's office did not prosecute.[7] The extent of the network revealed by the investigation offers a glimpse into the crony-corporate cabal that mobilized to capture a share of plantation wealth even before production commenced. Most villagers received little or no money for their trees. Some worked as day laborers during the plantation's establishment phase, but Natco did not hire them in permanent positions as it had promised. They continued to tap the rubber trees that remained in their tiny enclaves, but they could no longer grow rice.

Reformasi

Villagers we met in Malay and Dayak hamlets "enclaved" in and around Natco had no quarrel with oil palm, which they saw as a lucrative crop they wanted to add to their own farm repertoires. They had requested the government to supply them with oil palm seedlings to plant on their own land as early as 1985 but received no response.[8] Their grievance was with Natco, the corporation that had occupied their land and failed to provide them with decent jobs; and with its managers who did not treat them as social equals, people who should be consulted on plantation matters. A Dayak elder described the affects generated by the position they were placed in as "becoming ghosts in our own land," a phrase that suggests Natco and its government allies looked right through them, as if they were not there.[9]

After the fall of Suharto in 1998 villagers watched TV broadcasts about New Order corruption and the mobilization of people in all corners of the archipelago protesting against decades of land seizure and demanding *reformasi* (reform). A Dayak political movement emerged in West Kalimantan with the ambition of claiming a position for Dayaks that was equal to that of other ethnic groups in the national arena. No longer would Dayaks be treated as social inferiors, nor would corporations bearing concession licenses issued in Jakarta grab their timber or land. The immediate target of Dayak assertiveness was a migrant minority from the Indonesian island of Madura who had settled in Kalimantan over many decades. In 1997 and 1999 Dayaks united to evict tens of thousands of Madurese from towns and rural areas and there were hundreds of violent deaths. The Madurese were a small group and not especially powerful, but by evicting them aspiring Dayak political leaders sent the message that they planned to reclaim their land and authority, and they were ready to use violence to achieve their aims. It is a message they continue to repeat (figure 1.2).[10]

FIGURE 1.2 Dayak Warriors Parade in Pontianak City

In 2012 Pujo watched a Dayak parade featuring "warriors" in black-and-red costumes carrying bush knives, who took threatening poses and issued war cries. Pontianak City is the location of plantation corporation offices and the homes of plantation managers like the one pictured in the background of this figure, complete with a metal fence and two cars. The atmosphere during the parade was tense, and the sense of threat was so real that Pujo noticed onlookers step back when the warriors passed by. PHOTO: PUJO SEMEDI.

The climate of reformasi and Dayak assertiveness were the context for a dramatic confrontation at Natco in 1998, when a united front of Dayak and Malay villagers set up blockades at seven key choke points and demanded redress for the seizure of their land. These were unusual times when it seemed possible, briefly, to construct a new relationship between villagers and the state plantation corporation that was directly implicated in the greed and corruption of the New Order regime.[11] The confrontation involved fifteen Malay and Dayak villages led by their headmen with the support of the sub-district head—officials who had been complicit with the occupation until that point. Participants in the blockade recalled that village youth associations played a big role. For a week they maintained a twenty-four-hour guard of two hundred men drawn from participating villages in rotation. Meanwhile the headmen met to formulate demands.

The blockade was the first time the occupied population had mobilized collectively and forcefully, a significant event in itself, but the content of villagers' demands was modest. They wanted some land to be returned, an out-grower scheme, and plantation jobs. The dispute went before the district head in Sanggau town where hundreds of villagers demonstrated in the street; then it went to the province where officials brokered a settlement. "We were reformed (*direformasi*) in 1998," a Natco manager recalled. "Villagers said we were arrogant (*sombong*). We were really scared at that time because we had seen the attacks on the Madurese on TV. None of us in the plantation dared to confront them. The protestors demanded to see the company director, so he came from Pontianak. Dayak leaders killed a pig and put the pig's blood on their hands before they shook his hand—knowing he was Muslim."

Accusing plantation managers of arrogance and insisting on meeting the director in person were demands to form a direct human relationship with a person in authority; villagers were not satisfied with dealing with the giant's minions. To achieve this end they had used a show of force. But PTPN directors refused to give up any land at all, arguing that the corporation held a legal concession, and the blockade reinforced managers' conviction that Dayaks were wild and irrational people with whom negotiation was neither possible nor necessary. A Natco public relations manager confirmed his patronizing approach: "This Dayak guy came to my office claiming that 100 hectares of the plantation belonged to his family. He asked for a lot of hectares and palms as compensation. I asked him why he was making the claim now, not in 1981? He came back several times. I gave him *tuak* (rice wine) to drink. Others came too. After a while, they started to say I was a good man because I gave them tuak, and they forgot about their claims. It is an art to manage them." Another manager noted that pacification was hard work. "Making them understand things is the hardest part of my job," he explained. "They call me a colonial and a thief. It is OK if it is just a matter of cursing. I'm a Batak, I'm used to that. I tell them we came here to make a living, to make friends, not to create problems."

Managers commented that they missed the clarity that General Suharto's New Order rule once supplied. "When Natco began its work in 1980," a senior manager observed, "plantations were right, villagers were wrong." Since reformasi villagers had become bolder. "They say all this land belongs to them. If there is any small problem, they make demands or impose customary fines and put up blockades." He refused to concede ground. "If they want to be treated well, they have to cooperate with us. If not, I am ready for the big fight. We are outsiders here and if we give up too much, it will just get worse, because they will think we are afraid." The manager's explicit recognition that the plantation was an occupying force that villagers could be expected to contest ("we are outsiders here") was unusual. In other conversations he did not describe villagers as adversaries in a "big fight" but as anarchists and thieves. Several managers confirmed that all the plantations in Sanggau faced the same problems: blockaded mills and stolen palm fruit. They echoed the standard line that located the source of Natco's problems in the surrounding villages where lazy, ignorant, and ungrateful villagers failed to understand the progress the corporation had brought to their region.

At the time of our research, relations between Natco and surrounding villages were tense. Villagers were frustrated at the limited settlement they achieved with their blockade in 1998 and suspected that some of the headmen who had negotiated on their behalf had sold them out. Natco had promised to provide them with an out-grower scheme and more plantation jobs. These were formal promises, written on a document signed in 1999 by the village heads, the subdistrict head, and representatives of the army and police. The document and its signatures had affective force: they made villagers feel their demands had been heard and taken seriously. A copy was duly pasted on the wall of the out-grower co-op. But a decade later the promised jobs had not materialized, and the out-grower scheme was beset with problems.

The out-grower scheme was of the type called KKPA (Kredit Koperasi Primer Anggota, primary co-op credit) in which Natco took out a bank loan to pay for planting oil palm on villagers' own land, and out-growers had to repay the debt by selling their fruit to Natco through a co-op. But villagers squeezed into enclaves were already short of land and some had no land at all to convert into out-grower plots. Delay was another problem: the scheme was not implemented until 2005, allowing time for brokers to buy up land from villagers who were short of cash.[12] The co-op was dysfunctional and the financial arrangements obscure. Despite numerous requests Natco managers either did not or could not tell out-growers how much money Natco had borrowed from the bank for plot preparation, hence how much debt they had to repay. In protest, some out-growers bypassed the co-op and stopped repaying their debt. Confrontations again became physical. Managers attempted to block rogue out-growers by identifying choke points where they could install gates and guards to prevent the outflow of fruit except on designated harvest days. Pak Luwar, a leader in the Dayak hamlet of Batang Belian, noted that channels for making informal arrangements with people in power had closed down: "Before, the police would tip us off so we could sneak through and get our harvest out, but now they just make arrests. There is a real chance of clashes. The police should look at who is really in the wrong here and correct the company, not just us."

Occupation Renewed

Around 2010 a new site of overt conflict opened up: replanting the aging palms, and the renewal of the concession. Natco managers argued that they had no obligation to consult with former land holders about the renewal since the land had always belonged to the state. Village leaders were appalled that the occupation could be renewed without taking any account of their presence or perspectives. The renewal confirmed that the attempt they had made in 1999 to assert a position as interlocutors of the management team had achieved nothing. The unilateral format of the occupation was still intact, and they had no say in its terms. They pushed back on the managers' claims about law by citing law. They pointed out that Natco's own legal foundation was not solid: it had failed to pay them the compensation it had promised back in 1980; it had operated without a legal basis for five years before it received its concession license (HGU) in 1985; and it failed to deliver the out-grower scheme as per the 1999 agreement.

Villagers' deeper reason for renewing the struggle against Natco was a crisis of livelihoods and rising frustration in the enclaves where a new generation had come of age watching other people prosper while they had no access to oil palm wealth. The out-grower scheme had taken up much of the residual land in the enclaves, and there were no more rubber trees to tap. Villagers saved and borrowed to buy additional land for their children, but the price was astronomically high. As Natco started to replant its aging palms, it extended the planted area right up to the edge of the enclaves and alongside streams, closing off small spaces villagers had used to plant vegetables and graze cattle. The problem was especially acute in Batang Belian where the enclave was tiny. "Did you see the red signs on your way here?" Pak Luwar asked. "The company put them there to warn us: Do not plant, do not harvest." There were several cases of arson and one arrest, as irate villagers protested what they saw as a new enclosure. "We have to fight the company," Pak Luwar insisted, "they have to give up some land. We understand they can't give up all of it, but they have to give us some, so we too have a share." He was desperate and spoke with emotion: "I'm stressed all the time," he said. "I get panic attacks. Where will my children and grandchildren go? If you ask me that question, I can't answer it. None of us here can answer it. It was all set up wrong from the start. The company took all our land and gave us nothing. Now there is oil palm everywhere except the graveyard."

Pak Luwar was hoping for another mass mobilization against the concession renewal, but it was not clear that village headmen would unite to press their demands as they had in 1999. He said it was too risky for anyone to act alone. Action had to be coordinated, but time was passing. "Natco went ahead with replanting without saying a word. It shouldn't do that. This is our place. We are the original people here. Maybe we don't have documents to prove that the company promised to return the land to us in twenty-five years, but the old people remember it clearly. Now the company is saying it was thirty-five." For Pak Luwar "original people" meant the people on the spot who had a right to be consulted. He felt they should receive a "rightful share" of plantation wealth, which he understood as a share that would enable villagers to prosper for as long as the company was present in their midst.[13] For him it was not a finite amount, nor could it be covered by a one-off payment. Its horizon was future oriented and intergenerational. It meant that his grandchildren would not ask, "Why is the company so rich while we have nothing?"

Dayak leader Pak Jamin from Salimbat, who was active in the 1998 blockade and renowned for his tough stance, said that since replanting started, delegations from different villages had come to ask him when they would take action but he was reluctant. He confirmed that Natco's concession was indeed thirty-five years, so they had to wait until it expired in 2020. Pak Jamin's position was ambiguous: he led protests against Natco and Priva, and he was also paid by both companies to help manage tensions and keep villagers in line. He could be friend or foe to the companies, and his access to government officials combined with his bullying style of leadership made everyone a bit afraid of him. When we visited his house, he had many young men milling around, presumably on standby should a show of force be required.

Whether or not villagers succeed in mobilizing collectively to challenge Natco's renewal, they planned to continue to make demands. Pak Yusuf, a leader in the Malay enclave of Sei Tembawang, put his position thus:

> Just imagine if from the beginning the company had a good model. We wouldn't just be the audience. They think we're standing in the way of development. So until there is proper leadership and a good direction, we'll keep on making demands. They should give the people some land, one plot per household. I don't think it would be such a problem for them. People here are surviving with just half an out-grower plot; one would be even better. It would help. Like that the people could progress. But we have such bitter experiences. Now whatever Natco proposes we won't agree.

Pak Luwar, Pak Yusuf, and other Dayak and Malay villagers wanted respect— "a good model . . . proper leadership . . . a good direction." They knew they could not remove the occupying force, so they sought small, concrete improvements like additional out-grower plots to help with immediate livelihood needs. A return of some of their land would be even more helpful as it would enable them to regain their economic autonomy and grow oil palm independently, which farmers who still had some land were already doing enthusiastically.

Buying Compliance at Priva

Priva's mode of land acquisition was quite distinct from Natco, hinging more on compliance, both purchased and coerced. The privately owned corporation had its mill and office block directly opposite Natco across the Kapuas with a concession that reached 22 kilometers (13½ miles) into the hinterland along the Tangkos tributary. The owner was Pak Wakijan, an Indonesian of Chinese descent. We never met Pak Wakijan and we were unable to access Priva's archives, so we don't know the story of how or why this particular plantation came to be here.[14] Pak Wakijan's previous experience was in timber extraction. By all accounts he was eccentric. Twice a year he would arrive by helicopter to visit for a few days. He stayed at the plantation's executive guest house, visited the office, and drove around with the manager to inspect operations. If it was Sunday, he attended church. He came with pockets full of IDR10,000 (USD1) notes that he handed out to workers he met. This was strange in itself, but more so because he made the gift with his left hand, which Indonesians regard as unclean. According to multiple observers the behavior was consistent and deliberate: he withdrew the money from his pocket with his right hand but transferred it to the left before giving it away. One worker asked him why he did this: "He told me it is to get rid of bad luck. Maybe he'll give ten thousand and get back twenty." Pak Wakijan's conduct might have been superstitious or simply idiosyncratic, or it might signal his view of workers as objects whose bodies he could use to generate more wealth for himself just by handing them money the wrong way. His practice also implicated workers as they would say, "Hey, Pak Wakijan is here, let's go get some money!" The amount was not trivial. For a casual worker it was equivalent to half a day's pay.

In addition to the 38,810 hectares of this concession, Pak Wakijan's corporation owned another 5,000 hectare concession nearby, which he sold in 2016 to buy a location permit for yet another concession in another district, this one 17,000 hectares. We return to the story of the new plantation in chapter 5. Our point here is that Pak Wakijan had a huge area of land under his control, and he brought a "plantation life" to tens of thousands of people who—like us—did not meet him, had no access to corporate reports, and had few ways to hold him to account. Managers handled the day-to-day running of the plantation. Some of them were skilled professionals, others were Pak Wakijan's relatives, who workers said were not competent. Overall, managers and workers had a high turnover and they had less institutional memory or company loyalty than we found at Natco. They had no heroic story equivalent to Project Sanggau. For them, installing and sustaining the plantation was a job, not a mission.

Priva started its work in 1990 as a collaboration with the Ministry of Transmigration. It followed a format known as PIR-BUN-Trans. The plan proposed a total transformation of the landscape and the installation of a new form of life for thousands of villagers and transmigrants. The scale was vast. There would be a core plantation of 9,000 hectares worked with hired labor and 18,000 hectares of out-grower palm. Out-grower plots of 2 hectares were to be allocated to nine thousand households who would live in eighteen new settlements of five hundred households and organize their production and marketing through eighteen company-sponsored co-ops.

The plan seemed more attentive to villagers' concerns than that of Natco because it proposed to allocate half the out-grower plots to villagers who agreed to release land. Implicitly, the plan recognized their customary rights to the land—if it was not theirs, they would not need to agree to release it. But the devil was in the details. According to the rules of PIR-BUN-Trans, villagers had to give up their land on a ratio of 3:1. For each 7.5 hectares villagers released, 2.5 hectares would be returned to them in the form of an out-grower plot, a house lot, and a small wooden house, while the balance would go to incoming transmigrants (2.5 hectares per household), and 2.5 hectares to Priva for its core plantation, roads, and facilities.

Villagers who released land had to assume the same debt for out-grower plot preparation as incoming transmigrants who had not contributed land, conditions villagers felt were grossly unfair. They argued that giving up two-thirds of their land was a huge sacrifice that should be recognized and compensated. Making them pay for plot preparation denied the sacrifice. Although the scheme was not an outright grab it was consistent with the colonial chain of reasoning we outlined in the introduction, one in which the corporation and government planners deemed villagers to be people of lesser value whose current farming practices and land rights were not entirely overlooked, but severely discounted (3:1 + debt).

The Map, the Grid, and Company Men

Priva worked from a topographical map in which 1 centimeter represents 2.5 kilometers (1½ miles) without taking into account slope, land quality, or natural obstacles such as swamps. The variegated terrain was just one of many challenges that made the rather precise plan difficult to implement on the ground. Priva handled the process of land acquisition through officially appointed "land release teams," which comprised hamlet and village heads, customary leaders, company representatives, subdistrict officials, army officers, and police.[15] Village and hamlet heads are the representatives of the state at the local level, people to whom villagers normally turn for help in dealing with administrative and other official business. Their appointment to land release teams made them into "company men" (*orang perusahaan*). They became instruments of the occupation, degrading the citizenship of villagers who lost a crucial avenue for defending their interests vis-à-vis the corporation.

The first task of company men was to use both persuasive and coercive power to induce reluctant villagers to give up their land. They were well rewarded for their work. One company man received twenty-one out-grower plots; another received a salary but was not expected to show up for work. One elder who turned against the company when asked to do things he found improper was thrown out and ended up with nothing. Another, Pak Ibrahim, described his involvement with the company like this:

> I gave up my land in the end. That is because the subdistrict head called me to his office four times. He said to me, "If you give up your land you will be safe, but if you keep resisting, you and your family will be on your own." So I gave up my land, 40 hectares, and everyone else followed me. Before no one here had a motorbike and now you see they have satellite TV! The company offered me a job, but I chose to become a contractor for land clearing. First I hired fifty men, then one hundred and finally two hundred, working with bush knives to finish up quickly. It was so easy for me to get money in those days. I bought the wood and cement to build this house and I still had IDR30 million [USD3,000] in hand. In 1994 I moved into the transmigration area and opened a store. I was the village head there from 1994 to 2004.

In Pak Ibrahim's account subdistrict officials were part of the coercion: "If you keep on resisting, you and your family will be on your own." Only if Pak Ibrahim complied would the subdistrict head protect his interest, which he did by recommending Pak Ibrahim as village head. Pak Ibrahim's moral justification for complicity with the occupation was the idea that his neighbors also profited from it (they too got motorbikes and satellite TV). In his old age after he no longer received payments from Priva he turned against the company. He attempted to claim compensation for 20 hectares he said Priva had grabbed from him to use as a seed bed. His case went to court where the judge asked him to show his land title. He had himself used lack of title deeds as an argument to persuade his kin to release their land, but the table had turned.

> I said to the judge, "It does not matter whether you are Dayak or Malay, you know very well that our land title is the act of pioneering the forest. From my grandfather the land was passed to my father and then to me. We do not need documents." Ordinary people are always put in the wrong. The judge knew we didn't have documents, but because he was not fair, he kept asking for them. So we have to accept it. I'm just praying the company mill will burn down. Whether we give in to them or oppose them we still lose. The company is like the communists—they take what they want.

Pak Ibrahim used the label "communist" in the sense given to it by New Order propaganda, which cast communists as violent people intent on grabbing people's property. Seen from another perspective Pak Ibrahim was the villain because he had manipulated scheme memberships, using his position as a company man to enrich himself. Pak Ibrahim seemed to survive the disrupted social relations, but other company men ended up ostracized by neighbors who felt their leaders had sold them out. It was not only personal relationships that were damaged. The entire system of local leadership was thrown into disrepute. Leaders' words could not be trusted, and Pak Ibrahim was but one example. Neighbors pointed out that Pak Ibrahim had obtained nine out-grower plots, one for himself and two for each of his four children. Neighbors knew he had previously been a woodcutter with little inherited land. There was no way he had contributed 40 hectares to the out-grower scheme, as he claimed, still less 67.5 hectares as per the rule (9×7.5).

The planners' assumption that villagers had large areas of unused land they could release for a massive plantation-plus-transmigration program was incorrect. It turned out that the only villagers with landholdings bigger than around 10 hectares in the Tangkos area were rubber traders who had taken over rubber lands from clients who could not pay their debts. By our calculation, the average land area released per household in return for an out-grower plot was 3.5 hectares. Many villagers had only around 5 hectares, not enough for even one scheme membership (7.5 hectares) per the plan. Hence, they were complicit with hamlet heads in inflating the size of their landholdings. Hamlet heads took advantage of the extraordinary power they acquired through their official role as providers of information to Priva. They manipulated maps and lists, fabricated consent, falsified land measurements, and sold scheme memberships to government officials, plantation managers, and others with capital to invest. They both collaborated with the corporation and stole from it, and they stole from their own people. For Ibu Marlina, it was the intimacy of a village headman's betrayal that stood out:

> My mother was a widow. We were five children. She was raising us by tapping rubber and we grew our own rice and vegetables. Our family's rubber garden was right there by the bridge. Then the village head took the land. It was for himself—he ended up with lots of plots and he sold plots to other people. I was young, but I remember him coming to the house, asking my mother to release her land, and promising she would get a plot and other things too—food, sugar, while waiting for the first palm harvest. But it was not true. Only my mother's younger brother got a plot because he was the hamlet head and he insisted. My mother and her other brother received nothing. She didn't press her claim. What could

she do? That headman doesn't even live here anymore. We used to have something of our own, even though it wasn't much. Now this all belongs to the company. We just have to take orders from them and hope they give us work.

To take orders and hope for work is to live under corporate occupation but for Ibu Marlina it was a particular individual who had condemned her to this fate. There was a further, gendered dimension to the loss. According to local Malay and Dayak custom that gives equal inheritance to boys and girls, Ibu Marlina's mother should have received the same share as her brothers, but as a widow she did not feel strong enough to press a claim.

The land release process, which took more than a year, culminated in one crucial document: the list of out-grower scheme members. The company submitted the list to the district head for approval, then forwarded it to the bank that held the title to the out-grower plots until the debt was paid. The official out-grower list was also the basis for membership in the co-op, the key institution that was supposed to support out-grower production and funnel payments. Until they saw the final lists villagers did not know whether or not their names were on them, nor did they know which other names had been added—people who previously owned no land in the area. By then, however, the damage was done, and it was hard to prove who was at fault. Some hamlet heads covered their tracks by burning their copies of the maps and lists on which they had noted the size and location of lands their neighbors released. The copies that should have been stored in the district archive could not be found. Priva managers claimed to have no record of who had given up land. "We used a global system. If a hamlet released 750 hectares we gave them one hundred plots. The details were all handled by the hamlet heads," manager Budi insisted. "Villagers keep coming to us claiming they did not receive their share. We tried to settle the problem by giving out additional plots. We even gave up some of the plantation core. That is why it is so small." Indeed, the plantation core was only 3,800 hectares, not 9,000 hectares as planned, and Priva's final planted area including out-growers was not big enough to make full use of its expensive mill.[16] Budi felt that villagers had manipulated Priva, but the company could not retrace its steps nor buy an enduring peace. Twenty years after land release, villagers continued to protest, open new court cases, and mount periodic blockades demanding that Priva provide the out-grower plots they were due.[17] The complicities and obscurities of the land release process enabled Priva to establish its presence, but also rendered it fragile.

The spatial location of hamlets and their negotiating strategies made a difference to how much land they released. It was especially hard for villagers to retain land designated to become part of Priva's plantation core. In the Malay village of Muara Tangkos landholders who tried to resist by posting private property signs and standing guard over their rubber trees were met with company bulldozers. A collective effort by Dayak villagers in Salimbat was more successful. Salimbat's leaders refused to give up their prime land for Priva's core plantation and insisted that their out-grower plots be located by the Kapuas for ease of access. They also released much less land than scheme rules required, leaving them with plenty of land to plant with oil palm independently. Johan, a Malay from Muara Tangkos who admired the Dayaks' maneuvers, argued that the key to success in a protracted struggle was the first encounter: "This is how it goes in the early stage," he explained. "When a company arrives, it is a stranger. If the locals hang tough the managers will be afraid. But if the locals are afraid, they will carry on being afraid. Whoever wins the first bluff keeps on winning. If the locals win, company managers keep on obeying them." Salimbat's leaders continued to insist that they be treated as masters in their own land, and many Salimbat households prospered, earning enough to expand their independent oil palm holdings, build good houses, and send their children to university. Johan despaired at the poverty of villagers in Muara Tangkos, which he felt was the result of their collective failure to present themselves as a serious counterforce vis-à-vis the occupier from day one.

Villagers in interior hamlets used a different strategy in their attempt to hold on to their land. They took advantage of their remote location and Priva's poor-quality maps to release their sloping and infertile land or land that fell within the protected forest, while keeping the best land for themselves. Their aim was to offer just enough land to attract Priva to build a road into their area, a practice they called "fishing." The cost of their strategy, however, was that Priva was reluctant to maintain these roads because the production from upriver areas was too low to justify the expense. The total number of transmigrant households that arrived was 1,040, far less than the 4,500 in the plan, so Priva did not develop the full number of out-grower plots.[18] Villagers upriver reclaimed land they had previously released, but they feared Priva might seize it later to fill in the missing pieces on its concession grid: the full-scale occupation could still happen (figure 1.3). Alternatively, a different corporation could take over the unused part of the concession with the argument that Priva had failed to develop it. In 2015

FIGURE 1.3 Priva's Uneven Grip

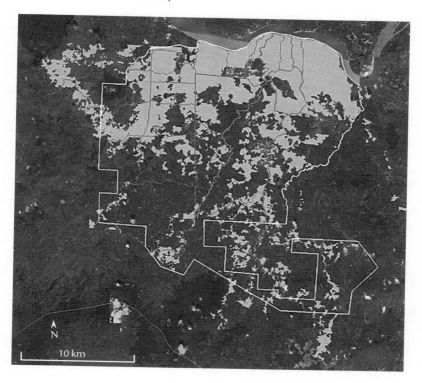

A Google Earth satellite image from 2016, painstakingly cross-checked by research team members with GPS, revealed Priva's uneven grip on its concession land. The white line is the official concession border. The light-colored blocks are planted with oil palm. The light area outside the concession to the left is Salimbat's independently planted palm. Dark areas inside the concession are rubber groves that were successfully withheld from the company by the original landholders. In the lower part of the image, dark predominates because upriver farmers only gave up land along the roadside. PHOTO: AJI PRASETYA.

some upriver village headmen had begun negotiations to see if they could strike a deal along these lines.

"Raining Bush-Knives"

Under the national transmigration program landless families from Java, Bali, and other crowded islands are given "empty" land in Indonesia's remote regions on which to establish model communities and productive farms and set an example for the local population. It is an internal colonization project founded on the assumption that villagers in less densely settled islands are socially inferior and less competent in farming.[19] For Malay and Dayak villagers in Priva's concession area the program rationale was insulting, and the facts were incorrect. They did not have land to spare for incoming transmigrants, and they were more skilled at farming than many of the transmigrants who came from Java's city streets. They resented the privileges transmigrants received as the government's "golden children" captured in the unfair terms of the land release: transmigrants received land for free, while villagers who had released their land still had to pay for plot development. The deduction of a third of their monthly income for debt repayment was a regular reminder of this insult, unfairness, and loss.

Villagers' resentment grew into anger when they realized that some transmigrants were manipulating the program. Many transmigrants left within a year, selling off the wooden houses, tools, cooking pots, and the supply of rice transmigration staff had issued them on arrival. Their more serious fault was to sell the rights to the land they had been given—rights that would result in a land title after the debt was paid off. A detailed review we conducted of five hundred households (282 locals, 218 transmigrants) in one transmigration hamlet showed that eighteen years after the out-grower scheme began, 49 percent of the transmigrants (106) had sold their land rights and 35 percent had left the area. Among local Malays and Dayaks, 72 percent still held their original plots. In the words of Pak Ibrahim, transmigrants "made our land into a business" and he was outraged. Selling assets allocated to them was a mafia practice: transmigrants used their privileged position to capture unearned wealth, a clear indication that they did not respect the sacrifices locals had made.

There were many reasons for transmigrants to sell up and leave: the palms were not ready to harvest, as the Ministry of Transmigration had promised; the price of palm oil was low in the early 1990s; some transmigrants could not adjust to Kalimantan's fierce heat.[20] But the mafia practices that emerged were not idiosyncratic. It is an open secret of the transmigration program that some transmigrants stay only until the plots are allocated, then sell them to other transmigrants or to plantation staff, government officials, merchants, rich farmers, or brokers who prowl new transmigration sites with cash in hand.[21] As a transmigrant explained to us:

> It is a scenario. It goes on all over Indonesia. Transmigration officials are just looking for project funds. They inflate the costs. They don't do a proper site assessment. The planning report is just made up—no one checks the

site. The officials who accompany the transmigrants, the company that transports them by boat, they are all in on it—it is a business. These officials have ordinary salaries but just look at their houses! One or two weeks after the transmigrants arrive at the site someone comes along and says, "I'll just have your land, you can go home now. Can you really stand it here? I don't think so." Brokers lure the transmigrants with money when they are feeling overwhelmed at the sight of all that forest and swamp that has not been cleared.

The purpose of the scenario, according to this observer, was to give outsiders the opportunity to grab or buy land in frontier areas where corporations were building infrastructure, perverting a program designed for the poor to serve the rich. The position of people who sell their allocation is ambiguous in this account: are they victims of false promises or are they knowing participants in the transmigration mafia system, seeking to capture a share of unearned wealth?

Locals could not risk overt protest against the transmigration scheme during the Suharto years, but around 2000 Abidin, a Malay villager from Muara Tangkos, took action. He gathered family members armed with bush-knives and blockaded an out-grower block comprising twenty-seven plots. The hamlet head held one of these plots, and Abidin wanted to force this man to take responsibility for failing to provide his family with the number of plots they were due, which he said was nine—a number that would have provided one plot for each of his siblings. Observers disputed this number, saying there was no way Abidin had really released 47 hectares of land as he claimed, still less 67.5 hectares in return for nine plots, as per the rule. But Abidin focused his claim on a different rule: the prohibition on land selling.

When we visited Abidin in his home he went to his cabinet to pull out a folder of documents. Among these was a one-page document signed by the director general of transmigration in Jakarta that listed five things transmigrants must not do: (1) sell or mortgage their houses, (2) sell or mortgage their land before ten years, (3) abandon the location, (4) gamble and extort, or (5) disobey transmigration rules. The penalty was confiscation of all rights and facilities. For Abidin the document confirmed that his act of repossession had a legal basis: if government officials would not enforce their own rule against land selling, he argued, he was entitled to enforce it himself. Another official document extended the no-selling rule to fifteen years. As he rifled through more documents, he pointed out signatures and ccs to the governor and head of the provincial parliament. "Look here," he said, "if these documents were not important why would high-ranking people sign them? I was brave to fight this because I was in the right." To buy peace the company gave him two extra out-grower plots, but the matter did not end there.

Abidin's forceful action terrified transmigrants at the receiving end. Sujak, head of the farmer's group whose land Abidin targeted, recalled the event as traumatic: "It was raining bush-knives, there was a real possibility of armed attack. I thought if they are going to kill me, so be it. If you want to hold on here, you have to be mentally very strong." Sujak said that if Priva had treated Abidin unfairly he would have helped him to seek redress, but it was wrong for Abidin to attack fellow farmers. While Sujak proposed a vision of comradely equality among out-growers, other transmigrants did not recognize Abidin's actions as a legitimate protest against officials and transmigrants who failed to abide by the rules. Instead, their explanations for Abidin's conduct drew on well-worn tropes about lazy natives prone to irrational outbursts. They attributed his actions to "social jealousy," a key term of the New Order that treated protest as evidence that inferior social groups had defective and childish ways of thinking. They also offered a different interpretation of the timing of Abidin's protest, linking it to the increased price of palm oil and the growing prosperity of transmigrants who had waited patiently and tended their plots. Sujak thought that locals should understand the pragmatics of the situation and not be so offended: "We came here to improve our lives," Sujak observed, "and one plot is not enough, so there is nothing wrong with buying extra." Reflecting further on the challenge of navigating these fragile personal and intergroup relations, he said, "Here we have to be tough; tough but not too tough, soft but not too soft."

The documents convinced Abidin that he was both adult and law abiding. His insistence on the no-selling rule inspired more locals to reclaim plots transmigrants had abandoned or sold to other transmigrants. A new informal rule emerged in the out-grower areas according to which transmigrants could sell their plots to locals but not to one another. The new rule enabled land transfers to take place but prevented land from becoming a commodity that transmigrants could buy and sell freely among themselves. Since none of the out-growers had paid off their debt, what was actually being sold was scheme membership that would become land ownership only when the bank released the land title, and the new owners paid to have their own names inserted on the title documents. Predictably, these informal land transactions enabled accumulation by hamlet heads, who harnessed the need for their signature on transfer documents as a toll booth, brokered deals, and bought the land of departing transmigrants to resell at a profit.

Many transmigrants who bought land had to pay for it twice—once to the departing transmigrant and again to the former owner, plus tolls.

Successful protest action and reclaiming by locals left transmigrants feeling vulnerable. They had to recognize that they were outsiders in someone else's land, but unlike the Natco manager we quoted earlier they could not retreat behind a guarded plantation gate. They had to live as neighbors and cooperate daily with local Dayaks and Malays who regarded their presence as illegitimate. Some were subjected to a form of confrontation called a "mass harvest" in which local thugs mobilized twenty to thirty people to harvest a transmigrant's disputed plot and sell the stolen fruit to Priva under their own names. Many transmigrants had their plots seized or decided to abandon them and seek a more secure and peaceful life. One family moved across the river to become workers in Natco: "When we were living in the transmigration area, we were sick all the time," the father reflected. "After we moved here, everyone was healthy." He hinted that the illness was the result of malevolence or ill will among neighbors, or perhaps a covert witchcraft attack. He recovered possession of his out-grower plot in 2005 when the provincial governor issued a ruling that land seized from transmigrants had to be returned to them. He decided to sell the plot anyway because he feared renewed violence, but he received only half the market value.

The source of tension in transmigration areas was not ethnic difference as such. Upriver communities had absorbed scores of spontaneous migrants who moved in over the decades (Javanese former plantation workers, single men, or entire families from other districts who came to tap rubber); many migrants married locally, and they abided by local customs, with the exception of Madurese, who kept themselves apart. Malays had their own ethnic map that caricatured differences: "Chinese gather money, Javanese work the land, Dayaks carry loads, Malays sit around and chat." It was a joke they told against themselves, a basis for intergroup acceptance not colonization. They could handle their own everyday differences (figure 1.4). The transmigration program was different because it made newcomers into agents of occupation. Transmigrants arrived under a government program that did not recognize the customary authority of local communities and fixed transmigrants into relations in which their advance was directly tied to local villagers' loss.

Tensions were especially high in Tapang Dacin, a transmigration settlement in which a group of Dayaks went beyond Abidin's insistence that transmigrants should abide by the no-selling rule to make an ethno-territorial claim. This group argued publicly that all the land allocated to Priva and to transmigrants should be returned to the customary landholders when the

FIGURE 1.4 Relaxing in an Upriver Hamlet

A mixed group of Javanese and Dayaks playing cards in an upriver hamlet. The Javanese here descend from contract workers on the colonial rubber plantation. Their parents moved to Dayak hamlets in 1966, when workers with Sarbupri affiliation were harassed. Their main income source is rubber tapping, which takes place roughly from 5 AM to 10 AM, leaving time for leisure. PHOTO: PUJO SEMEDI.

thirty-five-year concession expired. This way the entire occupation would end. Hearing these words transmigrants complained that they were living under mob rule. The same Dayak group was involved in extortion against fellow Dayaks as well. So were their attacks on transmigrants part of a campaign to end the occupation, or were the attackers simply thugs and thieves? Transmigrants wanted the government to step in to guarantee their safety and stabilize the situation by confirming that their presence in Dayak lands had legal status. In the words of Jikin:

> If the locals want to chase us out, they will have to pay fair compensation. And they will have to chase all of us, not just one or two. We are still in Indonesia, not in another country. There are rules. We came here under a government program and if they want to send us back, the government will have to organize it. The government wanted us to be united, one nation. . . . Since reformasi, since district autonomy, it is all about ethnic blocs. We shouldn't have a state within a state. . . . What happened to unity in diversity? It seems to have disappeared.

For Jikin the privilege that had once been accorded to him as a transmigrant was in danger of being reversed, making him a second-class (and unwelcome) citizen in Dayak lands. By recalling the national slogan "unity in diversity" he was making a claim for official, state-backed protection against people who did not seem to acknowledge the principle of common national citizenship or recognize the role of the transmigration program in national development. His own approach to this deeply uneasy situation was to keep a low profile and try not to attract attention: "If you are in a goat pen," he said, "you better bleat." Many transmigrants abandoned their assigned house lots in the new settlements where different groups were supposed to live together and regrouped along ethnic lines (figure 1.5). They formed a "team to protect transmigrants' rights" and agreed to defend their interests collectively and forcefully, should the need arise.

FIGURE 1.5 Hot and Lonely on the Transmigration Grid

Transmigration houses are built of poor-quality wood with a metal roof that makes them unbearably hot. Building contractors usually clear the land with bulldozers, leaving no tall trees for shade. Access to water is often problematic: Malay and Dayak hamlets are built near rivers or streams for good reason. The transmigrant family that owned this house was alone because they kept their house in its assigned spot on the transmigration grid. Most local Malays and Dayaks moved back to their home villages, and transmigrants rebuilt their wooden houses alongside the main plantation road for reasons of security and convenience.
PHOTO: PUJO SEMEDI.

Conclusion

In this chapter we asked: How did Natco and Priva become established in Tanjung and what novel relations did corporate occupation generate? The presence of Natco and Priva was underwritten by the colonial assumptions that villagers had large reserves of land, and by the legal regime that granted corporations access to huge concessions on the grounds that they could bring productivity and progress to a remote region. But establishing plantations was not simply a matter of following the law, the map, and the plan. Nor was it a one-off event, violent but complete. The two corporations took different approaches to establishing their plantations, sustaining political support, and dealing with former landholders. In the words of Mezzadra and Neilsen, there was, as always, "a backstory, a drama of frictions and tensions in which the efficacy of the operation appears far more fragile and elusive than might otherwise be assumed."[22]

Natco relied on its status as a state-owned corporation to carry out a unilateral land-grab, backed by an interpretation of land law that erased customary land rights and compensated farmers only for their fruit and rubber trees. Its operation was backed by coercive force in the form of bulldozers and the intimidating presence of government officials, army, and police. After the fall of Suharto, villagers challenged Natco and demanded the return of some of their land, but the corporation held the line and its political support remained solid. Managers refused to engage with former landholders as social equals who should be consulted on plantation matters and saw no reason to allocate them a share of plantation wealth. Natco was an occupier securely backed by state powers at the highest level; hence, it did not need to cultivate local collaborators. Natco managers simply overlooked villagers as if they were not there, a condition villagers described as "becoming the audience" or "ghosts in our own land." But the original landholders continued to insist they were entitled to share in plantation prosperity; minimally, they should not suffer a loss.

Priva established its plantation in partnership with the Ministry of Transmigration through a program known as PIR-BUN-Trans. The program assumed that villagers did have customary rights to their land, but their rights did not amount to ownership and could be severely discounted: villagers received back only a third of the land they released and still incurred a hefty debt for preparation of their out-grower plots. To persuade villagers to release their land the company worked though official "land release teams" that made village heads, customary leaders, local government officials, military, and police into collaborators. Although persuasion and partial inclusion might seem like a milder format for occupation than Natco's unilateral grab, it made village leaders into "company men" who could no longer fulfill their standard role as intermediaries through which "small people" seek redress vis-à-vis more powerful actors. The everyday relations that emerged were those of complicity, betrayal, and wiliness as individuals and groups sought to secure their own advance. Their maneuvers came at the expense of their own neighbors and kin, and at the expense of Priva, which had to keep on paying for the compliance it needed to keep its operation running.

Both corporations were an occupying force. They took over huge areas of land, obliterating villagers' rice and rubber fields and reducing a great many formerly independent farmers to near-landlessness. Priva's land acquisition process also fragmented families and sowed the grounds for enduring tension between locals and transmigrants. In different ways both corporations degraded the citizenship of the surrounding communities. Yet the change in citizenship that resulted from corporate occupation was not legally inscribed. The corporations had no official responsibility for people living in the enclaves and interstitial spaces outside the plantation borders who fell under the normal system of village government. Priva had limited responsibility for its out-growers, despite the total reorganization of their landscapes and livelihoods to secure palm fruit for the company mill. According to official narratives, the corporations were not occupiers but partners with the government in producing public benefits, and the spaces they occupied were large blocks on a map that happened to be sprinkled with some tiny squares. This format of occupation resonates with the one Makdisi describes in Palestine where the existence of a subject population is overlooked so it appears that no denial of their rights took place; denial is denied or simply not acknowledged as such.

The structure of denial that generated the position of the ghosts was supplemented in Tanjung's plantation zone by corporations' need to buy political support at all levels, from the national capital to the villages where plantations were installed. The result was hypocrisy and betrayal, as nothing was quite what or where it claimed to be. Mafia practices thrived on the plantations' obscure spatial and legal foundations. Sadly, our findings are far from unique nor are they confined to plantations that were installed in previous decades. The subdistrict official who unrolled his plantation map had just been asked to sign a document confirming that a new corporation had completed the proper procedures for land release, but he refused. The company had started land clearing without consulting villagers, a style commonly dubbed "clear first, talk later."

Odit, a member of our research team, spent six months in the new concession area and witnessed the land release process firsthand. He took on a participant role as assistant to the surveyor tasked with measuring farmers' landholdings and creating a record based on GPS. He spent his days riding on the back of the surveyor's motorbike and his evenings at the house of the customary leader, who offered lodging. From these locations he could see precisely how maps and lists were falsified, landholders were misinformed, and coercion was applied. Brokers acting on behalf of government officials, plantation managers, and other entrepreneurs acquired large areas of land. Some villagers were under the mistaken impression that brokers represented the company and accepted their word that their release of land would secure them membership in an out-grower scheme. Many studies have similar findings.[23] With monotonous regularity, the arrival of plantations in the Indonesian countryside degrades citizenship, entrenches mafia practices, and seeds conditions for uneven accumulation, impoverishment, and social disarray. This is the everyday face of plantation life where corporate occupation is not limited to the bounded space of a concession covered by oil palms but invades multiple practices, processes, and relations.

2

Holding Workers

In this chapter we ask, Who worked for Natco and Priva and why did they work there? Indonesia's contemporary plantation workers are not bonded so their involvement in plantation work offers insight into their assessments of plantation life. If plantations had nothing to offer them or they had better alternatives, they would not be there. So what drew workers toward these particular plantations and why did they stay? Just as plantations must be established in a specific place, the workers they employ must be recruited from somewhere, and enrolled in particular relations. Workers we met were differentiated by ethnicity, gender, and age, differences that managers instrumentalized but that exceeded their control. When sharing their assessments of the risks and benefits plantation work offered, workers highlighted their desires for a fair reward, security, and respect; their weak bargaining power; and their uneasy feelings about the mafia system in which they were inevitably involved.

Natco and Priva had quite different labor regimes (means of recruiting, rewarding, and holding workers), but the kinds of work and organizational hierarchy on the two plantations were identical.[1] Directors at their respective head offices located in the provincial capital Pontianak made key decisions on behalf of the corporation. Managers resident on the plantations oversaw operations. Office workers conducted tasks such as accounting and ordering supplies. Technical workers maintained machines and foremen supervised production. These high-status workers lived in central housing blocks, in houses ordered by rank. There were guards at the plantation offices, ware-houses, truck depots, the main plantation gates, and mills. The fields of palm were divided into blocks called *"divisi"* in Priva and *"afdeling"* (Dutch) in Natco. Each block had worker housing, a small office, a prayer house, and a childcare center. The housing and other facilities were of higher quality at Natco, which also had two government elementary schools and a private junior high school. Priva ferried resident workers' children to government schools in nearby hamlets and its locally recruited managers and workers commuted daily from their hamlets to their place of work.

Fieldwork roles for oil palm include harvester, truck driver and loader (all men), maintenance worker (mostly women, occasionally older men), and fore-man (*mandor*, mainly men, sometimes women for maintenance). The tools that workers use are very basic. Harvesters cut down the fresh fruit bunches using a sharp scythe attached to a pole that can be 11 meters (36 feet) long when the palms grow tall, making the task both strenuous and dangerous. Harvesters or their assistants transfer the fruit bunches to the roadside by basket or wheelbarrow. Each harvester puts his own mark on the bunch stem so clerks can count the number of bunches he harvested before it is col-lected by a truck and taken to the mill. Loaders spear each fruit bunch with a metal prong and toss it up to the truck where another worker stacks it neatly. Women use spray tanks for herbicides and pesticides, carrying the tanks on their backs and pumping by hand. They use huge baskets to carry fertilizer and smaller baskets, slung from their shoulders, from which they scoop fertilizer onto the palms. They use buckets for collecting the loose fruit that breaks off from the fruit bunch when it falls and hoes and bush-knives for clearing stubborn plants and vines that are resistant to herbicides.

In 2010, Natco had a formal, resident labor force of 883, of whom 80 percent were fieldworkers and 20 percent were office, technical, trans-port, and managerial workers. Workers' mean age was forty-five, and they had an average of twenty years of employment; 34 percent were women. Based on workers' names we estimated that 70 percent were Javanese,

12 percent Dayak, 7 percent Malay, and 8 percent Batak, the latter mainly in managerial and technical roles. There were thirteen managers: the head; five assistants for production, public relations, health, transport, and administration; and one assistant manager for each of the seven afdelings. There were thirteen staff in each of the seven afdelings (giving ninety-one in total). The staff lived in plantation housing alongside the fieldworkers and comprised the first foreman, first clerk, harvest foreman, harvest clerk, quality control clerk, accounts clerk, maintenance foreman, road foreman, fertilizer foreman, foreman for pest control, childcare worker, religious leader, and security. Natco had no resident mill workers as the mill it used was shared with another branch of the state plantation and was located some 20 kilometers (12½ miles) away. The shared PTPN mill employed 128 workers in two shifts.

In 2014, Priva had a permanent workforce of 527 workers for its 3,834 hectare core plantation and a further 180 workers at the on-site mill. Half the permanent plantation workforce comprised managerial, office and technical staff (121), foremen (109), and guards (37); one-third were male harvesters, mostly migrant; and some were female maintenance workers. In addition, there was an unrecorded number of casual workers, mainly Malay and Dayak women hired from the nearby enclaves for maintenance tasks. In 2019 a new online database showed that Priva had reduced its permanent workforce from 527 to 325 and increased its reliance on casual workers (357), a shift that followed a national trend.

Provision of jobs is a key argument used by plantation corporations and their supporters to justify plantation expansion. Annual corporate reports show neat rows of worker housing with cheerful children heading off to plantation schools. This glossy image is an accurate representation of the experience of workers at Natco in the period 1980–2005, but for Natco it no longer holds and for Priva it never applied. Across Indonesia, plantation corporations tend to shift toward more reliance on casual workers as soon as they have access to an abundant, proximate labor reserve. In Sumatra's dense plantation belt this shift was underway by the 1950s and in the 1970s, during Ann Stoler's research, it was well advanced.[2] Similarly, in Tanjung by 2005 five adjacent plantations saturated the subdistrict and consigned the former landholders to live in tiny, crowded enclaves where they were nearly landless and desperately in need of paid work. Managers at Natco and Priva recruited female casual workers from the enclaves but preferred not to employ local Malay and Dayak men for harvest work as they considered them to be lazy and demanding. Managers preferred Javanese migrants as harvesters, and by 2005 young Javanese men were easy to recruit, as they roamed the province in search of work. They were sons of Javanese transmigrants or plantation workers who had been born in Kalimantan but inherited no land. At the national scale too, cell-phone communications and improved transportation brought willing workers from across Indonesia to the plantation zone. The labor reserve had become both proximate and nationwide.

With an ample labor pool to draw on, managers at Natco and Priva found it less necessary to hold workers, and workers who experienced deteriorating conditions had to reevaluate whether or not to continue.[3] For reasons we explained in the introduction, workers had no unions to protect their interests or mobilize for a collective fight. Their conditions of work were shaped by a mafia system that pervaded both plantations from top to bottom, enabling superiors to prey on their subordinates and subordinates to siphon off small shares of wealth for themselves. These were the forms of everyday life for workers at Natco and Priva, and they left them with only two options: accept the situation or leave.

Seeking Security at Natco

In 1980 when Natco arrived in Sanggau, local Malays and Dayaks still had plenty of land. They sought jobs as plantation office workers or foremen, but they were not interested in becoming *kulis*, a label they reserved for pitiful people who have to take orders and do hard manual work for someone else. Hence to fill the plantation's labor needs, PTPN worked with the national labor bureau (Depnaker) to recruit migrant workers directly from Java. Corporate policy gave preference to young couples and granted both men and women full-time jobs, complete with housing, pensions, medical care, and other bonuses and benefits. These were good jobs, and most workers stayed until their retirement at age fifty-five. The aging of the core workforce coincided with the aging of the palms, which were so tall by 2005 that older men were not strong enough to harvest them (figure 2.1).

Instead of hiring new permanent workers as harvesters, a new corporate policy took advantage of provisions in the 2003 Labor Law to reduce the plantation's core labor force. PTPN's head office recruited 150 young migrant men on two-year contracts that came without most of the benefits the first set of workers had enjoyed: no pensions, no family housing, and no promise of permanent employment. Natco managers also outsourced tasks such as replanting the aging palms and refurbishing infrastructure, a lucrative source of contract kickbacks. Mafia practices proliferated among workers as well. To hold on to their production bonuses, aging harvesters used their

FIGURE 2.1 Harvester at Work

Harvesting palm fruit bunches weighing 15 to 30 kilograms (33 to 66 pounds) with a super-sharp scythe attached to a long pole takes extraordinary skill and strength. Harvesters are fined for cutting unripe bunches; if they cut one by mistake, they try to bury it before the foreman inspects. This plantation field is well maintained. In poorly maintained fields palms are overgrown and unfertilized, hence fruit bunches are small and harvesters, who are paid by the kilo, net low returns. PHOTO: D. LINTANG SUDIBYO.

privileged position as a toll booth: instead of doing the work themselves they hired young Javanese men whom they claimed were visiting kin, a practice known as "borrowing the worker's name." Some harvesters relied on their wives and children to pick up loose palm fruit. The popular idiom for all kinds of casual workers was BL (*buruh lepas*) but we also heard BL glossed playfully as outside worker (*buruh luar*) or wild worker (*buruh liar*).

"Flexible" labor arrangements meant that circa 2010 many of the workers we encountered at Natco were not part of its formal labor force. Although Natco prided itself on providing workers with facilities for a stable family life, its new labor regime fractured families by recruiting male harvesters and female maintenance workers from different labor pools. No doubt Natco saved money on benefits and facilities, but it lost out on productivity: a foreman complained that managers had not hired enough contract harvesters, and in his afdeling alone 10 tons of fruit per day rotted on the palms. To explore how workers navigated this changing labor regime we turn to the story of Godril and Monah.

Godril and Monah Hold On

The couple were among the first workers to arrive at Natco in 1980. After a period in a temporary barrack they were allocated a house in afdeling 5 where they still lived thirty-five years later. As Godril explained:

> I didn't have a regular job in Java. I was peddling ice water in town. The labor office came looking for workers, and told us we would get a salary, a ration of rice per person, housing, and health facilities. We both registered so we each had a salary. After just two years we saved enough money to go back to Java. My relatives said, "Are you back already?" I said no, we just came to visit, we're going back to the plantation. I told friends they should register as well, and one of my nephews came here. The promises the labor office made to us were all correct, they were not lying.

Godril and Monah appreciated the dignity and stability plantation work had afforded them. Although they did manual work they were not classified as *buruh* (worker) but as employees (*karyawan*), a term also used for foremen and office workers, elevating their status.[4] They noted that employment in a state corporation made them rather like civil servants (PNS). Their sense of dignity and security increased as they witnessed the gradual improvement of plantation facilities and worker welfare: "We used to walk everywhere in the heat," Godril pointed out, "now everyone has a motorbike, and some foremen have cars." Managers seldom fired people, punishing misdeeds such as gambling and theft with a reprimand or demotion. So long as workers kept their heads down and did not cause trouble, it was a job for life. Their principal source of insecurity was retirement. Godril and Monah were acutely aware that they would soon be on their own. Their anticipated pensions were low, around a quarter of the minimum wage, so they needed to make extra money to save. "Some retirees did not plan so they are still here, asking the foreman to hire them back as day labor," Godril observed.

For some of Godril's neighbors, housing had unexpectedly become a crisis. They had assumed that their children would be hired as permanent workers to take over their parents' jobs when they retired. They would all continue to live in the houses in which the children had grown up. But when Natco stopped hiring permanent workers it foiled this plan. Even the inferior two-year contract harvester jobs were hard to get. Natco managers had no mechanism to give preference to young men already living on the plantation, or to surrounding villagers who also felt entitled to these jobs. PTPN had centralized all hiring at the head office to reduce nepotism. Afdeling foremen let contract harvesters live in unused houses, but there was no official provision for their families. The men were bitter: "The company really wants to eat us up and throw us out," one harvester observed. In Godril's afdeling about half the houses previously occupied by worker families were empty and rotting away or having second lives as chicken coops. Contractors were building some new brick houses but far fewer than the wooden houses they replaced. These shifts in housing—who had access to a house, and whether a house was new or deteriorating—had affective force: they communicated to workers that plantation life would still be a secure, cradle-to-grave family life for a few privileged workers but for those recruited on a casual or contract basis that secure life was no more.

Godril and Monah had bought land for their retirement in another part of the district close to a transmigration area as they wanted to live among fellow Javanese. They had planted the land with rubber for income to supplement their pensions, but they had yet to build a house. Very few of their neighbors had retired to Java where the cost to buy land was high and supplementary income hard to find. Reflecting on his own approaching insecurity Godril observed that Javanese who came to Kalimantan as transmigrants fared better than those like him, who had come under the government's interprovince labor recruitment program. "At first the transmigrants' life is very hard, but in the long run they end up with some land and a future, while we who came as workers just have our savings and pensions."

He was resentful that local Malay and Dayak villagers who had blockaded Natco and made threats in 1998 had forced managers to provide them with out-grower plots, while workers like him whose labor had built and sustained the plantation for thirty years ended up with no oil palm plots of their own. He felt the outcome was grossly unfair.

Godril's official job was to maintain the afdeling generator, and he moonlighted doing electrical repair in surrounding villages. Monah worked in field maintenance. Although her official workday was 6:00 AM–2:00 PM, like most other fieldworkers she was usually home by about 10:00 AM. She completed her housework and took a rest before starting her second job planting oil palm seedlings for a contractor. Monah's foreman had no complaint about her short work hours because he doubled as the contractor, hence he preferred her to save her energy. The doubling of official and private roles extended right up the pyramid to plantation managers who took on contracts using the names of cronies, or had cronies do the work in return for commissions. Workers called this the network system (*sistem jaringan*), a term that confirmed the routine nature of these practices but was a bit less condemnatory than the term "mafia." In Sumatra, Ann Stoler reports that workers called the plantations' internal thieves *wereng.*[5] Wereng are plant hoppers that attack the stem of a rice plant and inject a virus, leaving the plant intact but unable to produce grains. It is a striking metaphor for thieves who work surreptitiously, extracting value from the inside while leaving the shell of the plantation intact. Stoler does not mention whether workers applied the term "wereng" to themselves or used it as a term of moral critique (like "mafia"). At Natco we found ambivalence: our interlocutors acknowledged their participation in the network system while expressing discomfort with a life in which nothing was quite what it claimed to be. The conceit that state-owned enterprises like Natco modeled high standards for technical excellence and rational management magnified the disjuncture.

A consultant from the College of Plantation Training (LPP) in Medan whom we met when we stayed at the Natco guesthouse was holding workshops for managers to teach them "best work practices." He was inspired by the quality of Malaysian plantations with yields that were much higher than Natco achieved. Although managers blamed poor soil and insufficient rainfall, the consultant thought these were merely excuses. He cited widespread corruption, excessive bureaucracy, poorly defined work tasks, fruit harvested too early or too late, and trucks jammed for hours at the mill waiting to off-load. Most of all he stressed that the "problem was the people." Natco managers concurred with this diagnosis but pointed the finger at fieldworkers not at themselves: "A plantation must be run like the army," one manager observed.

In addition to army discipline and obedience to command, he might have been thinking of practices like morning roll call that required workers to line up in rows and hear lectures on productivity, safety, and company loyalty. Roll call was a practice that Natco managers enforced sporadically, but since their own conduct set the tone for plantation life and they were often absent for days or weeks on end, discipline was a difficult problem to resolve.

On our last visit to Natco in 2015, the plantation was close to bankruptcy and Godril and Monah's loyalty to the company seemed to have evaporated. They were furious about Natco managers' greed and mismanagement that were so excessive they had jeopardized the livelihoods of ordinary workers.[6] They were no longer receiving an annual bonus. Managers had directed workers to stop fertilizing the twenty-year-old palms so the plants bore few fruits and harvesters who relied on per kilogram bonuses made little money. Replanting efforts had stalled and Monah said her maintenance work had become absurd: "During replanting we were told to plant vines (to improve the soil and suppress weeds). Now we are supposed to kill the vines with herbicide. That vine is OK if you control it, but it can grow 14 centimeters [5½ inches] in one night!" A glance around the plantation showed that vines were indeed smothering the young palms. The regular maintenance teams were decimated by retirement and could not keep up. Monah and her neighbors took on additional work on contract, but the pay was too low to attract casual workers from the surrounding villages. All four units of PTPN in Sanggau District were in the same sorry state.

Directors in the PTPN head office announced a plan to handle the plantations' financial crisis and the pesky vines: they ordered managers and office staff to help with fieldwork three times a week. Godril and Monah thought the plan was ridiculous. "When the managers and office workers showed up at the field you could see they did not know how to work. They were carrying bush knives and chopping about wildly, not doing anything useful at all. Their clothes were like people on a picnic. They did not want to wear their uniforms because they thought it was undignified for office workers to be seen working in a field." Godril's amusement turned to anger as he described how managers sent a bus full of office workers to help at another PTPN plantation as per head office directives, but the cost of the transport was IDR19 million (USD1,900). "Why didn't they just give that money to real workers who could get the job done?" he complained.

Godril and Monah were upset by managers' inefficiency, waste, and double talk. Godril pointed out the irony of the company's "pearly words," which were written on sign boards posted throughout the plantation: *When the company is healthy, workers do well.* "Now it seems the company has collapsed, so how about us?" Monah put the point more directly: "The bosses just think of themselves. We heard that the directors stole billions, but we pay the price." Her analysis did not highlight the routine extraction of the value of workers' labor by the corporation in the form of profit, which she accepted as normal. Nor did she question the hierarchical distribution of rewards: she expected managers to receive higher pay (and payoffs) than ordinary workers.[7] Instead she focused her outrage on the selfishness of managers and directors who took so much for themselves they put workers' livelihoods at risk. The couple agreed that some unofficial accumulation was necessary to solve the problem of low pay and future retirement. They did not treat workers who obeyed all the rules and depended on the company for everything with respect. They ridiculed them for their passivity and failure to take advantage of the available opportunities. Yet they thought excessive greed was unseemly. They mentioned a rumor that one manager's child was so obese he could not stand. This was an exaggeration, but the story made an important point: the manager and his family lacked judgment. In Monah's view it was not routine theft but gross excess that had caused Natco's decline.

Like many plantation workers and managers, Godril and Monah were surviving the decline by raising cattle that they set to graze among the palms. Cattle enabled workers to manage without their usual bonuses and to raise the lump sum they needed for large expenses such as buying a motorbike or paying school fees. One full-grown beast sold for IDR12 million (USD1,200), a huge sum for workers whose base pay was IDR1.4 million (USD140) per month. Godril was especially proud of his initiative in organizing a thirteen-person cattle-raising group that district officials had praised as an example of rural income generation. Hence, he was furious when a senior manager issued a unilateral edict that all cattle had to be penned because they were eating the young palm seedlings. Practically speaking, gathering grass to feed penned cattle would take too much time (figure 2.2). Owners would have to sell their stock—probably at a low price, since the forced sale of several hundred cattle would flood the market. This was not the first such edict, but the sanction announced this time was severe: unpenned cattle would be shot or seized. "It is the same as killing us," Godril exclaimed, showing his emotion.

For Godril the manager's edict was the ultimate betrayal because it cut off his means of survival. Also, the manager failed to understand that cattle-raisers were helping the plantation. "We are up all night. We take it in turns to guard the cattle from theft, so that means we are guarding the plantation as well. The company does not have enough guards for this huge area. We use

FIGURE 2.2 Cattle Thrive among Palms

Raising cattle among oil palms disrupts production when seedlings are young, and some Natco managers suggested that it disrupts the monocrop aesthetic: cattle and their manure are matter out of place. Another disruption concerns plantation hierarchy, as cattle bans are widely ignored and cattle raising puts workers and managers on the same economic plane. PHOTO: PUJO SEMEDI.

our motorbikes to patrol, and if we see a truck loading fruit in the fields at night, we use our cell phones to alert the guards." Godril used his description of the night guard to emphasize that his loyalty was intact; it was the plantation manager who had lost his way. For Godril the manager was defaulting on the moral bargain that had enabled Natco to recruit the first generation of workers from Java and hold them in place for their entire working lives: workers would be loyal to the plantation in return for a dignified livelihood. Godril and Monah could not leave the plantation because they had to wait for their pensions, so they held on, bitter and frustrated not only about the reckless conduct of their superiors but also about the sad condition of the plantation they had built.[8]

Self-Protection at Priva

Unlike Natco, Priva did not recruit its core workers directly from Java. The contractors who did the initial land clearing, planting, and construction hired Javanese transmigrants alongside locals in their work crews, but few transmigrants continued to do wage work in the core plantation after they received their out-grower plots. For the crucial, time-sensitive harvesting, work managers still distrusted locals and preferred to hire migrants. They sometimes asked trusted workers to help recruit harvesters from their home villages, but mostly they hired men who showed up at the office singly or in small groups looking for work. Many of them were Kalimantan-born Javanese; some were spontaneous migrants who came to Kalimantan directly from Java, Sumatra, and Nusa Tenggara Barat (NTB) to try their luck. Turnover was high, and few workers expected to receive pensions. Since security was not on offer their emphasis was on protecting themselves from injury and making sure that their investment of time and effort produced material rewards that went beyond daily survival such as motorbikes, house improvements, or funds to educate their children.

A period of turbulence in 2011–12 brought workers' assessments to the fore. The drama started in 2011 when Priva's owner Pak Wakijan fired two relatives who were supposed to be managing the plantation but had run it badly and stolen funds. He appointed a new manager who had experience in Malaysia and promised to restore order and profit. As the new manager tightened the rules, he faced opposition from workers at all levels whose formal pay and extra income streams deteriorated sharply. Assessing the new situation, many workers argued that Priva was taking too much from them for insufficient return. Some workers were concerned about their basic bodily well-being. Like oil palm harvesters in Sumatra in the 1970s who told Ann Stoler they expected to burn out after eight years, both men and women workers expressed a fear of being "eaten up" by Priva's excessive demands.[9] Sufficient return encompassed both pay and respect, as workers looked for evidence that managers appreciated their contributions. Although they were prepared to make sacrifices for the good of their families, they did not want the company to take them for fools.

Stealing from Priva was a mode of self-protection that supplied extra income and pushed back against extraction, but workers had no mechanism to launch a coordinated struggle. Flight was not an obvious solution either because even if they could find other jobs, conditions would likely be just as bad. To explore worker perspectives on the changing labor regime and the dilemmas it presented, we focus on workers occupying different positions: Iksan, a harvester from Java, and new recruits from NTB; Sarip, a Dayak security guard and his wife Mega; Johan and Agus, Malay foremen; Tagor, a Batak guard turned junior manager; and Tina and Desi, landless Malay women from the enclave of Muara Tangkos.

Iksan and the NTB Recruits

Iksan was the son of workers who had joined Natco in the 1980s, but he did not grow up there as his parents left him in Java with his grandparents. He did all sorts of work in Java after he left school—factory work, building labor, loading at the terminal, cutting wood in the forest. He came to Kalimantan with his wife in 2002, and since Natco was not hiring, his parents directed him toward Priva. He liked the fact that housing, electricity, and health care were provided, but his wife complained that food was expensive, so it was hard to save. His main goal was to educate his children so they would not have to do kuli work—the hard, low status work he had done in Java and was still doing on the plantation. He felt his pay as a harvester was sufficient to meet his goal, and he knew from experience that it was much more stable work than he could find in Java. His wife preferred Java since her parents were still there, but she agreed that steady work was hard to find. Iksan did extra work on contract within the plantation and some harvesting for outgrowers, but he was careful not to be absent too often and risk his job and the house that came with it.

When Priva's new manager changed the harvesters' pay structure in 2011, Iksan and other harvesters worried that they would be reclassified as casual workers and lose the protection of the 2003 Labor Law. Under the new rules they would no longer receive a base pay for meeting their daily target plus a premium for harvesting extra fruit. Instead they would be paid at a flat rate of IDR55 (pennies on the USD) per kilogram of fruit. With this change the company could pay less to older or less productive harvesters or those whose attendance was erratic. Iksan and other committed workers recognized that they could make more money with the new system, but they would bear all the risk: difficult terrain, dry weather, small or sparse fruit, and days of work lost due to illness or injury would reduce their pay. They had many questions. Since the labor law's provisions such as the annual pay raise and the annual bonus were calculated as a percentage of base pay, how would it work for them if they had no base pay? Would they still be entitled to pensions? Would the company still take responsibility if they were ill or injured? Injury was a real risk: a harvester died when a 30 kilogram (66 pound) fruit bunch fell on his head; thorns caused infection; and super-sharp harvesting knives and long poles could do serious damage.[10]

Harvesters demanding answers staged a wildcat strike for three days and demonstrated outside the office complex. Managers assured them that they were still classified as permanent workers and made some promises about paid sick days but put nothing on paper. The harvesters' summary was that the company's protection was unreliable. Some local harvesters left their jobs and pieced together income from part-time harvesting for out-growers or tapping remaining pockets of rubber. Fifteen harvesters left as a group, enticed away by another company that heard about the turmoil, sent recruiters, and organized minibuses to pick them up. Most married harvesters including Iksan stayed in place, unwilling to uproot their families and disrupt the school year. Significantly, managers made it clear that if the harvesters did not want the work they could be readily replaced. It was no idle threat. Managers fired "lazy" workers, mainly local Malays and Dayaks with inconsistent attendance, and renewed their efforts to recruit migrants from NTB. Company records showed that of 119 harvesters in place in 2014, two-thirds had been recruited since 2010.

As Iksan adapted to the new system he noted that the previous base pay system was not ideal. It produced a directly coercive situation as foremen watched over harvesters to make sure they exerted a full effort.

> We were under so much pressure to meet our daily targets. We were supposed to work seven hours, 7:00 to 2:00; but by 2:00 we might have only eighty bunches. Then the foreman would say, "Oh, why so little?" and I would say, "I was tired today because I worked so hard yesterday, I didn't get home until 3:00." I would become emotional, I was so sweaty and exhausted, then I would say, "What do you know, you just stand there talking." If I did not restrain myself it would be so easy to pick up an axe to swing at his head. . . . There have been cases.

The new pay structure made Iksan responsible for his own productivity since he was paid per kilogram, but it also presented foremen in collusion with managers with a new opportunity to cheat him. They manipulated the payment system by assigning an average weight of 15 kilograms (33 pounds) per fruit bunch, which Iksan said was quite wrong—the true average was 19 kilograms (42 pounds). This was a difference of around 23 percent, which generated his superiors a huge unearned revenue at his expense. The worst part was that he could not protect himself from this mode of predation—it was built into the new system and he could neither challenge nor avoid it. He thought the company's search for profit was quite normal but managers and foremen who used their positions as toll booths to impose a callous rate of extraction to enrich themselves made him furious.

Facing competition to recruit and hold skilled harvesters, in 2014 the company raised the per kilogram rate and reinstated a quota system but reorganized it to extract even more work from harvesters. The revised payment system combined a quota with "precipice" style all-or-nothing incentives. A harvester who met his daily kilogram quota for twenty-five days a month received a base pay equivalent to the district's minimum wage. If he exceeded his quota, he received a significant bonus. If he failed to make his quota or he missed a day of work for whatever reason (e.g., a sick child), his pay for the entire month reverted to a low per kilogram rate. Just 1 kilogram below quota on one day, or one workday missed, meant falling off the precipice: "It is as if we just did all that extra work for nothing," Iksan observed. "Priva has become really clever, they trick us so we don't give up, we keep going." There was no longer a foreman standing over him. Nor could he make his own decision about how many kilograms to harvest. Instead he had to pressure himself beyond the point of exhaustion in order not to waste his own efforts.

Iksan felt that the "precipice" was oppressive, especially when the palms did not yield enough fruit to meet the quota, but he was prepared to tolerate the pressure so long as the rate was set high enough for him to earn well. He felt he had become smart and calculating, just like the company had become smart and calculating. He was still strong. He proudly showed us his harvesting pole, 11 meters (36 feet) long (figure 2.3). He also showed us the certificate his daughter had won for high grades in elementary school that the company had rewarded with a IDR250,000 (USD25) prize. He was confident that he was doing the best he could for his family. Through his investment of time and effort and the bodily risk he bore, he was creating a future in which his children would not have to do kuli work.

Unlike Iksan, who learned to become more calculating as the company changed its payment system, incoming migrant harvesters from NTB arrived with a calculative mentality already entrenched. In conversations with us they presented themselves less as workers than as entrepreneurs who had taken the initiative to improve their situation. They had left their wives and children behind and they wanted to ensure that their personal sacrifice and investment produced a significant return. To finance their travel to Kalimantan they had borrowed money from village money lenders at an interest rate of 100 percent with no fixed term, a system they called "borrow one, return two." They described the debt as a necessary cost of doing business that would only become a problem if their initiative failed.[11] Some of them had previously worked in Malaysia and their goal in Kalimantan was finite: to save enough money to finance their return to Malaysia, where earnings were higher. Others had a target like sending a child to university. "If we stay in NTB," one harvester observed, "the most we can earn

FIGURE 2.3 Iksan's Harvesting Tools

Iksan's harvest pole reached from the dirt path in front of his small wooden plantation row-house, across the front concrete terrace, along the linoleum covered hallway through to the kitchen at the back, where he parked his motorbike at night. PHOTO: TANIA LI.

is enough to get by from day to day. . . . What we are looking for here is the possibility to earn more than we spend, to get ahead."

In 2011 new recruits were not sure their investment would pay off. Considering the height of the aging palms, the small size of the fruit bunches, the debts they had incurred for travel, the cost of the necessary equipment (harvest knife and pole), and the need to buy basic furnishings (a mattress and pillow, a cooking pot), they might just cover their costs. It would take months before they could begin to send money home. They worried about how their families back in NTB were surviving and whether their wives would remain faithful to them. NTB has a notoriously high divorce rate and a telling name, *jamal*, for women left behind. Jamal is a contraction of *janda* Malaysia (*janda* means widow or divorcee).[12] They kept in contact with friends at other plantations to find out if conditions elsewhere were better but every move cost them money and time, so they planned to stay where they were and try to make it work.

Priva promised to reimburse the travel costs of the NTB recruits and give them permanent status with medical benefits if they stayed for a year. The workers were encouraged by the experience of an NTB harvester who had arrived two years before them and already showed signs of getting ahead: he had bought a motorbike that enabled him to moonlight by harvesting for out-growers on his days off. But he still had to tolerate the dismal housing

FIGURE 2.4 Old Barracks, Two Men per Room

Priva assigned contract harvesters living space in an old wooden barrack. Four workers had to share a two-room unit with one light bulb and one drum of dirty Kapuas water per week for drinking, cooking, and bathing. Harvesters who had previously worked in Malaysia made comparisons: there the housing was better, and companies supplied furnishings including mattresses, pillows, and cooking pots. PHOTO: I. B. PUTRA.

Priva provided for them in an old wooden barrack building (figure 2.4). It was a hard life. Nevertheless, after Priva changed the payment system in 2014, Iksan and the best of the NTB harvesters were making IDR6 million (USD600) per month, which was three times the district minimum and double the average wage of a schoolteacher. Some of the NTB harvesters asked their wives to join them so they could pick up loose fruit to maximize their chance of earning a bonus.

Sarip and Mega Withdraw Loyalty

Sarip and Mega were a Dayak couple from another district. He worked as a security guard and she did maintenance work. Guard was one of the favorite tasks of Malay and Dayak workers who were reputedly unwilling to do kuli work, not because they were afraid of manual labor but because they hated to do such work under direct supervision. Sarip certainly valued his status as a guard and the powers it gave him: he could decide when and where to patrol, and he decided the fate of wrongdoers he apprehended. He had detailed knowledge about the different kinds of stealing that went on in the plantation. He suggested it was OK for people to steal from the company so long as they did not cause him too much trouble. He sometimes protected them, especially if they were people he knew. "There was massive theft here in 2010, mostly by workers," he explained. "Harvesters called their friends to come at night with trucks to pick up harvested fruit waiting by the roadside. They sold it through out-growers, so it all went back to the Priva mill. They tried to recruit me but I refused. It was dangerous. I told them, 'If you can steal, good for you, but don't involve me. If I know about it I will report you.'"

Mega had witnessed her husband's selective guarding tactics firsthand. The previous day her friends had taken some fertilizer and hidden it in a bucket when Sarip came by (figure 2.5). "Lucky you didn't report them," she observed. "I saw them," Sarip responded. "I knew what was going on, but I didn't say anything. Next time I'll take back the fertilizer, but I still won't report them. I'll say, 'Just be careful how you go.'" Sarip said the same to a truck driver he caught stealing herbicide to sell to out-growers. "He was my friend, a good friend. . . . If it is insiders the company doesn't report them to the police, it just takes back what they stole and fires them, that is the end of it." Anything—chemicals, fertilizers, fruit, fuel, spare parts—could disappear. "It is always insiders," Mega added, "not anyone else."

As evidence of long-term, systematic theft workers pointed to the small size of the palm fruit bunches. The palms along Priva's roads looked healthy, but a hundred meters (328 feet) inside the field the palms were stunted and unproductive, evidence that little or no fertilizer had ever reached them. Whether the problem was caused by managers who manipulated the fertilizer order, warehouse guards or truckers who stole fertilizer en route to the fields, or women workers who hid fertilizers in a ditch, the net outcome was captured in an embarrassing number: Priva produced only 14.4 tons of fruit bunches per hectare per year, well below the average reported by Natco (19.3 tons) and below the average produced by five hundred of Priva's own out-growers (16.1 tons), a point to which we will return.[13]

Sarip was upset when the new manager's rules restricted his overtime hours, reducing his monthly pay by 25 percent. The company also stopped supplying fuel for his motorbike. "There are not enough guards. I am supposed to guard 670 hectares of plantation fields all alone. It isn't reasonable. I have to confront people and they get mad at me. I only carry a knife." Sarip's mode of self-protection was to withdraw his labor and his loyalty. "I used to work all night and cover 100 kilometers [62 miles], but now I just sit at the guard post. If Priva does not respect my work, I'll just think of myself. That is

FIGURE 2.5 Loading, Guarding, Supervising

After the 5:30 AM roll call at the plantation office, women wait near the depot. They prefer to start work immediately, while there is still a cool mist, but they depend on company trucks to transport them to the fields, together with their buckets and sacks of fertilizer. They are led by a foreman (or forewoman) who checks that they spread the fertilizer correctly and do not bury or steal it. The daily quota is assigned to a group, so women who finish quickly help their friends; then they have to wait in the hot sun for the truck to take them back to the depot. PHOTO: ARITA NUGRAHENI.

the way to fight the company." He added, "If it supported me, I would think differently, ask permission if I took time off. But if the company doesn't care about me, I'll be the same way." He had a plan to plant oil palm on some land in his home village, but he had a gambling habit so he could not save. In fact, he had come to Priva after he was caught gambling during a crackdown in his home village and risked arrest. "Here the police all gamble, so no one reports," he added. Mega was pregnant and appreciated that Priva had transferred her from her normal job spraying chemicals to the less hazardous task of sweeping the office block, but she didn't like being constantly under the managers' eyes.

Foremen Johan and Agus Make Plans

Many of Sarip's observations about stealing concerned foremen. He told us about a test he had devised. "I knew that foremen's official pay was less than mine, so I asked one of them if we could swap jobs but he refused. That is because he makes so much money. . . . If foremen are clever, they can make as much as they want." Foremen's tricks included inflating the number of fruit bunches harvested and taking the additional money from the harvester's pay; reporting fictive members on a work team; and taking a cut from casual workers to include their names on the daily roster—a repertoire of tricks identical to those Pujo reported from the tea plantation he studied in Java. In the case of casual women workers recruited from the enclaves, the foremen (or sometimes a forewoman) could be their own kin, making the predation more personal.

Johan, a Malay from Muara Tangkos whose observations on the crucial first encounter between villagers and corporations we reported in chapter 1, said he hated foremen. In his view they were an arrogant breed who used their petty powers to extort people and show off. But not all foremen were the same, and several foremen we interviewed saw dignity in the role. Johan had worked as a transport foreman at Natco for two decades during which he took on several principled fights on behalf of the workers in his unit. "Why should the bosses have air conditioning while workers in the transport section didn't even have a fan?" He rejected invitations to join collusive schemes such as stealing diesel fuel: "Come on Han, it's just us, only for our four eyes." He was uncomfortable with the routine practice at Natco in which managers took a 7 percent commission from contractors and distributed some of the money to staff. "Here Johan, take it, it is your share."

After Johan retired, he continued to criticize Natco, Priva, and their village collaborators. Eventually he gave up and left Muara Tangkos, even though it was his home village: "I want to live in a peaceful place," he said. "It is not good to have conflict all the time." Johan advised his son, a junior manager for a transnational plantation corporation, to retain his moral standards: "They asked him to sign blank receipts and I said don't do it, just work and when you have saved some money, start your own business." Johan's acts of individual refusal and his eventual departure protected his sense of himself as an upright man. He regretted that he had not been able to fix the mafia system, but he said it was hopeless and he was tired of the fight. In 2011 when Tania stayed at Johan's house the TV news had daily reports about high-level corruption in Jakarta: "If our leaders behave like that," Johan commented, "you can't expect too much from ordinary people; it makes us ashamed to be Indonesian."

Agus was a local Malay who had obtained his job as foreman at Priva through the intervention of his wife's father, a Dayak leader and company man who had a close personal relationship with Pak Wakijan that included rides on his helicopter. Agus felt that getting the job was fair because his own family had given up land to Priva. He had a sliding scale for deciding what size of cut from a worker's pay packet was reasonable (*wajar*) as the "foreman's share," and how much was excessive or in his words, "impolite" (*kurang ajar*). The new manager's rules had tightened control over foremen: "It is so tight now," he commented, "if a pay packet is short IDR50 we will be fired. Everyone has to report for roll call at 5:30 AM. For maintenance work, the foreman gets a budget—so many worker days, so much material—and if the job is not finished the foreman has to pay from his own pocket. You have to show the identity card for every worker in your group, and they have to pick up their pay in person." The new rules created inconvenience for foremen but did not stop them from cheating the company or taking a cut from workers' pay (figure 2.6).

Agus said he liked the more professional management style Priva had adopted. He argued that the company's new reputation for being well run increased his own market value as a foreman, which could be useful if he needed a new job. But he had bigger plans. He was treating his work at Priva as a means to gain experience. He did not expect to stay there permanently because in his view, independent oil palm was the only way to make real money. He did not live modestly: his household expenses were at least IDR5 million (USD500) per month and his job at Priva barely covered them. He wanted to send his children to university and to prepare for the anticipated expense, he said he needed to get 8 hectares of independent oil palm into production. It was his family network that made his plan feasible. His wife's village had been the center of cattle raising by Madurese migrants until they fled in 1998. The tradition of cattle raising had continued, and he was raising cattle on his wife's village land to generate capital. He bought 5 hectares of former rubber land from his mother, paying her a third of the market price, but he still struggled to pay for high quality seedlings and fertilizer, costs he pegged at IDR20 million (USD2,000) per hectare. For workers without local links and family land, the move from foreman to independent oil palm farmer was quite out of reach.

FIGURE 2.6 Foremen at Work

Each division has foremen who intersperse supervising workers with office work in which they are sheltered from the hot Kalimantan sun and have time to snack and chat. Their clean, pressed uniform shirts, pens, and reading glasses denote their status. They keep track of each harvester's productivity (displayed on the pin board), a performance of transparency that masks the "foreman's share." PHOTO: PUJO SEMEDI.

Tagor's Progress through the Ranks

Tagor was a Batak who arrived at Priva in 2005, looking for work. His first position was in the mill, but he found the mill foremen unqualified for their role, creating dangerous working conditions that put everyone at risk. He had a low opinion of most of Priva's managers and foremen whom he said had insufficient education and were not competent to do their jobs. Many had been recruited through nepotism: they were the kin of Pak Wakijan or kin of company men who demanded jobs for their family members. While at the mill Tagor made some efforts to protect workers by insisting that Priva correct the way it counted overtime and holiday bonuses. His weapon was the 2003 Labor Law, which he often quoted: "The law says it should be like this. . . . . but they do it like that. . . . It has to be corrected." Surprisingly Priva did not fire him, but he moved to a different job as a mill security guard. He enjoyed the relative freedom of the shift work that enabled him to moonlight as a part-time schoolteacher in Muara Tangkos.

Tagor favored tight rules so long as they were fair and orderly. He was uneasy with Priva's poor management and the instability it produced, and he criticized the new manager appointed in 2011 for subjecting workers to new rules and reduced pay without warning or negotiation. In 2015 another new manager, a fellow Batak, recognized Tagor's qualities and promoted him to the role of junior manager. He embraced his new job with enthusiasm and shifted his position from that of company critic to wholehearted supporter. He was excited by Priva's progress under professional management: yields increased, and some mafia practices were stopped. Sadly the Batak manager only stayed for two years and Priva reverted to its path of decline. Tagor stayed on because his new managerial position gave him a good prospect of being able to finance his children's education. He looked into buying an oil palm plot but found the cost prohibitive. Meanwhile his rise through the ranks gave him more pay and perks, and he moved from the housing block reserved for mill workers and guards to a bigger house in the managers' block overlooking the Kapuas.

Tina and Desi

Tina and Desi were among around forty landless Malay women from Muara Tangkos and nearby enclaves who did casual maintenance work for Priva. Some of these women had lost their land to Priva; others had never owned land, but they lost their work as rubber tappers when their neighbors' rubber gardens were replaced by palm. Since few local men were employed by Priva, the women's incomes were crucial for household survival. Many of their husbands were absent, seeking work elsewhere in the district, but the women stayed in the village to anchor their families and try to keep their children in school.[14] "We have to hold on here, where else would we go?" Tina lamented. Lacking options, they had to accept whatever work Priva gave them. As casual workers they were not protected by the 2003 Labor Law, so Priva had the legal right to hire and fire them at will, lay them off when it was short of fertilizers or chemicals, and provide zero benefits. The women's position was further undermined by the fact that Priva could easily replace them. Managers could draw workers not only from the nearby enclaves but also from Tanjung town where there were many women willing to commute daily to work on the plantation. As at Natco, managers used contractors for replanting and construction, and the contractors recruited their work crews from across the province. Managers did not prioritize landless women from the enclaves and women worried that managers might start to outsource routine maintenance work to contractors as well, leaving them with nothing.

When managers imposed the new labor regime in 2011, Tina, Desi, and other women workers were unanimous in their assessment: Priva was asking them to work too hard and absorb too many risks for an unreasonably low return. Like the security guard Sarip, women workers felt Priva was increasing its extraction of their labor while reducing signs of care that made workers feel valued and respected. Sarip responded by withdrawing his effort, but women had fewer means of self-protection. Under the new regime Priva switched women who worked clearing undergrowth with a bush knife from a day rate to a piece rate and they lost out heavily. Since much of the plantation was overgrown, they could clear only ten palms per day, giving them an income of one-fifth the district minimum wage. It was mainly older women who did this task. Priva switched women who spread fertilizers to a fixed daily rate based on meeting a quota with no overtime, resulting in a 30 percent reduction in their average monthly income. Their work was extremely strenuous, especially on hilly terrain where they had to climb up and down multiple times to refill their buckets. As Tina described it, "sometimes when I'm carrying that fertilizer, I feel I just can't do it anymore, I'm so worn out. I get a headache from the smell. It makes my eyes swell up, and I cry until night." As with harvesters, after 2014 failure to meet the daily quota for fertilizing meant that the entire month's pay reverted to a low, per kilogram rate.

Workers tasked with spraying chemicals were highly vulnerable to injury. In addition to the strain of carrying buckets of water from the nearest stream, carrying tanks on their backs, and continuous pumping action with the right arm, they suffered burns where the chemicals touched their skin or if the tank leaked. They also experienced damage to their lungs, manifested in a burning sensation, shortness of breath, and chronic coughing. They did not wear masks that they said made it impossible to breathe. Instead, they tied scarves loosely around their mouths and noses. The effects of the chemicals were severe enough to disable women and stop them from working after fifteen years. Priva's response to the health risk was to provide women with two cans of milk per month. In Tina's understanding the purpose of the milk was not to boost their strength; rather, the women were instructed to drink both cans at once to make them vomit, so the poison in their bodies would come out.[15] The supply of milk was also erratic. After workers received none for several months they feared Priva had stopped providing milk, further evidence of its lack of care. Although women bore the highest health risk of all plantation workers, their casual status gave them no legal right to health benefits or medical care, nor to compensation for their injuries.

Women workers' attempts to push back against the reductions in their pay were limited by their casual status and the fact that they could be so easily replaced. The non-urgent nature of their work also limited their leverage. Around the same time as harvesters staged their wildcat strike, all twenty-four men who loaded the fruit onto Priva's eight trucks stayed home for three days and achieved a reinstatement of the previous pay system. Their success hinged on the strategic nature of their work: without loaders, heaps of harvested fruit bunches rotted by the roadside and the mill had to close. Women's maintenance tasks could be delayed without loss to Priva. A few women workers did strike for six days, but Priva managers threatened to send thugs to their homes to intimidate them. Tina and some friends tried a polite approach. When they noticed that some days were missing from their pay in the transition from the old system to the new one, they went to the Priva office to inquire. "If they say we are paid per day it should really be per day. How can they say some days were missing? We were just asking for our rights."

Tina said she hated the company. She was indignant about the callous treatment and theft of workers' pay. Her main demand was for balance: tighter rules would be fine if the pay increased to match. She also demanded care and respect, and she was alert to the problem of disposability because of her mother's bitter experience. Her mother suffered a workplace injury, an infection from a thorn that refused to heal and left her unable to walk for six months. "Priva paid nothing for doctors. They used her up then threw her out," Tina observed. A foreman told her mother, "If you're too old to work you should stop, we only need workers." Although Tina's mother had worked for Priva for two decades, her casual status enabled Priva to throw her out like old rags. She had become *manusia konyol*: someone induced to make a sacrifice that earns them neither recognition nor reward.

Desi's approach to protecting herself was to outsmart the company: "Priva wants to claim our hours," she said. "If we're not smart about it they will tire us out." Faced with an increased quota of spray tanks from twelve to fifteen per day she doubled down: "Who can do that much? We need our tactics, like emptying out some of the water." Desi's tactics protected not just her hours but also her self-esteem: as an older woman and experienced worker, she felt she knew how to handle the company's excessive demands. Young women workers' self-preservation took an expressive form as they rejected the layers of baggy clothing worn by older women to protect their bodies and came to work in fashionable jeans and T-shirts. They dressed as if they did not belong on a plantation and spent their breaks listening to Korean pop music on their cell phones, reminders of their school days and futures they still imagined for themselves somewhere far away from sweat and exhaustion.[16]

A Constitutive Absence

The absence of independent unions was a constitutive element of plantation life in Tanjung. Since the violent elimination of the plantation workers' union Sarbupri in 1966, there has been no union or party capable of organizing workers or protecting their interests collectively. Workers at Priva and Natco were chronically fragmented. At Priva workers' lack of collective mobilization seemed to arise "naturally" from their segmentation by gender, place of origin, language, ethnicity, and religion, and their different status and spatial orientation. The men were mainly permanent workers who lived in plantation housing while most of the women were casual workers who continued to live in their home villages. These two groups of workers—men/migrants/permanent workers/harvesters on one side, and women/locals/casual day labor/maintenance workers on the other—were all employed by Priva yet they had little or no interaction. When small groups of workers with particular grievances staged wildcat strikes they did not connect across worker groups, and in the absence of solidarity and organization they made little headway.

At Natco the political technology deployed to immobilize workers and form them as compliant subjects was carefully planned. Workers at Natco were not segmented by gender or ethnicity: most of them were Javanese and married to fellow workers. Yet when they had their bonuses cut, they did not mobilize to demand resolution; they simply worked fewer hours as if their relationship to the corporation was based on a tacit sliding price. They handled grievances by making personal appeals to superiors. Fear of being branded troublemakers and reassigned to marginal and less lucrative positions was enough to discourage more forceful individual or collective action. Although workers like Godril and Monah who had spent their working lives at Natco took these modes of conduct for granted, Natco had been careful about worker selection. Back in 1980 it deliberately sought workers from Java's towns and villages who had no previous experience of plantation work. Like all candidates for government jobs, workers had to provide police certificates confirming that their parents had no Communist or union links.

The new recruits were to staff a new kind of plantation that would be "clean" and union free. Whatever violence Natco workers may have witnessed in Java as children (they were around ten years old during the massacres of 1965–66), they had been schooled in the New Order mantra that it was Communists and their unions who brought anarchy and destruction.[17] Formally, all Natco workers were members of the state-employee antiunion KORPRI.[18] A new union formed after reformasi SP Bun (Serikat Pekerja Perkebunan) was little different: it was headed by company managers and designed to reinforce company hierarchy.[19] Under the 2003 Labor Law workers gained the right to form independent unions, but as of 2015 no new unions had emerged.

On arrival at Natco workers were further schooled in a New Order familism that framed the state plantation corporation and its workers, like the New Order government and its people, as members of one family—harmonious, hierarchical, and bound by a common interest.[20] They were told explicitly during regular Monday pep talks that Natco would protect them so long as they obeyed the family head. Managers did not treat workers as adversaries in a class struggle, nor even as a group with distinct interests; they treated them as unruly children in need of firm guidance.

Infantilizing workers was also a feature of colonial plantation life, as Ann Stoler reports. Sumatra's plantation managers characterized Javanese contract workers as lazy, dishonest, and childlike. The law classified workers who refused to work or attempted to abscond as criminals. When workers occasionally attacked or murdered plantation managers or their families, managers treated their actions as irrational outbursts that confirmed workers' childlike mentality. There was a partial shift in the 1920s when managers argued that their irrational, childlike workers had suddenly become dangerous because they had been infected by Communist and nationalist ideas. At no point did managers acknowledge that workers who were being starved, beaten, cheated, and driven too hard had a legitimate grievance; still less did they interpret their actions as skirmishes in a class struggle with labor on one side and corporate capital on the other.[21]

Contemporary workers who are treated as children are still in a colonial situation, albeit one reformatted along the New Order's familistic lines. For a brief period in the 1950s Sarbupri challenged this imperial debris, educating workers to think differently about their social position in relation to corporations and society at large. Workers were not children to be guided nor serfs seeking livelihood and protection, feudal style. They were participants in a production process who deserved fair pay and benefits. Lacking access to such education, workers we met in Tanjung had no framework for linking their sense of injustice to a broader analysis or collective struggle. Even the elimination of Sarbupri had left no apparent trace. Susan de Groot Heupner, a researcher who spent months on plantations in Sumatra working with organizers attempting to recruit members for a new independent union, Serbundo, also noted this absence: "During observation, not a single reference has been made to historical events, such as those between 1965 and 1967, or to past structures, practices or regimes." Instead, workers she met attributed their dismal working conditions and harassment by company thugs to present structures alone. The violence of the past was embedded in everyday plantation routines that they understood to be natural and inevitable.[22] Similarly, the plantation life experienced by workers in Tanjung, one in which they could be cheated and thrown out like old rags, was constituted by the elimination of Sarbupri and the order of impunity it enabled, but no one we met made the connection.

When we discussed the prospects for labor organizing with Godril and his friends they did not mention the history of Sarbupri in Sumatra, its achievements in improving worker conditions during the 1950s, or the fate of its members during the massacres of 1965–66, which they probably knew nothing about. They did not mix with local villagers, so they knew nothing about Sarbupri's local history either. Sarbupri was active in Tanjung and had members at NV Agris, the army-owned corporation that ran the rubber plantation from 1957 until its bankruptcy in the 1970s. Villagers recalled seeing union members in paramilitary uniforms being trained as volunteers for the fight against Malaysia; some mentioned that union members were suspected of burning some plantation rubber trees and worker barracks, but the identity of the perpetrators was never confirmed.

The story villagers told most often was about Rajab, a local Malay who was a foreman at NV Agris and an active Communist Party cadre. He hung a Communist flag in front of his house near the Tangkos River. This was not a risky move at the time because the Indonesian Communist Party was legal until 1966; it had 3.5 million active members and 20 million supporters, the largest number outside China and the USSR.[23] There were no massacres in Tanjung, but when the party was banned army officers arrested party and Sarbupri members. They singled out leaders like Rajab for brutal treatment: they stripped him naked and made him crawl on his knees like an animal with a rope around his neck. They accused him of raping his daughter, a common army tactic to cast Communists as animals and infidels. Villagers who told this story were appalled by it because they knew Rajab as a neighbor and a good man who would never hurt his family. Regular Sarbupri members were arrested and held in Tanjung town for some weeks, then released with orders to report monthly to the military base. None of them returned to the plantation. They moved to upriver areas where they could work as rubber tappers for local farmers, and their children married into the local Malay and Dayak population.

The absence of a union was constitutive of another overwhelming presence in Tanjung's plantation zone: the mafia system that operated as a mode of distribution, siphoning modest shares of plantation wealth into the pockets of workers, managers, and surrounding villagers. A mafia system was also rampant in colonial times when workers were similarly disempowered and lacked legal recourse. As Pujo discovered from the archives of a tea plantation in Java, the internal dynamic was predatory as people with more power extracted tolls from people with less, and it was hierarchically arranged: the higher the office, the bigger the opportunities to reap rewards. Theft and predation were not a formal component of colonial technologies designed to pacify workers, but they were tolerated within limits because plantation corporations benefited from them: mafia practices kept production moving and managers and workers firmly attached.[24]

Mafia practices at Natco and Priva had their uses, but there were frictions and fragilities on all sides. Stealing made many of our interlocutors uncomfortable. Johan hated foremen who preyed on their workers and was reluctant to accept his cut of the commissions that managers extracted. When he worked as a foreman, he tried to improve conditions for the workers in his unit—rather like foreman Rajab, who became a Communist cadre a generation before. After he resigned from Natco Johan continued to criticize the mafia system that he thought was a terrible way to organize corporate and public life, but he had no organization or political vocabulary to translate his fury into collective action. The discourse of corruption was the only one available to him, and it did not offer a comprehensive analysis of the role of impunity in shaping plantation life, nor a way forward. Recall also that some of the corporations' abuses were quite legal since casual workers are not protected under the 2003 Labor Law. Whether within or outside the law, it was the absence of an organized counterforce that enabled the abuse of workers and predatory extraction to continue unchallenged. Excessive predation can damage the goose that lays golden eggs as it did in Natco, where it pushed the corporation close to bankruptcy, and at Priva where unfertilized palms produced few fruit. Yet the goose may be kept alive because a great many people benefit from its presence.

Conclusion

In this chapter we asked, Who worked at Natco and Priva and why did they work there? In 1980 when Natco was established in Tanjung with the mandate to open up a new plantation frontier, local Malays and Dayaks were not interested in kuli work as they still had their own land to farm. Hence Natco worked with the government labor office to import workers directly from Java. In 1990 Priva hired transmigrants for day labor at the establishment phase, but in the long run it met its labor needs by recruiting locals and migrants who arrived spontaneously, looking for work. By 2010 the saturation of the subdistrict by multiple plantations had created a proximate labor reserve as Malays and Dayaks who had become landless and lost their rubber tapping income desperately needed plantation work. Managers hired women casual workers from the enclaves, but they still preferred to hire migrants as harvesters, and had no difficulty recruiting them from the abundant province-wide and pan-Indonesian labor supply.

Much of the classic literature on plantation labor concerns slavery, indenture, and coercion. In contemporary Indonesia workers are not bound by contracts or physically confined to plantations, raising the question of what attracts them to plantation work and why they stay. In one way or another the rewards of plantation work must be better than the alternatives, with "better" a multidimensioned assessment in which workers' long- and short-term goals and their evaluation of risks play a part. Our research coincided with a period of instability in which Natco was in decline and the security of long-term workers was disrupted by new hiring practices and a precarious retirement. At Priva an attempt to tighten rules pressed some workers beyond the point of exhaustion while others were able to earn good money, enough to hold them in place. These changing conditions brought workers' reflections to the fore, and some of our interlocutors shifted their positions from loyal to critical or the reverse, offering us some insight into their reasoning.

Natco workers who were initially recruited from Java in the 1980s stayed for thirty years because the company offered them a secure livelihood and provisions for a stable family life. These were good jobs, and they appreciated the dignity that decent working conditions provided. Their loyalty declined when new policies reduced their security and prevented their children from taking over their jobs as they retired. They were especially bitter about managers who reneged on the moral bargain that rewarded them for loyal service, but they stayed anyway, waiting for their pensions to start. The facilities provided to workers by Priva were always less extensive.

Workers there made fine-grained calculations about the balance of risks and rewards. They also sought evidence that their contributions were appreciated and were offended when managers treated them as mere instruments who could be lured to work but deprived of reward and thrown out when no longer of use (manusia konyol). Workers' feelings of security, loyalty, precarity, and fury entered their assessment of plantation work and informed their decisions about whether to leave or stay.

The absence of unions was a constitutive feature of plantation life in Tanjung and played a role in workers' practices and evaluations. After the elimination of Sarbupri in 1966, labor relations were shaped by New Order familism, a political technology deliberately designed to orient workers away from organized struggle based in class solidarity toward loyalty to a corporation envisaged as a family. The family idiom was itself imperial debris: rot that remained from colonial racial rule in which workers were treated as children, fit only to be guided or punished. Lacking means for collective bargaining, workers in both plantations took covert steps alone or in collusion with others to protect their interests and improve their economic situation.

Mafia practices helped bind workers and managers to the corporations but made many of them uneasy: Tagor wanted rules to be transparent and enforced; Iksan was appalled by the predatory claims his superiors made on his labor; Tina and Johan hated the petty tyrannies foremen imposed. Workers tried to protect themselves from excessive predation while taking advantage of opportunities, but something did not feel right. In different ways, workers indicated that it was not just the material conditions of plantation work that troubled them but the forms of life it generated as well. Those who left had better options, namely the possibility of becoming independent oil palm farmers for far higher rewards. Most workers had no better options. The crushing oversupply of labor forced them to tolerate plantation work as a crucial means of survival and, for some of them, as a means to finance education with the hope that their children's working lives would take a different form.

3

Fragile Plots

In this chapter we ask: What does it mean for farmers to be bound to a corporation? In Indonesia as elsewhere, the word farmer (*petani*) signals autonomy, self-sufficiency, and prosperity earned through hard work. In 2010–15 Dayak farmers in Tanjung's upriver areas still had some of these characteristics. They retained significant control over their land, labor, and decision making, although they were not entirely free. They cultivated rice and grew or collected other foods, but their ability to afford school fees, improved housing, motorbikes, and consumer goods was heavily dependent on the global price of their cash crop, rubber. They sold their rubber through local traders (called *tokeh* or *tauke*) with whom many were perpetually in debt. When debts became too large a trader might seize rubber trees in payment, but if this happened, farmers could recover their dignity and autonomy by opening new land on the forest frontier. Not all farmers prospered, but class differentiation among them was limited by the abundance of land and the relative scarcity of labor: traders and farmers with large rubber holdings employed their neighbors as tappers and paid them a high share (70 percent) that helped to spread wealth among villagers. Rubber tapping was democratic in another way too: young and old, women and men, healthy or not—anyone could do it, unlike oil palm harvesting, which favored young men.

The situation of oil palm out-growers attached to Priva was far more fragile. We sensed this fragility one day when we were sitting at a coffee stall in Tapang Dacin, a transmigration settlement with a mixed population of Dayaks and transmigrants from Java and Nusa Tenggara Timur (NTT). We were talking to the Dayak owner Sempon about his grievances with the company when his father-in-law Tasi drove up on his motorbike in a panic. The older man was not strong or skilled enough to harvest his own out-grower plot, so he relied on a hired harvester to do the work. But it was already noon, and the harvester had not shown up. Tasi risked losing an entire month's income if he could not get his palm fruit to the roadside on time for pick up. "Did anyone know someone who could do the work?" he asked in desperation.

The livelihoods of Tasi and his fellow out-growers were fragile because they grew a single crop; they were locked into a relationship with a single corporation, dependent on its roads and mill, its co-ops and credit; and they were subject to the endemic predation of the mafia system. They were also caught up in the transmigration scheme that promised landless migrants a future as independent and modern farmers and offered locals who released land an opportunity to become out-growers who share in plantation wealth. As a storyline the out-grower scheme was attractive to its members, but as a design it had three catastrophic flaws. First, it required the occupation of villagers' land by Priva and transmigrants, degrading their citizenship in ways we discussed in chapter 1. Second, the scheme locked out-growers and the corporation into a symbiotic relationship in which the survival of each side depended on the other, but the fragility of out-growers was more acute. Third, it allocated out-growers plots of oil palm of just 2 hectares, a size that was too small to support a family and guaranteed that many of them would stagnate or become impoverished. Without savings, a family emergency could force them to mortgage or sell their oil palm plot, a loss that enabled entrepreneurial out-growers to accumulate.[1]

Class differentiation among out-growers was not part of the transmigration plan that envisaged relatively equal farm households united in a co-op who prospered together with the support of a benevolent and responsible corporation. The reality was otherwise. Tasi was one of the original Dayak landholders in Tapang Dacin and as an erstwhile company man, he had managed to withhold some of his land when the bulldozers arrived and accumulate a few extra out-grower plots. His absent harvester Tomas was the son of Peter and Susi, transmigrants from NTT who were barely holding on to their original 2 hectare plot and had nothing to give their son. Tomas was himself married with children and supported his family by harvesting for different out-growers. Maybe his position as a skilled harvester gave him some bargaining power, and he used his absence to send Tasi a message; or maybe he was injured or sick.

We begin by examining the ambiguous position of out-growers who were dependent on the corporation for their survival yet formally classified as ordinary villagers. The form of occupation to which they were subject was in part territorial, as their land was part of the corporate concession and planted with monocrop palm; it was also dispersed in multiple practices, sites, and institutions that enabled the corporation to extract value from their labor while avoiding responsibility for their fate. We track how the relations that bound out-growers to the corporation were structured, and how they were experienced. Then we examine the practices that emerged among out-growers over the long term as some prospered and others stagnated or lost their land. Finally, we describe a prolonged blockade that demonstrated the resilience of Priva and managers' tactics for sustaining the plantation. Corporate fragility did not mean collapse or retreat.

Stepchildren of the Plantation

The Indonesian term for out-growers, *plasma*, suggests a vital link with a nucleus since in cell biology the nucleus and plasma are equally fragile, and one cannot survive without the other. Priva's out-grower scheme was so extensive it suggested a vital relation: the core plantation of 3,833 hectares would not be viable without 16,000 hectares of out-grower plots. But mutual dependence can be hierarchical and fraught. Out-growers described their relationship to the corporation as that of stepchildren. To be "made into a stepchild" (*kami dianaktirikan*) means to be part of an enterprise but treated poorly. A stepchild is made to work hard for the family but excluded from its benefits, given old clothes and leftover food, and not included in family conversations. By using this idiom out-growers suggested that the corporation was like a parent who exploited their labor but treated them callously and exposed them to suffering and ruin. As children they could not survive alone, hence they could not escape the parent's grip, but they were reluctant to accept cruel treatment. Their demand for fairness was undermined by the fact that—as in a family—there was no contract specifying Priva's obligations toward them.[2] Moreover Priva was not a person they could approach (like a stepfather or rubber trader); it was a shifting cast of characters (managers, public relations staff, company men) who engaged in contradictory practices, including mafia practices in which out-growers were complicit.

The out-grower scheme co-devised by the Ministries of Transmigration and Agriculture (PIR-BUN-Trans) envisaged a pathway toward farmer independence. That was the principal story line. Professional plantation managers would oversee the preparation of thousands of hectares of oil palm, then divide it into plots of 2 hectares per household; they would instruct novice out-growers on technical matters; and they would organize out-growers into co-ops that would handle the transportation of fruit to the mill and gradually take over responsibility for road maintenance. After they repaid their debt for plot preparation, out-growers would receive individual land titles and become formally free of their bond to the corporation, although the plan assumed that co-ops would continue their coordinating role.

In theory free farmers could sell their product anywhere, but if there was only one mill within reach the corporation would still be in a monopsony position. Dependence on one crop, one corporation, and one mill would be a fragile form of freedom, but for out-growers who joined the transmigration scheme with nothing, it was a huge step forward in their social and economic status and they embraced the dream gladly. What made them furious was that the corporation did not provide them with the means to achieve the promised independence. They would be stuck in the position of stepchildren indefinitely. To examine what this meant in human terms we unpack the elements of the out-grower system one by one, focusing on the nature of the bond between the two parties.

Autonomous Farmers or Bonded Workers?

Out-growers for Priva saw themselves as farmers, a status they thought was superior to that of kulis in the core plantation who were subject to the authority of a foreman standing over them, and the indignity of roll calls and constant surveillance. Their self-description as farmers and the promise of a fuller autonomy to come after they had paid the debt bound them to Priva.[3] In the meantime, however, they worked to produce palm fruit for the corporation. They performed the same tasks as other plantation workers, but they were not classified as workers under the 2003 Labor Law and Priva had no obligation to pay them the minimum wage. Priva did not need to worry about their welfare or living conditions nor did it provide them with pensions, health services, schools, or other facilities. Their livelihoods depended on the corporation but from the corporation's perspective they were ordinary villagers who had to take care of themselves.

Out-growers captured the ambiguity of their position in the term they used to refer to their payday (*gajian*): the day each month when they received payment from the company for their oil palm fruit. Payday suggests a stable salary, like the salary received by Priva's permanent workers or by government officials. Yet the amount out-growers received on payday was not pegged to the work they had performed; it was the monthly revenue from their assigned plot that hinged on the global price of palm oil, the condition of the roads, deductions for debt repayment, and other charges. When considered as captive workers the amount out-growers received on payday was meager. Even when the price of palm oil peaked around 2011 the net income from a standard low-yielding 2 hectare plot after deductions was IDR550,000 (USD 55), well below the district minimum wage of IDR925,000 and far below the provincial poverty line of IDR1,351,530; it was barely enough to buy rice with nothing left for other kinds of food, schooling, clothing, and so forth. Even the low income was insecure. Priva could refuse to buy their palm fruit if the price dropped so low it was not worth milling, or a receiving clerk at the mill might reject the fruit or grade it as poor quality because out-growers did not pay him a big enough toll to let it pass.

Entrapment in a situation that exposed them to exploitation and extortion might seem to make out-growers into ideal workers for a corporation intent on maximizing profit, but Priva managers saw the situation quite differently. They resented out-growers' residual freedom—the fact that out-growers could not be relied upon to cultivate their plots according to technical specifications, applied insufficient fertilizer, and achieved low yields. Out-growers made continual demands for road improvement and quick turnaround when unloading fruit, and when disgruntled they mounted protests and blockades. They were, in short, prickly subjects who were much harder to control than workers under a foreman's thumb. Low yields and disruptions at the mill reduced managers' production bonuses and challenged their self-image as technical experts who were firmly in charge.

Roads

Roads were a flashpoint in out-grower relations with Priva. When we visited Tapang Dacin in 2015 the road was impassable for trucks. Out-growers had formed a crew of volunteer and paid workers who were trying to insert palm trunks into the trenches dug by truck wheels. Only motorbikes driven carefully along the edge of the trench could pass. Building and maintaining roads in Kalimantan is expensive. The red clay soils erode easily and when combined with heavy rain and heavy trucks bearing tons of palm fruit, they can turn into mud ponds 2 meters (6½ feet) deep—deep enough to sink a truck. To harden and maintain the roads Priva had to import stones by barge from other Indonesian islands, but the cost was huge. It had built a total of 258 kilometers (169 miles) of roads within the concession boundaries to connect out-grower plots to the mill, but it neglected to maintain roads where out-grower production was too low to justify the expense. From a business perspective, the decision to prioritize areas with more production closer to the mill made perfect sense; from the perspective of out-growers it was the decision of a callous stepparent who willfully made them suffer.

Out-growers depended on Priva-built roads to send hundreds of tons of fruit to the mill daily and receive back fertilizers and other supplies. Unlike Kalimantan's previously dominant cash crop, rubber, which can be stored for months and transported on the back of a motorbike, oil palm fruit are so bulky and heavy they can only be sent to the mill by truck and their transfer is time sensitive: the fruit has to reach the mill within forty-eight hours or it spoils. That was why Tasi was locked into a tight schedule: if he missed his block's assigned pick-up date, he had no other way to get his fruit to the mill.

Out-grower frustration came to a boiling point during episodes when the roads were closed due to heavy rains. In 2011 washed-out roads blocked access to hundreds of out-grower plots for three months. Again in 2013, washed-out roads reduced the out-grower harvest reaching the mill from 2,735 tons in October to 989 tons in December. For Priva this was a problem, but for out-growers for whom oil palm was their only source of income, missed paydays were catastrophic. They had invested money in fertilizer and labor, costs they could not recuperate. They had to pay for food, school fees, and basic expenses. Many had to pay monthly installments for their motorbikes, an essential working tool for accessing distant plots. Some out-growers salvaged a small part of their harvest by using the old infrastructure—flat-bottomed boats on the shallow Tangkos River—but this route was more expensive, the tonnage capacity was limited, and few out-grower plots had river access. The entire out-grower scheme was built around a grid of roads, making washed-out roads a logistical nightmare as well as a financial one.

Out-growers could not turn to law to oblige Priva to take responsibility for the roads because Priva was not bound by a contract. Priva's agreement with the Ministry of Transmigration specified only that it should build the necessary roads—it said nothing about their quality or maintenance.[4] Priva managers insisted that the district government was supposed to take over road maintenance after a few years. District officials claimed that the company was still responsible because these were production roads primarily used by heavy trucks transporting palm fruit. Out-growers argued that as citizens, district politicians and officials should attend to their needs, but officials returned the problem to the company, arguing that corporations paid minimal taxes to the district, hence they had no funds to maintain the roads. Priva passed the problem back to out-growers, arguing that their co-ops had a role to play in road maintenance so they should increase the road levy they charged out-growers and coordinate with other co-ops along the route. To summarize, the ongoing maintenance of the most crucial element of the out-grower infrastructure, the roads, depended on the economic incentive of the company, the political capacity of villagers to make demands on the district government, and cooperation between co-ops. Yet none of the economic, political, and social relations necessary to secure the roads was actually in place.

Out-growers had limited access to government officials and politicians hence they focused their anger on the proximate target: Priva and its woeful neglect. Before each rainy season panicked out-growers organized demonstrations at the Priva office and blockaded access to the mill to gain attention. "We are not anarchists," a village headman who participated in these actions remarked, "but we need to use blockades to get Priva to take responsibility." Priva managers responded to protests but not comprehensively: they fixed one road here, another there, seeding more anger and the sense that they were choosing favorites, or they had been bought. Priva managers, for their part, felt that the company was being held hostage to mob rule as out-growers were never satisfied and always demanded more. Roads transported fruit to the mill; they also inserted mafia practices and feelings of anger and neglect into the everyday experience of out-grower life (figure 3.1).

Debt

Priva took out a bank loan to develop the core plantation and the Ministry of Transmigration (with support from the World Bank) secured a low-interest loan to pay for the preparation of the out-grower plots. Out-growers had to repay their share of the debt to obtain their land titles and break free from their bond to Priva, but there was a catch: Priva was the broker and guarantor

FIGURE 3.1 Sunk Truck

Dayak out-growers in Salimbat were notorious for taking a tough stand with Priva and get-ting what they wanted. In 2011 they demanded stones for road hardening, and the new man-ager expressed impatience in some careless words: "If they want stones so much," he said, "let them eat stones." He was speaking at an internal company meeting, but Salimbat leaders promptly received a report. They mobilized a crowd to find the manager and ask him to make amends for the insult. "We may be poor," Salimbat leader Jamin said, "but not so poor we need to eat stones." Fearing violence, Priva staff evacuated the manager and his deputy by boat to Pontianak City, and they never returned. Priva staff sent Salimbat IDR70 million (USD7,000) in payment of a customary fine, but hamlet leaders did not consider the matter resolved because the manager did not come before them in person to apologize. Priva staff complained about the Dayaks' excessive sensitivity: the manager had not meant the remark to be taken literally. From their perspective Dayak anger was irrational; from Salimbat's perspective, threats were necessary to keep their road from becoming a mud pond. PHOTO: PUJO SEMEDI.

of the loan. Unlike independent farmers who can select a source of credit based on criteria such as cost, transparency, and trust, out-growers bound to Priva and Natco had no control over the loan conditions.

At Natco, out-growers who asked managers to provide them with an account of how much money Natco had borrowed for plot preparation re-ceived no response. After endless delay they sent a "fact-finding team" to the bank's head office in Jakarta to try to find this information. The bank in Ja-karta told them to try the branch in South Kalimantan, and there they were told to go to Pontianak. After this frustrating and expensive runaround they finally obtained the information. When they saw the numbers, they were convinced that they were inflated: Natco had overcharged them. In protest some out-growers stopped repaying their debt, which meant bypassing the Natco-imposed co-op and selling their fruit through private traders. Both parties lost money through this arrangement: the private traders took a commission that reduced the price out-growers received for their fruit, and Natco lost control over the quality of its supply as traders mixed in fruit from multiple sources. For out-growers, however, it was a statement of independence. Debt that is manipulated or not transparent is part of the ILO definition of forced labor, and they would not tolerate it.

Priva and its out-growers encountered an even more intractable problem. The bank's record of debt payments received did not match out-growers' records, or the records kept by Priva. Apparently, some payments had never reached the bank. This put Budi, manager of the out-grower scheme, in a difficult position. He was a local Malay whose family were out-growers so while it was his job to represent Priva he understood out-growers' frustration.

> I went with the finance staff to visit some out-growers and they were really insistent. They said we took the money. I told them it was not us. They should go and make a police report, or take it to the subdistrict so we can all get to the bottom of it. My boss told me to get the out-growers to sign a document agreeing to the bank's numbers, but I told him I can't do that. Maybe the illiterate ones would sign but the smart ones will refuse. Do we want to take that risk? I showed him the data on my laptop that confirmed the amount the farmers had paid, and he said OK then in that case we won't force them to sign.

Budi thought out-growers should make a police report and try the legal route "so we can all get to the bottom of it," but they did not take his advice. They did not believe that Priva staff who had stolen the money would ever be held accountable. Entanglement with the police and the judicial mafia would only waste their time and cost them more money. But they did not want to be taken for fools who kept on paying a debt that they had already settled, so they too began to bypass the co-op and sell their crop through private traders. Their refusal salvaged their dignity but prolonged their bond with Priva as the bank would not release their land titles until the records showed the debt was paid. Without titles they could not obtain credit from a bank or credit union to replant their aging palms. Priva's internal mafia was preventing them from obtaining their promised independence.

Co-Ops

All the co-ops in Priva's out-grower scheme were fragile, but the one in Tapang Dacin was especially fraught. Different Dayak factions as well as transmigrants jostled for control over the co-op, which was a central node in both the formal organization of the out-grower scheme and its mafia practices. The co-ops were established by Priva as compulsory one-stop portals for flows of money, materials, and information. Each block of five hundred households had a co-op that was supposed to supply fertilizer and other chemical inputs, maintain roads, organize trucks to collect and transport harvested fruit, funnel payments on payday, and update out-growers on the balance of their debt. Like colonial systems of indirect rule, the mediation of co-ops enabled managers to issue commands and exercise "power without knowledge": they took no responsibility for out-grower welfare or resolving out-grower problems, and individual out-growers had no mechanism to approach them to get grievances resolved.[5]

Co-ops were usually run by company men. When an out-grower with an independent approach managed to get elected to the co-op committee the result was a stand-off, as happened in Tapang Dacin. Markus, an outspoken transmigrant from NTT, studied the district bylaw that spells out how co-op members should elect their leaders and hold them accountable through practices such transparent bookkeeping. He was a fierce critic of the Dayak group who had run the co-op for two decades. He held them responsible for missing funds, impassable roads, and unreasonable fees charged to out-growers with no proper accounts. He campaigned to get himself elected to the internal auditing committee (*badan pengawas*), but when he attempted to check the books, co-op leaders sent thugs to ransack his oil palm plot. This experience and a general climate of intimidation discouraged other co-op members from taking action. Wardiman lost 10 tons of fruit worth IDR15 million (USD1,500) when the road was impassable. "We paid an extra levy of IDR200 per kilogram to the co-op to fix the road, but where did the money go? There are no accounts," he said. "If I ask co-op leaders for clarification, I'll be the one in trouble."

Although Markus and Wardiman characterized the struggle in ethnic terms, as one between Dayak strongmen and vulnerable NTT and Javanese transmigrants, elite capture is a routine problem in Indonesia's state-imposed village co-ops and not unique to multiethnic or remote locations.[6] Yet despite this well-known problem the co-op format is always used for out-grower schemes and seldom questioned. Many Indonesians believe that

TABLE 3.1

Out-Grower Pay Slip

Farmer	Kartono
Co-operative	Raja Ketapang
Month	2010 February
Harvest/kilograms	1,087

DEDUCTIONS	IDR
Transportation	93,786
Road maintenance	8,696
Co-op fee	3,261
Farmer association fee	13,044
Credit payment	550,000
Farming tool payment	–
Fertilizer payment	23,000
Saving	5,000
Photocopy	300
Truck crew consumption	83,000
Grading	–
Mosque/church contribution	–
Bereavement contribution	–
Co-op office building	10,000
Weighing fine	30,000
Weighing cost	33,000
Total deductions	**853,087**

Price/kilogram	1,301.73
Gross revenue	**1,414,980.51**

Net income in receipt	IDR550,384.50 (USD55)

The monthly pay slip the co-op issued to Kartono shows the weight of his harvest (1 ton from a 2 hectare plot), valued at IDR1.4 million (USD140). His credit payment was 39 percent of the gross revenue. The co-op charged him fees for transportation, the co-op building, road maintenance, meal expenses for the truck crew, and unspecified costs and fines for weighing that totaled around 23 percent of gross. Adding up these numbers, his net revenue should have been IDR561,893.51 (USD56), so IDR11,509 (USD1.15) was obviously missing, but all the fees listed were potentially inflated or specious. He paid additional tolls to truck drivers and mill clerks.

co-ops embody national cultural values of mutual assistance and a preference for working together in groups. This idea was popular among colonial officials who conjured an image of a collectivist East in contrast to an individualist West; it was taken up by the nationalist leader Muhammad Hatta, who promoted co-ops as the "economic pillar of the nation"; it was also favored by the Indonesian Communist Party as a means to promote farmer welfare.[7] Under the New Order and its successors, state and corporate sponsored co-ops became instruments of predatory extraction; they lock millions of out-growers into an imposed structure they cannot avoid.

In Tapang Dacin and throughout Priva's out-grower scheme circa 2011, co-ops no longer provided a full slate of services. The minimal function they retained was that of a conduit for money and paper: out-growers could only receive payment through the co-op, and only through the co-op could they pay off their debt. The co-ops' monopoly over the flow of funds made them into highly lucrative toll booths, as a close examination of an out-grower pay-slip reveals (table 3.1).

The Mafia System

Co-ops were not the only toll booths in the out-grower scheme. There were multiple choke points that provided opportunities for theft along the route that palm fruit traveled from out-grower plots to the mill and beyond, and everyone was involved. Markus shared with us his analysis of the mafia system as he had observed it operating in Tapang Dacin over a period of twenty years:

> I will take you from bottom to top, starting with the out-grower plot. The fruit stem should be 2 centimeters, but the farmer keeps it long, to increase the weight. The farmer is already mafia. Then he adds in fruit that is dried up, or rotten. That is mafia.
>
> Now let's go to the farmer group. The group has a head, a secretary, a treasurer. The scales they use are wrong [when they weigh the fruit at the roadside], and some fruit goes missing on the way to the mill. That is mafia. Moving now to the co-op. The co-op leaders collect fees from members to fix up the roads, but they never let members check the accounts. They say they paid the bulldozer for seven hours, but it only worked for four hours, so they kept the money.
>
> Next, to the mill. I experimented with this. Even if everything is correct, the clerk says one palm fruit in ten is below quality, so the company won't

pay for the bad ones. I say give me back the bad ones, but the clerks refuse. That is mafia. Then when the price dropped in 2008 Priva refused to buy our fruit. They said they had no money. We came from far [to join the transmigration scheme] so if we have a problem with the company the government should step in to help resolve it. Some people manipulated the price and made a lot of money, but who suffered? It was the people. Finally the governor understood the problem and fined Priva, but who got the money? It wasn't farmers, it was officials. Then we get to the local government mafia. They misuse the funds they get for organizing Independence Day events so when they have to close the gap, they get money from the company, and Priva charges us for it by paying less for our fruit.

Concretely, Markus explained, out-growers knew the rules: they knew how long the fruit stem should be, and they knew that if they left it too long, the mill would reject it. So they attempted to get the length just right—a bit over regulation length to increase their incomes without being rejected. Out-growers also had a backup system: they paid IDR250,000 (USD25) per truck to the mill clerks who inspected and graded the fruit. Mill clerks assigned a low grade to a batch of fruit if the out-grower did not pay them, or they might assign a low grade because they were under pressure from mill managers to acquire fruit that did not enter the official books. The oil from this off-the-books, uncounted, unpaid fruit added to the total yield, which made the mill seem more efficient and generated a legitimate, on-the-books bonus for managers.

The mafia practices Markus identified were not idiosyncratic, nor were they aberrations: they were built into the out-grower system and entwined around its formal structures. If there was no bureaucratic requirement for the farmer group to note down the weight of the fruit at the roadside, or for the co-op to submit reports, those particular toll booths would not be there (figures 3.2 and 3.3). The key to the mafia system in the out-grower scheme and throughout the plantation zone was the absence of countervailing forces: competing mills, free farmers who could by-pass toll booths, farmers' unions strong enough to insist on fair treatment, and legal redress for co-op members when their leaders abused their power or company staff failed to deposit their debt payment at the bank.[8]

Although it was routine, the mafia system made many of its participants uneasy, and some were explicit about the moral dilemmas it presented. As with mafia practices among workers and managers in the core plantation we examined in chapter 2, stealing could be interpreted as a mode of pushing back against the corporations' extraction of value, but the predatory element set it apart. Occupants of toll booths were often stealing from their neighbors. Bujang, a Malay out-grower, noted that Fredi, the head of the weighing team for his farmer's group, made an extra IDR500,000 (USD50) per month by manipulating the weighing report—a significant sum in Bujang's eyes, "enough to pay the credit for a new motorbike." Bujang could see why Fredi was tempted, but he did not want to be robbed by his neighbor, so he decided to bypass the weighing group and sell his fruit through a private trader. His refusal to submit to theft rescued his dignity—he did not want to be taken for a fool. But he paid a price since bypassing the co-op meant he would not obtain his land title.

Corporate occupation in the out-grower scheme did not set up a uniform system of bureaucratic order, panoptical surveillance, or authoritarian control. Instead, it produced a proliferation of small monopolies and petty

FIGURE 3.2 Weighing Palm Fruit by the Road

The basis of fruit payment is weight, hence weighing out-growers' fruit by the roadside is a crucial step. The head of the weighing group is elected by out-grower block members but distrust prevails. Here the farmer (crouching in the front) is keeping his own record to guard against manipulated numbers, but he has no way to check the accuracy of the scale. The government service for weight verification does not reach the out-grower zone. PHOTO: PUJO SEMEDI.

FIGURE 3.3 Recording Weighing Slips at the Co-Op Office

The head of the weighing group brings the weighing slip from each out-grower's field to the co-op secretary, who records the details in a ledger and fills out another form to send to the Priva office to generate payment in cash. PHOTO: PUJO SEMEDI.

tyrannies at multiple choke points from bottom to top. Individuals who felt morally compromised by the mafia system had the three options outlined by political theorist Albert Hirschman: exit, voice, or loyalty.[9] Markus sold up and left Kalimantan to return to his home district in NTT where he planned to start a fish pond business. He said he was tired of fighting. Loyalty was not an option for him—he thought the mafia system was a terrible way to live. He had tried voice at some risk to himself and without success, so exit was his only option. He worried that fellow out-growers from NTT would suffer intensified predation from local thugs after he left, because they did not fight back. "They better be ready to become like those women who go to work as maids in foreign countries (TKW)," he said, "to keep on submitting, keep on losing, because that is what will happen. If someone asks them for money, they will have to pay up." The price Markus paid for his exit was material: he sold up under duress and did not receive full value for his plots. Budi, the locally hired Malay manager who refused to force out-growers to sign a document that misrepresented their debt, was appalled at the prospect that his kin and neighbors would regard him as a thief. After many unhappy years during which he tried to solve problems for Priva and for his neighbors, he resigned to focus on his own farms where he said he felt at peace. His exit from the company was enabled by his accumulation of oil palm plots that provided more than enough income to provide for his family and send his children and a niece to university. For those who could not or did not exit, the mafia system produced a world of fragile and broken relationships. They had to live among thieves, submit to theft, and become thieves themselves. So long as they remained part of the out-grower system and in the absence of countervailing powers, stepchildren were condemned to reproduce some elements of the stepparents' callous treatment.

After the 2 Hectare Plot

The transmigration program's standard size for an out-grower plot, 2 hectares, is a pivotal number: it renders the livelihoods of households that have only one plot chronically fragile and sets in motion a process of differentiation through which some become landlords and others become landless workers.[10] The size derives from the Java-centric premise that 2 hectares per household is enough to support a family. This is true in Java where fertile volcanic soil enables intensive cultivation and high yields, but it is not true for Kalimantan. Poor soils cause most transmigration programs in Kalimantan based on intensive rice cultivation to fail, and even with oil palm, a far more tolerant crop, the 2 hectare allocation per household is insufficient to cover farm inputs and family living costs.[11] It sets out-growers up for failure, if not within the first generation then certainly by the second, since they have no capacity to provide land for their children. Out-growers cultivating only oil palm calculated that they needed a minimum of 6 hectares: 2 hectares to cover monthly expenses, 2 hectares to cover farm inputs, and 2 hectares to cover saving for emergencies and investment in education or land purchase for the next generation.[12] With only 2 hectares they needed additional income sources such as rubber tapping, pig raising, or wage work to survive. Insufficient fertilizer on their oil palm plots kept yields low, a vicious cycle. Taking fertilizer on credit could increase yields but was risky as the investment could be lost when roads washed out. Households with only 2 hectares were chronically exposed to the risk of having to mortgage or sell their precious plot as they had no savings for emergencies. Whenever an out-grower plot was up for sale prosperous neighbors were eager to buy it.

Losing a 2 hectare plot was easy: illness or accidents, a failed investment, low prices, or chronically insufficient income and unmanageable debt would do it. Holding on to a plot took resolve; transmigrants held on if they could because owning a plot confirmed their status as farmers even if most of their income came from wage work. Accumulation was a more varied process as out-growers started with different assets and adopted diverse strategies to acquire extra plots and hire and hold workers, as we show with some examples from Tapang Dacin.

Jikin and Ani—Successful but Ill at Ease

Transmigrant couple Jikin and Ani made very effective use of their original 2 hectare plot as a base from which to build their fortunes. They arrived in Kalimantan from Java with nothing at all. Jikin's father was a gambler so Jikin had to drop out of primary school to work. From 1978 to 1985 he was in Sumatra working as a coffee sharecropper, but he made barely enough money to live on. He returned to Java and worked as a road laborer, the lowest status kuli work. When he and Ani joined the out-grower scheme they left their children in Java so they could both focus on income. They were determined to get ahead. They planted vegetables and did day labor for Priva, saving money to buy an additional plot of land. Twenty years later they had accumulated nine plots and were able to send their three children to university. They became skilled farmers and achieved high yields. They obtained land titles for some of their plots and used banks and credit unions to finance further investment. Ani sold dry goods from a small stall in the front of her house, but that was the extent of their diversification: their main focus was oil palm.

Jikin and Ani's advance was enabled by the fragility of their out-grower neighbors. Whenever neighbors fell into debt or faced emergencies, Jikin and Ani were ready with cash to buy their land. Failing out-growers were also their main source of labor. Managing a 2 hectare plot took about eight days of work per month, four for maintenance and four for harvest, a task that had to be carried out twice a month. So their nine plots required a minimum of seventy-two work days per month. This was clearly too much for the couple to handle alone so they became farm managers and hired a regular workforce of five men, among them their transmigrant neighbors Peter and his son Tomas.

Peter and Susi had many children and struggled to make ends meet. They held on to their plot, but their yield was very low. For them, Jikin's success was helpful: it gave them access to steady paid work nearby. Peter did a regular fifteen days of work per month for Jikin. Many out-growers survived in this way. Abidin from Muara Tangkos, the man who fought so hard to obtain one out-grower plot for each of his siblings, ended up with just one plot himself and survived by doing regular harvest work for four of his out-grower neighbors. He earned around IDR1.6 million (USD160) per month, enough for his family to live modestly at 2011 prices, and three times the amount he earned from his own plot. Skill was a crucial element. Many out-growers could not do harvest work. We estimate that around 8,000 hectares (half of Priva's out-grower area) was harvested by hired workers; if each harvested around 8 hectares (twice each month), out-growers employed around a thousand harvesters. Out-growers paid their harvesters well, about double the rate on Priva's core plantation, but access to harvest work was gendered and age specific: it was only for healthy young men like Tomas. Peter was getting too old.

Despite their economic success the daily life of Jikin and Ani was strangely empty. They kept relations with their NTT workers businesslike and did not visit their homes. Their children were away at schools and universities and when they were present during holidays, they hung about the house, rather bored. Jikin and Ani wanted their children to obtain government jobs for prestige and did not want or expect them to become farmers, even though the income the family's oil palm generated far outstripped a government salary. The couple's house was simple, not too different from the original transmigrant house they had been allocated on arrival, and they did not bother with furniture. They saw their lives in Tapang Dacin as temporary, and they feared their Dayak neighbors, who had shown they could be violent. To avoid provoking them Jikin and Ani lived modestly and built a fine house in Pontianak City where their children stayed during their studies and where they expected to live in their old age.

Ani found her life in Tapang Dacin dull and she spent much of her time in Pontianak with the children. She came back with boxes of supplies, especially vegetables. She had stopped growing her own vegetables because of the wandering pigs kept by her neighbors from NTT: she was Muslim, but they were Christian and did not have a taboo against handling pork. If no vegetable peddler made the trek to their housing block, the menu in Ani's house was rice and instant noodles. "This place is just for earning money," she explained; it did not feel like her home. Thin and extractive relations with the place and their neighbors left Jikin and Ani feeling ill at ease. Ani handled this by withdrawing; Jikin's approach was to keep a low profile and focus on his farms.

Omar—2 Hectares plus Initial Capital Make a Home

Omar's parents were originally from the city of Semarang, Java. They moved to Sumatra as transmigrants and had some success with their rice field but stagnated with debt, and he did not see a future for himself. He observed that transmigrants in Sumatra's oil palm out-grower schemes were prospering and decided to make an application. He was eventually accepted for transmigration to Kalimantan. He arrived at Priva in 1997 in the last batch of transmigrant out-growers, and the company allocated him a poor quality plot in an isolated block. Like Jikin and Ani, Omar started by doing day labor and growing vegetables to augment his income, but his economic rise was more rapid because he had capital to invest. After two years checking out the situation, he sold family land in Java to buy an additional two plots. This had always been his plan: to find a place in which he could accumulate. For him the initial 2 hectares was a foothold, not the end point. He said he was business oriented, like his mother, who had supplemented her farm income in Sumatra with trade. He moved to the center of Tapang Dacin where he opened a store selling dry goods, household items, and farm supplies. His wife managed the store, a task she could combine with the care of a small child. His main accumulation strategy was mortgages and moneylending. He took over out-grower plots for five to ten years, splitting the revenues with the owner fifty–fifty after expenses; and when his neighbors could not wait for payday, he bought their fruit ahead of time at a discounted price.

Omar's approach to hiring workers balanced intimacy with distance. Through his kin he recruited young men from Semarang city who had been doing odd jobs, "people who had nothing," he said. He sent them money for their travel expenses and met them at Pontianak port. He provided a small barrack for his workers. In 2011, he had two workers recruited directly from Semarang, and three recruited locally from the out-grower scheme—young married men like Tomas who had not inherited out-grower plots. The intimacy was built on his provision of travel funds, housing, and his willingness to lend money. His workers often dropped by his house and store to chat and check in. The distance was in his management style. Instead of supervising his workers directly and meeting their diverse needs and demands, he gave them contracts for specific tasks. "With day workers we are responsible for everything, their cigarettes, food, health. . . . If they are tired, we have to tell them to rest. If they are sick, we must provide medicine. With a contract it is different. If they want to work hard, fine, if they want to sleep or do nothing, it is up to them. They are free."

Omar and his wife felt they had made a home in Kalimantan. They said it was more peaceful than Sumatra where violence and crime were pervasive. They were proud of the upward mobility they had achieved. Omar had little education and invested heavily in university education for his two daughters who lived in Pontianak. He hoped education could save them from becoming overseas women workers (TKW) whose sad fate he had seen on TV. Omar's perspective on the status of transmigrants was quite different from that of locals who complained about the unfair privileges bestowed on Suharto's "golden children." In Java, he said, "they call transmigrants 'thrown away people' (*orang buangan*); if you have nothing your neighbors push you out to a place where there is land; they think you are a person of no value." The stable life he had built in Kalimantan by treating the transmigration program as a starting point for accumulation was a source of pride to him, and proof he had made good decisions.

Ekay and Efi Reach Their Limit

Dayak out-grower Ekay was one of the original landholders in Tapang Dacin. At the time of the initial land release he managed to retain around 20 hectares of his rubber land in a prime location near a plantation road and gradually planted it with independent oil palm. His neighbors said he was pro-company, a position they thought aided his economic advance. His own story emphasized his enterprise and willingness to do hard manual work, elements that he thought his Dayak neighbors were sadly lacking. We visited him in 2015 when he had just spent several hours trying to hire some workers to do emergency repairs on a washed-out road on behalf of the co-op. He had offered what he thought was a good wage—double the day wage at Priva—but he could not find anyone willing to do the work.

> They say you lose if you become a kuli but I say the important thing is a pocket full of money. They sit around all day at the coffee stall. They laugh at me when I come home tired out. . . . I've been like this since I was a bachelor. I had nothing. I built a hut in the middle of the forest. It was just 2 × 4 meters [6½ × 13 feet]. I raised pigs, I grew rice, and I planted a whole lot of rubber. . . . I'm not ashamed about earning money. If the guy who loads my oil palm fruit doesn't show up, I go with the driver and

do the work myself. Once we arrived at the mill to unload and the clerk at the gate didn't know I was the owner of the fruit *and* the truck. When the driver told him he was so surprised! If you're used to suffering like me, you're OK doing any kind of work.

Ekay had no capital to buy out-grower plots when they were still cheap in the 1990s, but by 2011 he had accumulated ten plots. He acquired two of them from his siblings as payment for loans he had made over several years, but he did not like to lend money. His main strategy for accumulation was to buy neglected out-grower plots and bring them into full production. He boosted his capital by taking a formal bank loan, using land titles as collateral. He also took loans from a credit union. His aggressive expansion meant that he had to budget carefully to make the monthly interest payments on his debts and meet other costs.

Access to labor was Ekay's principal constraint. Many local Malay and Dayak out-growers used the traditional labor exchange (*royong*) system in which groups of two to thirty neighbors joined forces once or twice each week to do the maintenance on one another's plot in turn. A plot owner could also buy a royong to complete a big task—a practice that remained a royong in name but was effectively hired group labor. A group of ten women in one Malay hamlet formed a royong that hired themselves out to spray herbicides. Another group of thirty people, men and women, specialized in clearing heavily overgrown plots. We often saw small royong groups assembling outside the house of a farm owner at 7:00 AM, ready to head off to the designated plot on a fleet of motorbikes, bearing tools. The plot owners followed with panniers filled with food and kettles to boil water to make coffee for the workers. The royong system worked well for owners of just one or two plots, especially if they were short of cash to pay workers and they had enough people in their household to reciprocate days of work. But it did not meet Ekay's needs: his ten plots demanded a stable workforce.

Ekay's solution was to hire kin and neighbors, but he found them unreliable. He could not adopt the contract system like Omar because the yields from his neglected plots were too uneven to attract contract harvesters paid by the kilogram. He was also worried about quality control: he supervised his workers very closely to make sure they did not damage the palms by cutting immature fruit. He wanted the plots to be cared for as assiduously as if he had done the work himself, so often he did it himself to the point of exhaustion. He blamed his labor troubles on his wife, Efi, who was short-tempered. "If we want to be in business, we have to know how to keep workers happy," he said. "They ask for fuel for their motorbikes, cigarettes, and expensive energy drinks, as well as lunch and snacks and we have to give them what they want." He gave one worker an advance so he could make a down payment on a motorbike, but still the worker did not stay.

There was more to the couple's problem than Efi's sharp tongue. With the previous cash crop rubber, payment was based on a share system (30 percent to the owner, 70 percent to the tapper) that reduced the need for direct supervision. Neither side referred to tapping as a wage relation, still less as personal subservience or "becoming someone's kuli." Faced with the need to hire workers, Ekay suggested it was better to hire kin so the money stayed close, but kin could be too sensitive: a sharp word could be taken as an affront. For some locals it was awkward to become the kuli of someone who was their social equal, especially if that person demanded high standards and kept close watch. Ekay's alternative was to hire migrants with whom he could perhaps establish a more businesslike relationship. This approach left him socially rather isolated, but he said he was not bothered by sour relations with neighbors and kin; he just focused on his plots.

At ten plots (20 hectares of oil palm) Ekay and Efi's enterprise had reached the limit for smallholder accumulation. Efi was a full partner in their oil palm enterprise and an astute manager of their farms and funds, but she too was exhausted. They needed both stable workers and a manager to oversee them: they could not be present all the time to ensure the work was done correctly. But they were not ready to hire a manager, the first step toward forming a small plantation. So long as they maintained direct supervision, if workers stole from them or were lazy, they knew exactly what had happened. Conversely if Ekay or Efi were stingy or thoughtless they damaged social relations and risked losing their workforce. High demand for skilled and reliable harvesters combined with social proximity kept both sides honest (figure 3.4). Beyond 20 hectares and with a hired manager, a mafia system was sure to emerge.

Reluctant Kulis and Disposable Income

Ekay's observation that some of the people around him were reluctant to do kuli work had some truth to it. For transmigrants from Java and NTT whose families had always been landless, being forced to sell their out-grower plots and ending up landless again was the end of a dream of independence. Holding on to their plot—however unproductive—was a point of pride. For locals who had always had access to abundant land inherited from their ancestors,

FIGURE 3.4 Plot Owner Supplies Harvester with Snacks and Drinks

A young harvester takes a smoking break and tanks up on coffee with sweetened condensed milk while the plot owner looks on. The harvester has just mixed up some Extra Joss, an Indonesian branded energy drink containing caffeine and ginseng that is heavily promoted to men with images of a clenched fist and sporting activities. Although plot owners complain that they have to pamper their workers, who demand expensive treats, harvesters say that they cannot continue their strenuous work day after day without Extra Joss. From their perspective, the drink is not a luxury but an essential support to their bodily strength, which is their main source of livelihood. PHOTO: PUJO SEMEDI.

or the opportunity to clear new land on the forest edge, the idea of becoming landless and forced into kuli work was distressing. It was the main reason why upriver Dayaks had refused to release their land to Priva: they wanted their descendants to be farmers not kulis. Rambak, an upriver Dayak, divided his single plot into four, one slice for each of his three children and one for himself, which he soon sold to pay hospital expenses for a grandson who had a motorbike accident. For Rambak the shame of losing his plot combined with failed ambition was enough to bring him to tears, and he withdrew from his hamlet to live in the forest, away from daily interaction and gossip. He did not have to become a kuli because he could rely on his wife's rubber tapping, an income source still available upriver. For Malays living in the enclaves who were unable to withhold their rubber land from corporate occupation, selling their single precious out-grower plot meant a significant loss of status. In Muara Tangkos in 2012 around 47 percent of households had no land at all because they did not receive an out-grower plot or had been forced to sell their plot under duress.

Healthy young men were in high demand as harvesters, and they did their best to distance themselves from the kuli category. They often worked in pairs or teamed up with their wives to get the job done faster (figure 3.5). Married men like Tomas and Abidin just made ends meet, but young harvesters without families to support had time and money to spare. Like young women in the core plantation who handled their low-status work by dressing well and playing Korean pop music on their phones, young male harvesters dressed up. They also smoked expensive brands and drove around their hamlets on their motorbikes, public displays of their disposable income and freedom to enjoy leisure (figure 3.6). Some older men with multiple plots also had money to spare; pyramid and get-rich schemes proliferated, as large sums of money flowed in and out of (some) out-growers' hands.

FIGURE 3.5 Husband-and-Wife Harvest Team

This Malay couple moved into an out-grower hamlet from a crowded enclave where they had inherited no land. They built a wooden house on a borrowed corner of someone's house lot. They made a steady income doing harvest work full time, rotating between multiple out-grower plots. The husband harvested, and the wife hauled heavy baskets of fruit to the roadside on her back or by wheelbarrow where the terrain permits. They considered their motorbike an essential work tool. In the background of the photo are some oil palm seedlings belonging to villagers who planned to plant them independently on their own land.
PHOTO: PUJO SEMEDI.

FIGURE 3.6 Young Men Enjoy Disposable Income and Leisure

Young men on display are conspicuous in the plantation zone. Some are sons of prosperous out-growers; others are harvesters who set aside their work clothes and dress up on their days off. Money comes more easily to them than to young women and older people, who are excluded from lucrative harvesting work. PHOTO: JAMES BIRCH.

Capitalizing on the spare time and funds of prosperous out-growers and young men, drinking and gambling that had been organized only during Dayak festivals and holidays became routine in out-grower areas. Prostitution was also more brazen. This behavior made women furious for two reasons—they were embarrassed by the behavior of their husbands and sons; they also resented the waste of money that was needed for family subsistence (figure 3.7). Most out-grower plots were registered in the name of men as the assumed head of household, even if the origin of the plot was the wife's family land; the exceptions were women who had been registered as owners by their parents before their marriage.[13] Some women lacked access

FIGURE 3.7 Dancing Girls from Pontianak City

At the 2011 Dayak Harvest Festival, sponsored by Natco, organizers brought dancer–sex workers from Pontianak City to provide entertainment. Malay and Javanese men who had prospered as out-growers joined the festivities, which continued for more than a week. PHOTO: JAMES BIRCH.

to a share of the money from payday at the out-grower co-op if their husband picked it up. Student researchers who lived for months in out-grower households reported that some men handed the cash over to their wives who served as family treasurers, or couples sat together to work out their budget for food, credit payments, and school expenses, and set the money aside in labeled envelopes; but some men went off to the brothels of Tanjung or Pontianak and kept much of the money to themselves. In one upriver Dayak hamlet a group of women fought back:

> To celebrate Independence Day, we hosted a week-long soccer tournament. We women were having fun because there was a nice crowd. After the tournament the festivities continued into the night. People were playing *kolok-kolok* (gambling with dice) and dancing on a stage. It was lively! A lot of men were crowded into the lap-coffee stall (*kopi pangku*). The servers were young women from town wearing miniskirts. They were allowing the men to grab them. Then the men asked the women to sit on their laps. They went off in pairs, into the oil palm fields. The men went home very late. Some slept out on the soccer field because they were so drunk. We women didn't like what we saw, and we told them to stay home the next day and not join the festivities, but they kept going. We all got mad at them. One evening we got together and ran to the soccer field screaming at our husbands and sons to go home. We were so mad we knocked over the lap-coffee stalls and ripped down the tents and yelled at the girls to go away. Then it stopped. If the men want to play soccer that's fine, but just soccer, no more lap-coffee.

Collective Action?

Whether they had one plot or many, all out-growers depended on Priva for their livelihood. If the stepparent mistreated them or abandoned them with impassable roads, they all suffered. Hence out-growers periodically engaged in collective action to attempt to hold Priva to account. Their main tactic was to blockade the mill to force managers to address grievances such as poor roads, arbitrary fruit grading, and long waits to off-load at the mill. The mill was the choke point at which protesters had most leverage (figure 3.8). It was both a spatial funnel and a temporal one: if palm fruit is not milled within forty-eight hours of harvesting, the oil content drops. To avoid loss, managers were anxious to settle disputes quickly. Hence, they called in blockade leaders to offer them partial, ad hoc settlements (some money, a promise to resolve grievances, a small grant from the "corporate social responsibility" fund), only to have the cycle repeat a few months later. Managers called this mode of handling recurrent protests "applying Panadol."[14] It was a temporary fix that cooled temperatures and made a headache go away but left underlying problems unresolved. Managers also claimed "operational expenses"

FIGURE 3.8 The Mill

Mills are key sites for confirming the corporate mandate: only a corporation—with its capacity to combine capital, technology, and expertise—could build something so imposing in a remote area. Mills have both brute functionality and a modernist aesthetic: note the landscaping and the sign, "Keep the area clean." Mills can also be a site of embarrassment for plantation managers. Priva's mill was built to handle 60 tons of fresh fruit bunches per hour but operated far below capacity because the company's planted area fell short and the palms' productivity was low. The mill gate is a particular point of tension because of its position as a choke point. For out-growers, the gate is the point where trucks bearing their fruit have to wait to off-load and where mill clerks inspect the fruit to decide whether to accept it and which grade to assign for its quality. Out-growers' monthly income depends on that encounter. For corporations, the gate is the weakest link in the production machine as out-growers can mount blockades there, stopping fruit from entering and forcing the mill to shut down. The flow of funds needed to keep the operation moving and generate corporate profit are pegged to an open mill gate. PHOTO: JAMES BIRCH.

for their trouble. Hence for both protesters and managers, collective protests could be transformed into toll booths.

The unity needed for collective action was fragile, hence blockades were difficult to sustain. Mill closure not only caused losses for Priva but also for out-growers whose fruit rotted by the roadside. Blockade leaders who were reluctant to settle faced pressure from out-growers who questioned whether anything useful could be achieved. Out-growers in different blocks and co-ops did not trust one another nor did they trust co-op leaders. Since the co-ops were mafia nodes and set up by Priva, it was not easy to repurpose them as vehicles to advance a common cause. Out-growers suspected blockade leaders of seeking fame as a prelude to running for election at the village or district level or thought they were double agents who claimed to be advancing a common cause but were actually working in league with Priva managers to extort the company.[15] Proving bona fides could be expensive. Priva managers reported one protest leader who "caused them inconvenience" to the police, obliging him to pay a hefty bribe to avoid arrest. He had to use his own money because fellow out-growers who suspected his motives did not support him.

Unusually, a blockade in 2013 lasted four weeks because Priva's owner, Pak Wakijan, decided to let it run its course. The mill stopped production. Managers instructed harvesters and other Priva workers to join the security guards and armed police protecting company property and called in scores of additional police from the surrounding areas. Sarip, reassigned from field security to help guard the mill, recalled that it was "high drama, like a movie." He was uncomfortable with the role he had to play: "We were told to go inside before the gate was sealed. It was not that we wanted to fight the out-growers, it was just to make them realize that we also need to eat. If we protect Priva it is because we need to eat. We need the company so we can eat," he repeated. Although workers and out-growers both had grievances against Priva their different positions in the plantation zone dispersed their struggles and left them without a common platform.

Around two thousand out-growers from the eighteen co-ops participated in setting up the blockade and witnessed a ceremony conducted by customary leaders from nearby hamlets to seal the gate: if Priva breached the gate it would have to pay IDR2 billion (USD200,000) in customary fines. Throughout the month the co-ops took turns to maintain the blockade, which was covered by the media.[16] Merchants in Tanjung town suffered. They called up Budi and other Priva managers to complain that out-growers were not making monthly payments for motorbikes they had bought on credit, and business in town was terrible. Pak Wakijan bore a huge financial loss and some loss of face from the media coverage. The impasse was not resolved at the district level and had to be settled by officials from the provincial governor's office at a meeting in Pontianak City. Pak Wakijan hosted the meeting at a hotel, attended by leaders from the affected villages, subdistrict, and district, as well as "customary" authorities. He bore all the expenses and paid a "customary" fine. The political support he needed to protect the corporation materialized but it was very expensive. He could have avoided these costs by settling quickly with the out-growers—the Panadol solution—yet his management team supported his decision to hang tough. They thought out-growers had become too demanding and needed to be stopped.

On this occasion out-growers' grievance was focused on the queuing system and rejection of fruit. In 2013 the mill started to process fruit from Pak Wakijan's new 5,000 hectare plantation nearby and prioritized this fruit over that of Priva out-growers. Managers argued that out-grower fruit was of lower quality because they were adding fruit produced by independent farmers to their own harvest batches. Tagor, who was still working as a mill security guard at the time, explained what happened. "The queuing system was a mess, then suddenly without warning managers had a metal divider installed in the road with out-grower trucks on one side and Priva trucks on the other. It seemed like a small thing, but the result was huge because 80 percent of the fruit comes from out-growers. So they were the ones who had to wait, sometimes for two days."

In the final settlement brokered in Pontianak, out-growers were made to promise not to send unripe or undersized fruit to the mill, stop intimidating workers at the unloading dock, and stop "anarchic" behavior at the mill gate. All the out-growers gained was a partial reinstatement of previous arrangements: a queuing system in which their fruit was off-loaded more quickly, and the right to submit fruit from private growers, although it would receive a lower price. Pak Wakijan also agreed to rehire a Batak plantation manager whom out-growers thought had treated them fairly, but the manager did not stay long.

Tagor understood the out-growers' grievance, but on this occasion, he saw Pak Wakijan as a victim of out-growers' dishonesty and extortion. He commented on Pak Wakijan's generous spirit: "After the settlement he said to us, 'Come on, let's get back to work; the out-growers are our family, our children after all. The important thing is to open the mill so our children and grandchildren can make a living.'" Neither Tagor nor Pak Wakijan saw the protest as a confrontation between adversaries with opposed interests: the corporation on one side, out-growers locked in unfair arrangements on the other. For many managers out-growers were crooks who used blockades as a mode of extortion; for Pak Wakijan they were unruly children who needed to be reintegrated into harmonious and hierarchical family life. Out-growers were forced to comply with the settlement conditions, but they longed for the day when they could break the bond with Priva and farm and sell their harvest freely.

Conclusion

In this chapter we asked: What does it mean for farmers to be bound to a plantation corporation? For out-growers at Priva it meant a position of acute fragility in which their livelihoods depended on a single crop, a single corporation, a single road and mill, an imposed co-op, and nontransparent debt; it also meant subjection to the endemic predation of the mafia system. Their fragility was linked to the hope instilled by the transmigration scheme that promised locals and transmigrants a bright future as independent and modern farmers who shared in oil palm wealth. It was hope that bound them even when the rewards did not materialize. Unlike workers who could leave and perhaps find similar jobs elsewhere, out-growers were bound to their plots as well as to the corporation. They had to stay put if they were to reach the goal of independence; meanwhile they had to tolerate harsh conditions and try to hold on to their land.

Out-growers described their position as stepchildren of the corporation. They were part of its operation, but they were treated poorly and did not receive fair rewards. Considered through the lens of occupation, their position was ambiguous. Transmigrant out-growers were an integral part of the occupying force as Priva could not sustain its expensive mill without the fruit they produced; but they were a subordinate part that could be sacrificed when expedient. On these occasions the corporation repositioned out-growers outside its arena of responsibility and treated them like ordinary villagers who had to survive on their own. Yet they could not survive on their own because the material infrastructure of the occupation—the corporation's roads, mill, co-op, and credit system—was built into their mode of survival. Nor did they have citizens' normal means of recourse: politicians and officials ignored their pleas for help. An occupying force controlled their fate and the occupier had political support.

Out-growers were subject to the predations of the mafia system and to a further source of fragility that was built into the transmigration scheme from the start. The standard 2 hectare plots were insufficient to sustain farm and family and build up emergency or investment funds. Hence out-growers with only one plot were doomed to stagnate with low incomes and many had to sell their land. Those who managed to hold on to their precious plots salvaged their status as farmers, but they depended on wage work to survive and had no way to secure a farming future for their children. Men's harvest work was relatively well-paid, but it was very hard for young families to save enough to buy additional land or pay for their children's education. The pattern that emerged over the twenty years since the scheme began was one of class differentiation as some out-growers prospered and acquired additional land while a large number became landless or stagnant.

In addition to growing palms, thriving smallholder communities can generate opportunities for off-farm income in enterprises such as selling clothing and housewares, building materials, motorbikes, cell phones, and fertilizers; owning trucks; building houses; installing and repairing generators; running coffee and dry goods stalls; and peddling cooked food and snacks. There are two conditions for a thriving off-farm sector: out-growers must prosper, which means they have enough land, decent prices, and good infrastructure; and the money must circulate locally. In Priva's out-grower scheme the two conditions were not met. A few out-growers prospered but most stagnated; and prosperous transmigrants like Jikin and Omar spent much of their money building houses in the city and educating their children elsewhere. Some out-growers who invested locally chose to develop oil palm–related businesses such as trucking and fertilizer supply, but most focused on accumulating more oil palm because the crop brought them high returns.

In contrast to the acute fragility of out-growers bound to a corporation, the livelihoods of farmers in upriver areas were more robust. They still maintained their rubber and rice. During the time of our study in 2010–12 the price of rubber was very high, and they felt prosperous: they improved their houses, bought motorbikes, and began to save through credit unions. Some were eager to join the oil palm out-grower scheme should Priva extend the roads to their area, but they worried about losing land to the corporation. Where would their children farm? It was not difficult for them to see the problem that so many out-growers had run into: excessive dependence on an unreliable stepparent, and 2 hectare out-grower plots that were not sufficient to cover the needs of the present or future generations. The ideal pathway, in their view, was to plant oil palm independently on their own land, giving up none to a corporation and maintaining flexibility. They calculated that they could manage the expense of seedlings and plot preparation; it was roads and access to a mill they lacked, and these were firmly under corporate control.

4

Forms of Life

In this chapter we ask: What were the forms of life that emerged in the plantation zone? In previous chapters we explored core elements of Natco's and Priva's production apparatus—how they acquired land, recruited and held workers, and managed their out-grower schemes. We also paid attention to the political technologies they deployed to govern landscapes, form subjects, and secure compliance. Here we deepen our analysis of forms of life by taking up the line of inquiry proposed by David Scott in his discussion of colonialism. Rather than ask whether or not corporate occupation was resisted, we ask how it "transformed the ground on which accommodation or resistance was possible in the first place, how it . . . reshaped or reorganized the conceptual and institutional conditions of possibility of social action and its understanding."[1] We start by examining the set of legal and institutional arrangements that emerged throughout the plantation zone at the nexus of formal law and everyday practice, embedding the order of impunity at intimate scales. Then we turn to daily life inside Natco, the site of a modernity project that deployed the vehicle of a state-owned corporation quite deliberately to produce subjects with new dispositions. Finally, we explore forms of life in the Malay enclave of Muara Tangkos, a zone in which former landholders experienced a double jeopardy: they were both occupied and thoroughly abandoned. Neither the plantation corporations that occupied village land nor their government collaborators paid any attention to their fate. Villagers could observe the modern lives of Natco's privileged workers and witness the children of prosperous out-growers head off to university, but they had no means to access such lives, a predicament they dubbed "becoming the audience."

Law and Citizenship under Corporate Occupation

Plantation corporations are legal entities with official status, rights, and obligations. They are also dependent on support from bureaucrats and politicians who smooth their way in return for a flow of funds. In the introduction we outlined the order of impunity within which crony-corporate cabals operate in Indonesia but as in other "dirty money states," impunity does not mean anarchy. Rather, it means the emergence of a set of legal and institutional practices in which the role of law is mutable and contradictory. In the plantation zone we found that law was neither suspended nor consistently applied; it created toll booths; it protected corporations and exposed them to extortion; and it produced a form of citizenship in which rights were formally intact but rendered ineffective. Law and citizenship are fragile everywhere in Indonesia, but their fragility was intensified by corporate occupation.[2]

Local Government

In Sanggau a tight link between corporations and local government is legally prescribed in the District Plantation By-Law 3/2004, which stipulates that government officials are to facilitate corporate operations, and corporations may pay them for services rendered. In chapter 1 we described the formally constituted "land release teams" comprising civil authorities, customary leaders, and the heads of the police and army at each administrative level (village, subdistrict, district). After land release is completed these teams are renamed "coordination teams" and tasked with facilitating corporate operations for as long as the plantation exists. The Plantation By-Law formally positions team members (and their networks) as collaborators of corporations, making it difficult for any part of the local or district government to enforce laws that interfere with corporate interests. Corporations pay team members a monthly honorarium as a retainer and make additional payments according to workload, for example, if team members are called upon to help resolve a dispute. In a political system where local officials are expected to act as intermediaries who help citizens to solve problems involving powerful actors that as "small people" they cannot address on their own, the enrollment of officials on the side of corporations leaves citizens without recourse. Their legal rights as citizens are formally intact, but their capacity to claim those rights or to seek personally mediated protection is degraded.

Corporations further undermine villagers' access to recourse through another legal practice: donating to the election campaigns of district and village heads and members of the district parliament. Unsurprisingly, corporations prefer to work with leaders who can be counted on to support their plans.[3] In the Suharto era this was not a problem since district and village heads were selected on the basis of their loyalty to the ruling regime and its cronies, and district parliaments had a limited role. Since 1999 when village and district heads began to be elected, corporations fund the campaigns of strong candidates, hoping to secure their future cooperation. The purpose is not to fix the election result, but to ensure that whoever wins is loyal to the corporation.

While the payments they receive from corporations may be welcome, some government officials in Sanggau indicated that contradictory mandates to protect corporations and protect citizens put them in an awkward position. Subdistrict officials who had to mediate between corporations and villagers were on the front line, constantly exposed to conflicting demands. At a seminar we held at the district head's office in 2012 several current and former subdistrict officials spoke critically about corporations that failed to meet their legal obligations and expressed discomfort at their own role in assisting them. Here is one account:

> I was there, those promises came from my mouth when we met with villagers, but the company did not deliver even one of them. According to the signed agreement the company should supply out-grower plots within four years but seven years later villagers still had nothing. That is why I said to the manager, "If you say my people are ransackers, I say the company is a thief because you are three years late."

When we asked another subdistrict official whether our research could be helpful to him in any way, he responded: "Please tell me how I can make companies obey the law." He was exasperated by plantation managers in his subdistrict who refused to come to his office when he called them in. He witnessed numerous infractions of land release rules, for example, but could do little to stop the process. He refused to sign a document confirming the completion of land release for one corporation because it had made no effort to comply with legal requirements: "There is supposed to be an out-grower scheme, but the company has not made any commitments to the villagers. There are no documents at all, although company bulldozers have already cleared the land. The managers need to have more discussion with the farmers with witnesses from our office." In fact, there were documents concerning the land that villagers had released since the corporation needed these documents to secure its bank loan, but there were no documents concerning the out-grower scheme on which villagers' livelihoods would henceforth rely. Corporate commitments, if any, were verbal and vague; villagers accepted them on trust because they had no capacity to insist that corporate promises must be legally enforceable, and the subdistrict officials whose job it was to oversee the process did not or could not perform their task.

"The law is not implemented," another subdistrict official observed. In two cases he was handling, villagers who were skeptical that the corporations would deliver on promised out-grower schemes had sold their scheme memberships to brokers who prowled new plantation areas looking for opportunities. Brokers bulked villagers' land and resold it to government officials, plantation managers, police and military, some of whom acquired large areas (50–200 hectares) in areas intended for out-growers.[4] "The limit should be 25 hectares per person—more than that they should have a plantation license," he explained. He faulted both the corporations and his own colleagues who used their official positions to tap into plantation wealth. He had tried to cancel the permit of a plantation that reneged on a written commitment, but a senior district official undermined his effort by issuing a new permit to a company that bought the defaulted company's assets. Since both companies belonged to the same owner, selling the troubled asset was a tactic to evade responsibility. The outcome was that the subdistrict official was unable to protect villagers' interest and by irritating a senior official he risked becoming sidelined and even less effective.

Corporations in firm possession of plantation concession licenses granted by the national land agency often ignored officials who attempted to mediate or solve problems. The Sanggau District head tried five times to compel the PTPN director to meet with him, but he sent only junior staff, so nothing was resolved.[5] The village head of Muara Tangkos complained that Natco and Priva, which together occupied most of the village land, treated him with contempt. "If we talk to the managers about law, about regulations, they say they don't know about the law," he complained. "They think the land is theirs, they can do as they wish. The top managers never meet with us, they just send their public relations officer. . . . We never get any replies, no decisions, no clarifications." He argued that plantation managers were village residents, hence they should respect village authority. He also referred to his role on the official coordination team. "My role is to guide the company and help form a bridge between the company and the people. If a business like a minimart wants to open in the village, the owners need our permission, and they have to follow village rules, or we can throw them out." There was a theatrical element to his rhetoric. He knew that a plantation was quite unlike a minimart, and he had no capacity to throw it out. Corporate occupation degraded his legally defined authority as village head; he couldn't even talk to anyone who could make a decision.

Rightly or not, the fact that the village head received regular payments from Natco and Priva exposed him to the suspicion that his tough talk was a quisling's performance. So too for the Sanggau District head. In 2010 he complained publicly that plantation corporations did not contribute enough money to the district and demanded that the state plantation corporation hand over 30 percent of its profits.[6] The land and building tax paid to the district is miniscule, and article 7(3) in the Sanggau Plantation By-Law, which requires corporations to donate 5 percent of their profits for community development, is not enforced. Hence the district head's demand for 30 percent of profits to fund district development had popular appeal. Examined critically, it called his sincerity into question: If corporations did not bring public benefit to the district, why did he continue to issue new location permits? In Sanggau suspicions of hypocrisy and betrayal were integral to life under corporate occupation; even earnest village, subdistrict, or district heads seeking justice for their people were seen as actors in a staged drama, and their position as collaborators undermined their oppositional stance.[7]

The Envelope Guy

While government officials complained that law did not help them to control corporations that were huge, entrenched, and unresponsive, Priva managers complained that the law did not protect the company from extortion by government officials or by out-growers and villagers mounting blockades. Priva paid the legally mandated retainers to officials and company men on its "coordination teams" yet whenever something went wrong their political support evaporated—witness the long blockade in 2013 and the extra money Pak Wakijan had to pay to resolve it. Supplementing official retainers by making additional payments was routine but it was a fragile solution.

After Budi resigned from Priva and was able to talk more freely about his working life, he told us about the year he had spent as the company's "envelope guy." His job was to stuff cash into envelopes for government officials, journalists, people's organizations, and anyone else who could cause trouble for the company. Demands came in two formats. One was brazen and quasi-official. Each year during religious festivals Priva received written requests for "holiday bonuses" from various government ministries. The requests were printed on official letterhead and signed by the department head. They listed the names of staff in the relevant unit (e.g., the police; the army; the district-level agriculture, labor and environment offices; the village office; ethnic associations; and youth groups) together with the "suggested" bonus amount for each person, according to their rank. The second format was ad hoc demands for "motorbike fuel" (*uang bensin*) by journalists, officials, or NGOs who presented themselves at the plantation office. A journalist could write a negative report; an activist from an NGO could provoke a demonstration; a government official who arrived waving a regulation could always find infractions. To avoid trouble Priva found it expedient to pay.

Budi was under instruction to negotiate but he had to tread carefully. When he tried to reduce a "supplement" demanded by the police chief, the chief protested and Priva ran the risk that he would be slow to respond if the corporation needed his help, as it did during the long blockade. Priva previously paid local Malay and Dayak leaders to form "mediation teams" comprising young men in matching T-shirts who could be mobilized to protect company property, but Budi said the new manager had discontinued the practice because local strongmen were not reliable: they also caused the company trouble.[8]

A routine event underpinned by envelopes occurred in Muara Tangkos during our stay. It was a seminar in the village meeting hall presented by staff from the District Environment Department and sponsored by Priva. The objective was to persuade villagers to respect the environment and company property. More specifically, the problem was this: Priva had imported several very expensive owls from Sumatra to control the rats that eat palm fruit, but villagers caught the owls to eat or to sell them. Villagers' delinquent conduct is the standard alibi for officials to leave their offices in town to communicate official policy to the people, a practice called *sosialisasi*. Predictably, no villagers showed up to hear the message about the owls—the only participants in the seminar were Priva managers and government officials, recognizable by their uniforms. Behind the story of the owls was another sort of theft of the routine "We both know what's going on here" (*tahu sama tahu*) variety. The presenters were being paid twice: once by the Environment Department, which paid their salaries and travel costs; and again by Priva as Budi gave each visitor and the attending village officials an envelope of cash. There was also a theft of time (and money): although the seminar was budgeted to run for two days it folded after lunch and everyone went home.

Budi's normal envelope limit was IDR1 million (USD100), but he was sometimes instructed to draw cash from the bank to make payments up to USD 2,000. His superiors instructed him to enter these amounts in the account book under "maintenance of infrastructure." This category of expenditure was plausible because Priva's 258 kilometers (160 miles) of plantation roads needed constant work; but in the unlikely event that auditors made a site visit it would be hard for them to track whether the materials were up to standard or the work was actually done. Priva's head office in Pontianak handled larger demands from more senior actors such as visiting parliamentarians who asked for free hotel rooms when they visited the city, or aspiring politicians who asked for donations or the loan of trucks. Priva's owner Pak Wakijan had sunk his capital in the ground; he could not leave so he had to pay.

Out-Growers Outside the Law

The fragile position of out-growers as an occupied population was extreme. Their entire livelihoods depended on a legally inscribed debt-bond to a corporation with which they had no enforceable contract, hence no legal means to protect themselves from neglect and abuse. As we explained in chapter 3, out-growers bankrupted by washed-out roads could not make legal claims because it was not clear which party—the corporation, the district government, or the co-ops—was responsible for road maintenance. Nor could they appeal to government officials to convey their grievances to the company or mediate disputes, since officials' positions on coordination teams oriented them to take the company's side.

Even everyday policing for crimes such as theft or assault was inaccessible to out-growers.[9] In 2011 when someone stole the monthly pay of two hundred out-growers from a co-op leader who was transporting the cash, a police investigation produced no result. Out-growers speculated that the co-op head and the police were in cahoots. Markus made a police report backed up with photographs when thugs ransacked his plot and threatened his life, but the police did nothing. Abidin was successful in enforcing the law that transmigrants could not sell their out-grower plots but only because he backed up his reference to law with a violent reoccupation of the disputed land. He was charged for the crime of issuing threats and later released; the people whom Abidin terrorized in the incident involving "raining bush-knives" had no redress.

Transmigrants in Tapang Dacin who were being intimidated or faced with ransacked crops said they had nowhere to turn. "So where are we supposed to go with our grievances?" Wardiman inquired. "We are really squeezed here. The government has no reach. If the police come in without permission, they have to pay a customary fine." Wardiman had tried to have his grievance addressed through the customary Dayak dispute resolution system, but he said the system did not work. The customary leader was a company man, and kin to some of the thugs who were intimidating him. Wardiman invited the customary leader to a mediation meeting where the problem could be resolved, but the leader refused to attend. Hence it was not only vis-à-vis the corporation that out-growers were vulnerable but also vis-à-vis one another. The occupation had undermined the capacity of customary and civil authorities to mediate disputes; hence any settlements they brokered were fragile and often expensive.

"Like Crackers in a Plastic Bag"

Inside Natco too legal and institutional arrangements both sustained the corporation and threatened its existence. They degraded citizenship in ways that were quite different from those experienced by villagers or out-growers at Priva. State plantation workers are among a very limited group—only 6 percent of the Indonesian workforce—who are classified as formal workers and have potentially enforceable labor rights.[10] Yet when Natco's liquidity crisis stopped it from paying them what it legally owed, Godril and his coworkers did not even consider making a complaint to the district labor office. They said they did not know where the labor office was, and they had no contacts there. They knew how to navigate the administrative system of the plantation, but they had no mediators to connect them to outside authorities.

However clear their legal rights, Natco workers still saw themselves as "small people" who could not approach a site of authority without someone to speak on their behalf. They said they expected government officials—including officials in the labor office—to side with managers because they were members of the same social group, that is, people of power. They had another reason to be silent about managers' misdeeds: "We too have done things," Godril acknowledged. Workers' complicity in theft even in small ways like returning home early from work made it difficult for them to launch a legal challenge. But there was more to their reluctance to seek legal redress.

As a standard part of their legal mandate corporations are entitled to establish rules to govern their internal affairs, creating zones of exception in which "normal" law is suspended. Natco organized its internal affairs along New Order lines, which specified that state-owned corporations should be run on family principles. As we explained in chapter 2, New Order politicians promoted familistic idioms to counter class-based politics: workers did not need a union to protect them because the state as a parent would take care of their needs. Natco managers and workers shared a common understanding that law was not relevant to solving the company's internal problems. Families demand loyalty, and everyone is expected to help guard the family's reputation. Hence managers handled "problems" such as theft by their subordinates as family matters. They gave the culprit a warning, a cut in benefits, a delay in promotion, or a suggestion that he or she should quietly resign. Managers did not take internal theft to the police. "It is all wrapped up like crackers in a plastic bag sealed tight, so they don't go soft," Godril's friend explained.

Disgruntled managers and workers had the option of making anonymous reports about the misconduct of their colleagues or superiors to the corporation's internal audit office, but they were explicitly discouraged from invoking the law or reporting misdeeds to outside authorities. Workers used gossip to enforce tacit rules about workload and acceptable commissions (that is, a reasonable percentage for the foreman's share), but they did not report predatory practices to their superiors or lodge formal complaints. Reporting managers' abuse of power to outsiders could boomerang. This was the unhappy fate of two state plantation workers whose story was reported in a national newspaper in 1998. The corporation's board of directors punished the workers for reporting corruption in their workplace to the attorney general's office. "Their action was a breach of company discipline, because they revealed company secrets to an outside party," the company's head of security explained. The sanctity of company secrets was so obvious to the security head that he made this statement to journalists without a hint of irony or apology. The news report noted only that the government's anticorruption effort was being undermined.[11]

On an everyday basis, familism at Natco offered workers like Godril some protection; their superiors might intercede for them if they had a problem;

they could steal from the corporation and from one another without going to jail. But as we noted in chapter 2, major theft by senior staff jeopardized the corporation and put workers' livelihoods at risk. In 2006 the district attorney found that the corporation had been defrauded of IDR30 billion (USD3 million) through manipulation of a contract to build a new mill in Tanjung. A senior PTPN director was the prime suspect, but after years of investigation and legal procedures the supreme court in Jakarta cleared him and no one else was charged. The court ordered the provincial attorney's office to pay the suspect IDR100 million (USD10,000) in damages.[12] PTPN suspended its Tanjung production and milling operations in 2018 due to financial insolvency and its directors were put under investigation for corruption, but a year later no charges had been laid.[13]

The price for not enforcing civil or criminal law was paid by workers like Godril and Monah, who did not receive the wages they were due. It was also paid by local villagers who had forced Natco to provide them with an outgrower scheme because when the PTPN mill closed for more than a year they had nowhere to process their fruit.[14] All Indonesians paid a price when a national asset that should have produced revenue was run into the ground. The same legal and institutional arrangements that protected Natco robbed it of productive crops, production activities, and profit.

After his election in 2011 President Joko Widodo made promises to eliminate corruption and politicians spoke often on TV about the problems caused by individual rogues (rogue officials, rogue corporations). But they did not acknowledge the order of impunity that enables corporations to act irresponsibly, supported by politicians and officials who are paid by corporations both above and below the table. Nor did they recognize the multiple harms that result from corporate occupation in the plantation zone. Instead, politicians continued to issue new plantation licenses, and in 2019 they mobilized to rescue the struggling state plantation corporation by reorganizing the units into a giant national holding company and injecting fresh capital.[15] The geese were revived, in sum, so they could continue to lay golden eggs.

Making Modern Subjects at Natco

When it moved into Kalimantan in 1980 the state plantation corporation's mandate was not only to produce palm oil but also to serve as an exemplary site of modernity in Kalimantan's backward interior. President Suharto liked to be called the "father of development," and the New Order regime made use of state plantations to further the development agenda in multiple ways: in addition to generating streams of rent for crony cabals, plantations brought dramatic transformation to the landscape; they were directly productive, generating flows of commodities the Ministry of Agriculture could proudly announce; and they enabled the regime to set aside big problems while demonstrating its capacity to form modern subjects within enclosed plantation worlds. Here we examine how managers and workers at Natco engaged with this modernity project and the novel practices it generated.

Discipline, Hierarchy, Prosperity

Natco took comprehensive control over the space, time, and daily activities of its employees. The plan went beyond the demands of efficient industrial production and corporate profit. It was an attempt to create modern subjects of a New Order kind, disciplined, prosperous, and attuned to the hierarchy of a state modeled on the family. For this purpose, Natco's facilities were quite complete. In addition to housing, there were childcare centers, primary schools, places of worship, and a medical clinic. Fieldworkers had to live in the housing block located in the afdeling where they worked, and their foreman served as the block head, extending workplace discipline to home life. A bell awoke fieldworkers at 5:30 AM so they were ready for the 6:00 AM roll call. In the 1980s before family houses were built, foremen used to check the barracks to make sure workers were asleep and not gambling. By 2010 it was the electric generator that regulated workers' leisure and sleep. In his block Godril was the one responsible for turning the generator off at 10:00 PM and on again at 5:30 AM. All workers wore uniforms.[16] At Friday prayers or Sunday services, company-appointed religious attendants reminded workers of plantation rules about cleanliness and punctuality, and the prohibition on gambling. Gambling is illegal in Indonesia, though widespread. As a measure to demonstrate their seriousness about discipline, during our research in 2010–12 managers backed up the prohibition by taking the unusual step of reporting gamblers to the police. This was one matter they did not "wrap up tightly" or handle with internal sanctions.

The hierarchy of Natco's plantation order was expressed in housing location and style. Fieldworkers' housing was neat but modest (figure 4.1). Managers and technical and office staff lived in the central housing block called by the Dutch term *emplasmen*. Unlike fieldworkers they were not required to attend morning roll calls. Their housing quality mirrored their rank: managers occupied bigger houses on slightly elevated ground, and they had access to electricity twenty-four hours a day, supplied by the national grid. Their official modes of

FIGURE 4.1 Natco Worker Housing

Natco's modernity project requires workers to keep their rowhouse yards tidy, plant vegetables and flowers, and paint the picket fence white. Workers are not supposed to modify their houses, although the family assigned to this house added an extension at the back for use as a kitchen and storage space. Workers display their wealth and modernity in the form of furniture, clothing, jewelry, and satellite TV. PHOTO: ENDANG PURWASARI.

transportation also mirrored rank. The head had the newest four-wheel-drive vehicle; the lower ranks used motorbikes. Individuals who purchased private vehicles followed Natco hierarchy because to outshine their superiors would be disrespectful. Offices were graded by size and the provision of air conditioning or fans. The higher ranks had coffee brought to them; those of lower rank had to get it themselves. Managers played tennis on the Natco court, which was close to their houses; lower-ranked office workers played soccer.

Managers' enactments of hierarchy were most visible in their interactions with fieldworkers. In the 1980s, one worker recalled, managers expected feudal-style subservience: "When a manager passed by, all the fieldworkers had to stop their work, face the road, and salute until he had gone. If it was the top manager only the foremen stood there, ordinary workers ran to hide. The manager thought it was disrespectful if we looked at him, and we didn't dare. Managers were forbidden to socialize with us."[17] These feudal-style relations echoed the racialized hierarchy of Sumatra's colonial plantations, a hierarchy that morphed only slightly after foreign-owned plantations were nationalized in 1958 and was embodied in the conduct of the Batak managers, originally from Sumatra, who founded Natco.

In the early days at Natco some foremen still meted out physical punishments such as beating workers with a stick. In the 2000s managers still expected fieldworkers to bow when they passed them in their cars, and fieldworkers who had to visit the central office did not dare to sit on chairs. Noting these bodily comportments one manager expressed his disapproval: "Some managers here still have 'the colonial' in them," he said. "We learned at the state plantation training school that we have to be more egalitarian. We can't be colonial or militaristic. Now we have to be persuasive and familial." In his understanding, to be an exemplary site of modernity in the New Order style the hierarchy long embedded in plantation life had to take a new form: it should be a combination of technocracy (the training school) and paternalism (persuasive, familial). The familial required a balance of proximity and hierarchy embodied in new practices. For example, Natco afdeling foremen started to invite managers to family weddings, which meant that managers had to be present in spaces not designated for them—their underlings' modest plantation homes. But hosts respectfully reinserted distance by allocating managers a separate time slot and better food, arrangements that protected these honored guests from the social obligation to mingle with lower-status workers.

Breaches of order and hierarchy help shed light on the character of "normal times" when everything and everyone is in place. We reported one example in chapter 2 when managers and clerks were asked to do fieldwork. Godril found the scene both ludicrous and upsetting: managers were the wrong people in the wrong place, with the wrong clothes and the wrong tools, involved in the wrong activities, and they produced no useful results. The incident drove Godril to assert the specificity of his own expertise: managers should leave field work to fieldworkers; managers and clerks—like fieldworkers—were not competent when they stepped outside their bounds. Another example relates to Priva where we noted that Tagor was upset by the lack of education of some managers and foremen that Pak Wakijan had appointed. For Tagor, administrative hierarchy had to be backed by technical competence or it did not hold. We gave examples where the meaning of familism was in dispute: workers like Godril and Monah readily accepted the hierarchy and paternalism of a plantation styled as a family but they demanded proper family care. A parent would not undermine their livelihood. These breaches became occasions on which workers readily discussed the other faces of the corporation that employed them: the one dedicated to profit in which workers were merely instruments to be used and cast out, and the predatory one in which greedy superiors treated workers as prey.

At Natco as in other state institutions, corporate familism assigned a particular role to women, especially wives of managers, who were expected to model loyalty and discipline. Natco had a formal women's organization, Ikatan Keluarga Besar Istri PTPN (Association of the Big Family of Plantation Managers' Wives, IKBI) headed by Farida, the top manager's wife. IKBI organized activities for the improvement of women of lower ranks, a program of benevolent intervention made easier by the presence of so many women in need of uplift living in the afdelings, within easy reach. To celebrate Kartini Day (Women's Day) in 2011, IKBI organized three competitions that were attended by Anti, a student researcher in our team who was asked to participate in the role of judge. The first was a cooking contest that all plantation women of any rank could enter. The second was a contest for public speaking in which the competition was controlled in the name of fairness: only women from the afdelings (fieldworkers or wives of fieldworkers) could enter. Farida explained that they excluded women from the emplasmen (women office workers, or wives of office workers or managers) because they assumed emplasmen women were more educated. If they competed, they would likely win, so excluding them showed sensitivity toward inferiors.

The third event was an interafdeling cleanliness competition judged by managers' wives. Here is an excerpt from Anti's field notes:[18]

> On the appointed day we piled into a van and went around the emplasmen collecting the managers' wives. Farida told us that our evaluation should be low key. Workers' houses did not need to be fancy because there were no fancy houses on the plantation, but they should be clean and neat, with a system for garbage disposal, clear drains, flowers and fruit trees in the yard, and windows open for ventilation. We also had to check out the public facilities like the daycare center, the prayer house, sports field, fishing pond, and garden for medicinal plants.
>
> In one of the afdelings there was a well-kept vegetable garden. Farida asked who did the work. The afdeling foreman's wife, who was in charge, replied that they all helped but Farida and the other judges did not believe her because right there in the garden was a hut with an elderly couple resting. It turned out that the afdeling paid the couple to maintain the garden. I just grinned, watching those women with their hands on their hips like big bosses. The afdeling foreman's wife kept on talking,

explaining all about the vegetables. Meanwhile the elderly couple stood quietly looking scared.

Anti's notes suggest she was uneasy with the hierarchical assumption that the wives of managers should judge the conduct of women workers and inspect the cleanliness of their homes. But the competition also produced other effects: inter-afdeling rivalry, pride in winning the competition, and gratitude toward the managers' wives for spending the day visiting parts of the plantation they did not normally see, thus showing that they cared about worker well-being.[19] For the judges there was the camaraderie of a day's outing and the care they took to mark the special character of the occasion and its out-of-doors location by donning an agreed uniform of matching track pants, bright pink tops, and sun visors.

Prosperity was integral to Natco's modernity project: workers should not only be disciplined and productive, they should also be prosperous enough to participate in modern consumer practices. In Indonesia key practices that demonstrate a family's prosperity are the provision of education for children, the lavishness of family events like weddings, and the standard of housing and material possessions. Natco workers of all ranks invested in their children's education; a common ambition was for children to stay in the plantation world but as managers, a status that fieldworkers who had barely completed primary school could not achieve. But education was a long-term and uncertain investment: children might drop out or have other plans. Saving for retirement was also important. Some office workers planned to retire in Pontianak City and paid a monthly subscription to a plantation retirees' housing scheme that would enable them to maintain friendships and the habits of hierarchy and formality to which they had become accustomed.

Since workers and managers were forbidden to renovate their assigned houses, the arenas with ample room for demonstrating prosperity were family ceremonies and the acquisition of consumer goods. Workers could send pictures of lavish events to relatives in Java and elsewhere to confirm that the decades they had spent isolated in the Kalimantan interior had produced tangible results: they too lived by urban standards of fashion and furnishing, as shown on TV. But the ready audience for their achievements was their neighbors, other plantation workers of similar rank. In the tiny, relatively closed social field of the emplasmen, the families of technical staff and office workers competed fiercely for status. Wives who had no employment led the way, perhaps because they had less opportunity than their husbands to develop workplace identities and limited arena for self-expression. Student researchers from Java were surprised by the intensity of the competition and its unapologetic character that offended their sense of decorum. If one family bought a new sofa, students reported, others immediately bought the same sofa or a better one if available. Families staged elaborate celebrations for circumcisions, weddings, birthdays, and graduations. When Endang, another student researcher from our team, was first invited to an emplasmen wedding she made the mistake of thinking that the plantation was like an ordinary village so she should be careful not to show off with city styles:

> I wore a simple outfit to the wedding to fit in with the other guests. When I arrived at the party, I was really surprised at the luxury of it. The decorations were satin cloth embellished with gold colored beads. There was a low stage with two gold-painted chairs. On each side were artificial flowers and an umbrella like you see in a Balinese temple. Next to it was a money box in the form of a traditional house from West Sumatra also wrapped in gold satin to make the stage even more shiny. It was really something! The guests were not as I had imagined. Every one of them wore jewelry. They had brooches, necklaces, something everywhere on their clothes, arms, and necks.[20]

Weddings of office workers and foremen cost from IDR10–40 million (USD1–4,000) with hundreds of guests and lasted seven to ten days. Circumcisions, birthdays, and funerals were also elaborate (figures 4.2 and 4.3). They were financed from wages, side earnings, loans, and donations from neighbors and coworkers through a system of reciprocity.

For Natco managers the plantation was not a relevant arena for social competition, and its rural and remote location jangled with their social status. Some of them kept their families in Pontianak City where they built fine houses, and they spent as little time as possible in their place of work. They hosted family weddings in Pontianak where their guests included business partners, officials, and other social equals. Managers did invite mid-level plantation staff whose reports on the food, entertainment, decorations, and fashions were eagerly awaited on the plantation, but the interest was not reciprocal. In Indonesia official positions yield networks, networks yield land, and land yields capital. Hence the most important asset for plantation managers to acquire was an elite politico-bureaucratic network that could help them to acquire land cheaply, together with the documents they needed to secure bank loans. Fancy weddings in Pontianak were one way to build such networks; linking up with local elites was another. One manager who prospered had acquired 120 hectares adjacent to Natco in the 1980s before villagers in the enclaves fully understood how scarce and valuable land would become. He married a local Malay woman who became a member of the district parliament for the ruling party Golkar. Two other managers acquired plantations of around 300 hectares. A young Batak manager without networks locally or in Pontianak confessed to doubt about his potential to accumulate and explained his predicament thus: "We can't go home to Sumatra if we don't take gold. So we are going to die here."

Difference, Separation, Superiority

As we explained in chapter 1, the presumed superiority of the plantation as a system of production was a precondition for the presence of Natco in the Kalimantan interior. Project Sanggau's inaugural document made assumptions about the backwardness of the local population explicit, noting their inadequate skill and knowledge, their low "index of motivation" and

FIGURE 4.2 Performing Modernity at a Plantation Reception

The decor for this celebration feast mimics a street-food stall, making a familiar scene orderly and beautiful, Disney style. The people serving the food in portions ready for pickup are members of a committee organized through a reciprocal labor system. Guests include workers of lower status, as having a wide social network is a sign of prestige. PHOTO: ENDANG PURWASARI.

FIGURE 4.3 Staking Prestige at a Circumcision

The decor and equipment for feasts is rented, so the same items reappear numerous times. Guests place their financial contributions in covered boxes by the stage. The money is in envelopes with the donor's name, making the amount both hidden and known, and thus controlled by gossip. For workers on tight budgets who receive multiple invitations each week, the celebration season is stressful: they must send money, even if they do not attend in person. Hosts take a risk as donations may fall short, leaving them with debts. This mode of financing celebrations and demonstrating the reach of social networks is common in both urban and rural Indonesia; the additional pressure among resident plantation workers is the relatively closed social world within which prestige may be gained or lost. PHOTO: ENDANG PURWASARI.

"low demand for necessities." Local Malays and Dayaks were caricatured as the mirror image of the disciplined, prosperous modern subjects the state plantation was designed to produce. But attention to the uneven spatiality of corporate occupation reveals a crucial limit: despite the claim that "with the opening of big and modern estates in the remote area of West Kaliman-tan there seemed to be an improvement of the people's way of thinking and living,"[21] Natco's modernity project did not extend to the local population. It had no plan to make surrounding villagers into modern subjects, nor even to expose them to the exemplary world of the state corporation. They were not invited to be participants; even as an audience they were confined to the side-lines, kept out by guards who questioned their presence if they deviated from the main plantation road. Natco workers also kept their distance. Although they were free to move in and out of the plantation and went regularly to Tanjung town, workers who had spent decades at Natco told us they had never visited Dayak villages upriver nor the Dayak enclaves nearby. They had developed a strong sense of their own social superiority and had no interest in mixing with villagers whom they thought were backward and possibly hostile.

Exceptionally, Godril and Monah formed a close social relationship with the family of a Dayak elder, Doan. It began in the early 1980s when Doan's wife Liling went to the afdeling to sell vegetables. "The workers were afraid of us," Doan recalled, "they thought we Dayaks killed and ate people, but that isn't true, we in Kalimantan don't do those things, it is not allowed." Liling noticed that Monah looked exactly like her daughter. They formed a fictive kinship bond as Doan and Liling "adopted" Monah, and the two families started to help out at each other's festivals and events and engage in casual visiting. Godril and Monah were the only couple in the afdeling to have such an intimate link. Fear of Dayaks based on rumors of cannibalism persisted and some Dayaks played with this story: "Aren't you afraid of us? Don't you know we eat people?"[22] Workers recalled that Dayak women who came to sell vegetables in the 1980s were bare breasted and the hunted meat they peddled included monkey and snake, foods Javanese found strange. Workers combined their sense of superiority with pity as they gave Dayak women vegetable sellers their old clothes.

The element of pity in workers' views of Dayaks receded and their fear intensified from 1997–99, when Dayak attacks on Madurese were shown on TV, confirming Dayak people's capacity for violence. The 1998 blockade of Natco we described in chapter 1 one infuriated workers including Godril, who argued that they were the ones who built up the plantation from nothing, hence local Dayaks had no right to make demands. Workers did not recognize that the coming of Natco had robbed villagers of crucial livelihood resources because they accepted the official narrative that the plantation was built on state land. They attributed Dayak actions to social jealousy and to defects in Dayak culture and personality. Several workers warned student researchers to avoid all contact with Dayaks because Dayak people were overly sensitive: the smallest misstep in social interaction could trigger a violent reaction or a customary fine. Hence the safe path for anyone who had no business with local villagers was to avoid interaction. If there was business, it would be hard to handle.

An event recorded by Lintang, a member of the research team, illustrates the strains of physical proximity and social distance. A group of Dayaks from the enclave of Batang Belian decided to pump out a stream so they could catch fish. Their hamlet is very close to afdeling 1 Natco, and the diesel pump ran all night, keeping workers awake. The Dayaks caught a lot of fish, but workers complained: "After they finished they didn't share any with us as compensation for our disturbed night's sleep, not even one fish as big as a finger." Attracted by the catch, some workers tried the same method, but after spending a lot of money on diesel, their catch was very small. So they decided to put poison upstream, a method guaranteed to produce a big catch as the half-dead fish are easy to scoop up. They knew poisoning was against Dayak customary law, but the foreman gave them tacit approval. "I am not saying yes, but I won't stop you," he texted. The catch was bountiful, and since the stream passed through Batang Belian, Dayaks also grabbed baskets to scoop up fish (figure 4.4). Afterward, Dayak elders threatened to impose a customary fine, but workers refused to reveal who had poisoned the stream. Workers argued that the Dayaks should have been fined for their noisy pump. The outcome was a stalemate in which each side believed the other had broken rules of etiquette—failing to share, poisoning a river, and not taking responsibility for one's actions.[23]

The social separation between workers at Natco and their Malay and Dayak neighbors was extreme. It formed their practices and subjectivities and was built into institutional and spatial arrangements. Ironically the gulf between the plantation and its surroundings, and between workers and villagers, was less marked in colonial times. Institutionally, the rubber plantation that preceded Natco was more integrated. Its Dutch managers lacked the dense networks of political and social support that managers in Sumatra's colonial plantation belt enjoyed. They were pioneers in Kalimantan, out on their own, and they operated the plantation in much the same way as local Malay and Chinese entrepreneurs who also had rubber holdings of more than 100 hectares. They borrowed from local moneylenders when they were short of funds during the Depression. The colonial regime supplied them with Javanese contract workers, but they had limited means to discipline their workers or hold them in place. Socially, the Javanese workers did not see themselves as superior to the local Malay and Dayak population. They learned survival strategies from them like how to grow swidden rice, an essential skill whenever the plantation faced financial difficulties and could not pay their wages. Workers envied villagers' autonomy. Those who did not return to Java after their three-year contract aspired to emulate the locals and become farmers in control of their own land.

FIGURE 4.4 Night Fishing and Other Pleasures

Young Dayaks dividing the catch after using a generator to electrocute fish. Fishing by night or day is a popular hobby for young men. The campfire suggests they planned immediate consumption. Young men also like to travel as a group to visit hamlets where there is a festival or soccer game to watch. To participate in this activity, they need access to motor- bikes and money for fuel. Those with ample funds to spare make group trips to Pontianak to take in the city lights. Youths in one Dayak hamlet were fortunate that a neighbor had installed a pool table, a ready source of low-cost entertainment. Opportunities for interac- tion across ethnic boundaries are limited. Natco workers hold their own soccer tournament, separate from the tournaments organized by villagers, to mark Independence Day. The main interethnic contact zone for young people is Tanjung town, where they attend junior and senior high schools and hang out in internet cafes to play computer games. Access to these activities is more limited for young women, with the exception of school, which could be a reason why they stay in school longer and are more likely to graduate. To keep in touch with friends in other hamlets, young people rely on their cell phones, and a new ritual has emerged: wherever they travel they immediately seek a high point to test the cellular-signal reception. Buying cell phone minutes is their first priority whenever they have funds.
PHOTO: A. D. YOGA PRATAMA.

From the perspective of villagers, the old rubber plantation was not an oc- cupying force. It took up only 600 hectares and left villagers with sufficient access to farmland. Its managers were friendly and offered villagers rubber seedlings, so they too could prosper from the new crop. Managers also per- mitted villagers to sell vegetables, clothing, household supplies, cooked food, and entertainment on plantation grounds. Poniman, a grandson of the first generation of Javanese contract workers, remembered his childhood in the 1950s when his parents had moved out of the plantation to live in Muara Tangkos. "It was so lively here in those days. There was a big gathering at the plantation every payday. There was Javanese horse dance, Chinese dragon dance, and drama at night. My mother and grandmother had a food stall selling Javanese salad and chicken soup. I was a spoiled kid, I never had to work, because my parents made so much money." Many Javanese workers left the plantation to tap rubber for local landholders on a share basis, and some married into local Malay and Dayak families. The name they gave for moving into Dayak areas was "going upriver." It was an attractive option when the plantation was failing. It was also important in 1966, when plantation workers who had joined the Communist-linked union Sarbupri were harassed and found refuge in upriver hamlets.

Poniman's account revealed the flow of people, money, and food between the plantation and surrounding villages before Natco arrived in 1980 and a rigid spatial and social separation became entrenched. Natco workers did not buy their monthly household supplies locally. The company transported them by boat to Yatan town, and later by truck to Tanjung town until they had motorbikes and could make the one-hour trip on their own. By 2010 the road to Pontianak City had been upgraded and there was a regular taxi service from Natco so workers could make the five-hour trek to the city whenever necessary. The new transport infrastructure directed the flow of plantation workers' wages away from surrounding villages toward progressively larger urban centers. Former trade and entertainment centers like Muara Tangkos lost their access to plantation wealth. Natco shipped its crude palm oil by barge directly from the mill to Pontianak port, a route that cut out another social group, the Chinese rubber traders who previously collected rubber from scores of upriver hamlets and shipped out hundreds of tons of rubber monthly. Younger generations of Chinese moved away, leaving only old people in a row of rotting shop-houses by the river. Corporate occupation robbed the village of Muara Tangkos of its farmland and its position as a trading center, a double blow that explained the poverty and hopelessness we encountered there in 2010.

Occupied and Abandoned

From the river the enclave of Muara Tangkos looked like any other Malay village with wooden houses on stilts clinging to the riverbank, a modest mosque, and makeshift jetties lining the shore (figure 4.5). By contemporary Indonesian standards the village was poor: it had no paved roads, only muddy trails and very few of the concrete houses that express social status in rural Kalimantan. Some houses still had palm thatch roofs and little or no furniture. Richer families had private wells, but most people drank polluted water from the Kapuas when their stored rainwater ran out and they used the river for all their other water and toilet needs. Poorer families did not own motorbikes and could not afford to connect to the electricity grid.

Natco and Priva occupied almost all the village land, and village leaders had tried to persuade the companies to provide funds for village infrastructure without success. An enterprising hamlet leader who read the 2004 Sanggau Plantation By-Law (article 7:3) discovered that corporations were supposed to donate 5 percent of their profits for "community development." Legal justification in hand, he made a request to Priva for funds but received no response. Natco agreed to give the village IDR25 million (USD2,500) to repair the police post, which stood empty most of the time. Johan made it his mission to extract funds from the two corporations to rebuild the almost-derelict village mosque, but he too failed: letters of support he obtained from

FIGURE 4.5 Muara Tangkos

This photo of the enclave of Muara Tangkos was taken from across the river at Natco. Plantation professionals would appreciate the view of a hillside densely covered with oil palm. For villagers, the hillside view means something quite different: the palms occupy land they previously used for growing rice, tapping rubber, gathering wild vegetables, and trapping small game. Some enclaves have a bit of land for village use, but in Muara Tangkos the palms come right up to their houses, leaving them with no land at all. PHOTO: PUJO SEMEDI.

the district office of religious affairs had no traction. Priva did not even support the building of a road bridge across the Tangkos River to link the Priva mill and office to the village center. Workers who traveled daily from the village to Priva, and children from Priva attending village schools, had to use a narrow wooden suspension bridge built with private funds donated by a Chinese trader. Village leaders complained that Priva made use of village facilities like schools and the health clinic to serve the needs of its workers but did not contribute to their upkeep. Priva managers argued that these facilities were already provided by the government for all villagers, so they did not need to duplicate them. As we noted earlier Priva already faced a heavy bill for maintaining out-grower roads and was beset with demands for "envelopes." Managers felt the corporation had already done enough to deliver prosperity, and it had no special responsibility for the people of Muara Tangkos, even though it occupied their land.

Access to livelihoods in Muara Tangkos was very constrained. Half the households in surveys the research team conducted in 2010–15 were landless, and the number increased each year as young couples set up households of their own. Villagers who had received just one out-grower plot found the monthly "pay" insufficient. Jobs were also scarce. In a survey that covered 117 households (roughly 240 working-age men and women), fewer than 20 percent had plantation jobs (twenty-three permanent, twelve men, eleven women; twenty-three casual, nine men, fourteen women). Many villagers struggled to find work of any kind. As we noted in chapter 2, managers at Natco and Priva were reluctant to hire local Malay and Dayak men, whom they regarded as lazy and troublesome. The village's riverside location enabled some men to work as fishers, as loaders at the makeshift dock, or as boatmen providing ferry service across the river. Many men sought work elsewhere in the district in mines and plantations, leaving their wives behind. The biggest losses were suffered by the poorest women, who were stuck in Muara Tangkos but could no longer earn a steady income from rubber tapping because all the rubber was gone. The variety of foods they could gather was much reduced, and the need to find cash to buy food was a daily stress (figure 4.6).

Some families had so little cash they could not afford the basics. Ibu Marlina's daughter Sara was married with a toddler, and when we visited Sara in her leaky one-room rented house, the child was crying. Sara was waiting for her husband to return from an odd job digging sand with IDR10,000 (USD1) so she could buy the child a can of condensed milk. Lacking money to buy a motorbike, or even a scythe on a pole, her husband did not have the means to join other young men who harvested for out-growers upriver.

Sara thought he would probably have to leave to find work elsewhere, but it would be temporary, casual work with no housing, so she could not accompany him. She would have to stay in the village where Ibu Marlina and other family members provided moral support though no material help, as they were equally poor. Many families were in a similar situation (figure 4.7).

For people who are near-landless, education might seem to be a pathway toward a better future, but the challenges are huge. Our survey confirmed that education levels were low: from 117 households, only seventeen had a family member who had completed high school; only seven people had been

FIGURE 4.6 Family Supper in Muara Tangkos

We went to visit Tina in the late afternoon. She invited us to stay for supper and made her provisions stretch for two extra guests. Her mother dropped by. "Too bad I did not know you would be here," she said. "I collected ten bunches of fern today and sold them all. I could have brought some here for supper." Tina's job at Priva was to spray herbicide on weeds, including ferns. "We don't spray all of them," she remarked, "or there would be nothing left to eat." Malay villagers eat bats, owls, and ferns, the tips of young oil palms, a fungus that grows on rotting palm fruit, and tilapia that survive in the toxic waters of the mill's waste pond. In Dayak enclaves the menu includes rats that feed on palm fruit and pythons that feed on rats. Most rivers and streams have very few fish, and the palm rats are so numerous they devour any vegetables the villagers try to plant. Villagers buy vegetables and fish in Tanjung town or from motorbike peddlers if they can afford them; if not, they make do with plain rice and instant noodles, which they optimistically call *sayur* (vegetables), perhaps because of the tiny flecks of red and green in the packaged flavoring. PHOTO: TANIA LI.

to university, three of them from Johan's family, funded by proceeds from his independent oil palm.

Tina and Desi took different approaches to the education of their children. Tina was determined to keep her daughters in school, even at the expense of her own health as her lungs were badly damaged by the chemicals she handled at work. When her older daughter asked about continuing her studies beyond high school, Tina told her, "We better think hard about this because I am really tired, but if you want to study, I will keep working." Tina showed Tania the bill she had received for extra school fees for her second daughter who had just enrolled in senior secondary school and asked her to help figure out what all the fees were for. She suspected that the school mafia was stealing from parents and had openly challenged the principal at the parents' meeting, with no result. "We are small people, what can we do?" she lamented. Tina's husband had worked for Priva for a few years before trying to make money as a door-to-door salesman, without much success. Tina's mother was doubtful of the wisdom of Tina's education plan. She was widowed in 1995 and made the decision to sell her single precious out-grower

FIGURE 4.7 One Oil Palm Plot, Three Generations

Datuk Adit distributed his three out-grower plots to his three married daughters. One daughter lives with Datuk Adit to take care of her sick mother. Her own children will inherit just one plot between them. To make ends meet, the daughter's husband, Mistam, works as a harvester for neighbors and Datuk Adit catches fish in the Tangkos River for family consumption. PHOTO: PUJO SEMEDI.

plot to keep Tina's younger sister in school—a failed investment. She raised her daughters by doing casual day labor for Priva, but she was bitter. She felt she had invested too much money and too much hope in her younger daughter's education.

Desi deliberately discouraged her daughters from aspiring too high for education, reasoning that even if they completed high school, the outcome would be the same. She pointed out that girls from Tanjung town with high school diplomas commuted daily to work in the plantation. In town girls could only work in shops or food stalls where the pay was even worse.[24] The few young women who left Muara Tangkos chasing city lights soon returned. So Desi took her daughters to work with her at Priva during school holidays as a form of training and as a lesson in the value of money: "Otherwise they just ask me for money all the time; they don't know how tiring it is to work." Desi's husband organized gambling at local festivals. She sometimes accompanied him to do sex work to augment her casual plantation wages, an arrangement with which she was at peace although she tried to discourage her older daughter from following the trade: "She is already quite clever at this. Men like her and ask her to be their wife for one night (*isteri satu malam*), but I tell her to send them to me, I know how to handle them."

Successful investments in education took a great deal of money. Tina's mother sold her land to pay for Tina's sister's education, with no result. Johan, one of the richest men in Muara Tangkos, invested most of his money in his children's education: "I'm poor now," he said, "I can't even finish building this house, but the children had everything they needed for their studies in Pontianak—nice lodgings, a laptop, motorbike, complete!" Johan was able to finance his children's successful exit from Muara Tangkos. Most villagers who left for education or tried to find work elsewhere came back empty-handed; the children of Chinese traders were the exception because they had wider kin and trade networks to ease their exit path.[25]

"It Is Not Our Job to Reduce Poverty"

Villagers in Muara Tangkos and the other enclaves aspired to a modern form of life and would have enjoyed the facilities Natco provided for its permanent workers—decent houses, clean water, electricity, and steady incomes sufficient to buy nice furniture and educate their children. They did not think a return to the status quo before Natco and Priva arrived was possible or desirable. Their demand was for access to a "rightful share" of plantation wealth, a share that would enable former landholders and their descendants to live well and prosper for as long as the two corporations occupied their land. Their leaders also demanded "proper leadership, a good model," one in which managers recognized their sacrifice and treated them with respect. But managers were convinced that villagers had no right to make demands, nor were they obliged to negotiate with them or ensure that they prospered in the short or long term.

The massive, collective mobilization of villagers in 1998 that began with a demand for Natco to return village land had ended up with Panadol. As we explained in chapter 1, Natco had agreed to provide villagers with an out-grower scheme with plots located on villagers' residual land and charged them the full cost of plot preparation. Managers we met in 2010 still resented the out-grower scheme that they had been forced to provide under duress. They viewed out-growers as troublesome and inefficient. They described the scheme as "a never-ending problem" (*kapan kapan permasalahan ada*), their play on the scheme's initials KKPA (Kredit Koperasi Primer Anggota, primary co-op credit). They also complained about the low capacity of the people, using another wordplay to convert the acronym SDM (*sumber daya manusia*, or human resources) into *sumber dari masalah* (the source of problems). They were more convinced than ever that villagers were incompetent farmers and social inferiors, quite unfit to be partners of a corporation. They were fit only to be subdued, guided, or ideally ignored.

Ignoring villagers became difficult for Natco in 2011 when its unilateral decision to replant its aging palms and extend its concession license brought villagers' anger back to a boiling point. Managers knew they had to repair relations or risk an embarrassing repeat of mass protests that drew media attention to the corporation's troubles. Repairing relations was also expedient because PTPN directors had announced a plan to expand the state corporation's holdings in Kalimantan and needed a different public image. The pioneering rhetoric of Project Sanggau would no longer work, nor would the New Order tactic of simply grabbing people's land in the name of national development. A promise of shared benefit was the only way for the corporation to move forward, but managers were adamant that only a technically competent, business-oriented corporation could grow oil palm efficiently, hence they had to maintain their control.

A new model for out-grower schemes introduced in the 2000s provided Natco with an opportunity to repair relations with villagers, expand its plantation area, and maintain corporate control over cultivation at the same time. The new model was known as the "partnership system" (*pola kemitraan*), the "one management system" (*pola satu manajemen*), "one block system" (*pola sehamparan*) or the "one-roof system" (*pola satu atap*). Under this model villagers who released land could become shareholders and receive a monthly dividend from plantation profits, but they had no role at all in growing oil palm, leaving managers and technical experts fully in charge. There were no more out-growers cultivating their own plots like the ones we described in chapter 3, hence no more struggles over roads, access to the mill, fruit quality, or debt payment. One-roof scheme members had nominal rights over a portion of the plantation land but no farm plot to visit and no tasks to perform. As in previous out-grower schemes, members of a one-roof scheme were formally represented by a co-op, but the co-op's only task was to oversee the deposit of monthly dividends into members' bank accounts.

For managers of Natco the one-roof system offered an ideal solution to the never-ending problem of delinquent out-growers as it restored their monopoly over production. They also hoped it could solve a very immediate problem: one hundred villagers had still not received the out-grower plots Natco had promised to provide them under the agreement it signed in 1999. Instead of allocating them out-grower plots, managers wanted to allocate villagers one-roof shares in a new plantation it was establishing sixty kilometers (37 miles) away from Muara Tangkos—too far for them to manage themselves. But the one-roof solution was only ideal if managers could persuade villagers to accept it; if not, villagers would keep on making demands. The attempt to guide and goad villagers to accept this plan set the stage for a two-act dramatic performance staged in Muara Tangkos while we were there in 2011.

ACT ONE—Eight managers from Natco plus the village head, all of them in uniform, sat behind tables at the front of the village meeting hall. The village head gave a welcome: "The purpose of this meeting is to open our thinking so we can be good oil palm cultivators. The company is making efforts for our welfare." He introduced the managers one by one, noting their job title and emphasizing their qualifications. Then one of the managers took over the microphone:

We want to have a happy and prosperous family. The state plantation corporation has a new vision. We are an agribusiness that grows and develops together with the people in a sustainable way. It is part of our social responsibility. Our old vision did not have this. True, we are a bit late. But now we have funds for this purpose. We can't give you money, but we can provide knowledge to empower you. The basis is partnership. We have to make a profit so we can keep our social development programs going.

We are going to provide you with practical training that will be useful for your daily life.

Off-stage, a plantation manager who was bored by the proceedings grumbled to us about wasted time. All he wanted to know was this: Would villagers accept the one-roof scheme or not? One of his colleagues corrected him: "We can't talk about the one-roof scheme now; first we have to build trust and the people need to be empowered." Another manager mentioned the need to act fast to forestall interference by NGOs that had started to criticize the one-roof model and caused trouble in other districts. After lunch the Natco managers went back across the river and three days of empowerment training began.

ACT TWO—The empowerment training was run by an outside expert hired by Natco. The trainer had spent the preceding afternoon trying to ensure that at least thirty village men and women would attend and making arrangements for food that should be modest so participants would feel at home, "whatever they usually eat, nothing special," he insisted. The training covered topics such as household budgeting and planting vegetables, repetitive themes in village development programs that link villagers' poor economic conditions to their imprudent spending. The principal focus of the training was trust and unity, which the trainer argued were the key to successful farming and village development. The training did not address Natco's relations with villagers or the reasons why they distrusted the corporation. It did not explain where they fit in the corporation's new vision of a "happy and prosperous family." It suggested that their future prosperity lay in their own hands (figures 4.8 and 4.9).

FOLLOW-UP—We asked the consultant why villagers needed to learn how to work together for a one-roof scheme in which they had no tasks to perform, but he had no answer. The participants enjoyed the games and were pleased that Natco had given them some attention: it was the first time eight officials had visited the village and organized a training for them. They accepted the envelopes of cash the trainer handed them as a reward for attending all three days. But they were baffled by the purpose of the training and remained thoroughly skeptical of the one-roof scheme. Experience had shown them that the state plantation was arrogant, corrupt, and not to be trusted. They did not believe that Natco would ever supply transparent accounts so they could verify the share due to them—the only

FIGURE 4.8 Empowerment Training Sponsored by Natco

To deepen villagers' commitment to trust and unity, the empowerment consultant used group games and exercises drawn from multilevel marketing. These included drawing pictures, writing slogans, singing songs, hugging, and a grand finale in which the consultant encouraged everyone to recognize their selfishness and brought the whole group to tears. The techniques were designed to create collective effervescence, a shared emotional intensity from which unity and trust were supposed to emerge. To our skeptical eyes the consultant's performance was similar to that of a snake-oil seller in Tanjung market: both the diagnosis of ailments and the prescription to cure them were fake, but for a brief moment the crowd was drawn into a fantasy of a bright future. PHOTO: TANIA LI.

mechanism available to members of a one-roof scheme to keep a corporation honest. Some of them had asked around, and they were aware that monthly payday in one-roof schemes was lean: less than even the lowest yielding out-grower plots and far below the sum earned by efficient out-growers.[26] Villagers wanted the company to return some of their land in the form of actual out-grower plots so they could recover their position as independent farmers. The one-roof scheme offered them no autonomy at all. They certainly did not see it as a solution to the problem of being trapped in an enclave with no land and little work. The two-act drama failed to persuade them that the corporation was starting to take them seriously.

Although Natco managers talked about empowerment, those we talked to had no interest in empowering people to challenge the terms of the

FIGURE 4.9 Trust and Unity, Unity, Unity

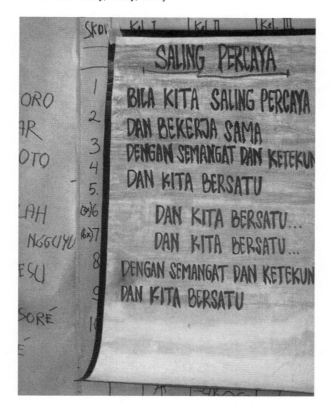

The mantra repeated throughout the three-day workshop was "Mutual Trust: When we have mutual trust and we work together with energy and diligence, and we are united, united, united." It suggested that the solutions to participants' problems were to be found in their own conduct, not in their relationship with Natco. PHOTO: TANIA LI.

occupation. Nor did they acknowledge that Natco had brought villagers far more harm than good. One manager informed us candidly that Natco had no obligation to improve villagers' livelihoods due to an official change in mandate: the state-plantation corporation's mission was no longer to relieve poverty (*mengurangi kemiskinan*) but to create prosperity (*meningkatkan kesejahteraan*). The shift might seem merely semantic, but the difference between the two concepts was significant. It freed managers from responsibility to address the needs of any specific group of people and legitimized the use of corporate resources to create prosperity for cronies and members of the regional elite. These people were peers and allies of plantation managers, people for whom power yielded access to land and for whom land was a business proposition, not a prerequisite for survival. The one-roof scheme was the ideal vehicle for cementing corporate-crony alliances as anyone could become a member of such a scheme: all that was needed was to enter their name on the list of members of the co-op and money flowed monthly into their bank accounts. "It is OK for us if the partner is a big landowner," the manager confirmed, "then we can be happy, and they can be happy too." With corporate allies as co-op members plantation managers' task would be easy: members would be grateful for the monthly payments they received. They would not be like villagers, "the source of problems," convinced that they had suffered losses and forever making demands. Far from giving villagers compensation, a place at the table, or a share in plantation wealth, Natco's new direction further marginalized them. It would "create prosperity" for the corporation's strategic partners but not for the people who lost most and gained least from its presence as an occupying force.

Under Indonesia's Plantation Law, state and private corporations are expected to bring benefits to the population, but the law specifies no obligations toward any particular people. So long as jobs are created it doesn't matter who has access to them; so long as new infrastructure is built, it is not necessary to know who uses it; so long as there are signs of prosperity—some people have motorbikes—no one monitors who has them or how they were acquired. The Investment Law includes a provision on "Corporate Social Responsibility," but there are no implementing regulations or standards for what corporations must accomplish.[27] In sum, corporations are not held responsible for bringing benefits. Nor are they held responsible for the harms they create, especially structural harms like the undermining of law and village government, reduced ecological and economic diversity, and the exclusion of millions of rural Indonesians from farm-based livelihoods now or in the future.

Villagers in Muara Tangkos and the other enclaves in Tanjung lived under corporate occupation: their former land was physically occupied by plantations and their village institutions were subordinated to corporate interests. Everything about their lives had been transformed yet no one took responsibility for their fate: they were both occupied and abandoned. Yet they were still classified as ordinary citizens (*rakyat biasa*), as if it was possible for them to live as they did before. Neither government officials nor corporate managers collected data to monitor what was happening to them or proposed solutions for how they could survive when confined to tiny enclaves shorn of farmland. The lack of data contrasts sharply with the situation Marina Welker describes at Newmont's mine in eastern Indonesia. There, social development experts sought numbers to demonstrate that jobs and other economic opportunities provided by the mine together with its community development interventions yielded measurable improvements in infant mortality, literacy, and gender equality in surrounding villages.[28]

At Natco managers' wives fussed over the proper arrangement of flowerpots, but they did not extend their benevolent surveillance to the enclaves where filthy drinking water was routine. Workers at Natco were encouraged and enabled to lead exemplary family lives; families in the enclaves were fragmented as men had to leave to seek work elsewhere. The extreme contrast between living conditions in Natco and the enclaves produced divergent senses of place. For Natco managers and workers the contrast confirmed their conviction that they were radically different from and superior to backward villagers who continued to live in the vicinity but failed to progress. We found no hint that managers or workers recognized their employer's role in producing destitution in the enclaves, hence it did not make them uneasy; it was just the way things were. Makdisi's writing about Palestinians under Israeli occupation offers a way to make sense of this affective disconnect not in terms of the occupiers' bad faith but as a specific kind of racism that produces a "genuine blindness . . . the inability— the absolutely honest, sincere incapacity—to acknowledge that a denial and erasure have taken place."[29]

For local Malays and Dayaks, in contrast, the sad state of their villages was ample confirmation that they had been denied, erased, and consigned to the position of an audience. The share of plantation wealth they were able to access was miniscule and disproportionate to their losses. Worse, the beneficiaries were outsiders who did not recognize their sacrifice, an occupying force that did not recognize itself as such. Villagers had become modern subjects who wanted to live decently and educate their children but were stripped of the resources they needed to achieve their goals. The resulting affect was less "social jealousy" than a deep sense of betrayal and anger that they had so little power to change their situation. What were the proper channels to communicate their concerns? Who would listen? Who was accountable for the damage done? The people to whom they might have addressed these questions were collaborating with the other side.

Conclusion

In this chapter we asked: What were the forms of life that emerged in the plantation zone? To answer this question we drew inspiration from studies that examined the transformations wrought by colonial rule and the deployment of political technologies that formed new subjects and profoundly reordered the grounds for social action. Forms of life in Tanjung were multiple. We examined how corporate presence shaped the everyday operation of law throughout the plantation zone before delving into two sharply contrasting sites, Natco and the enclave of Muara Tangkos, each visible to the other across the river.

The novel legal and institutional arrangements set in place by the occupation had contradictory effects. Impunity did not mean anarchy. Law was neither suspended nor was it consistently applied. For corporations, legal arrangements that favored them also exposed them to the depredations of the mafia system. Villagers were formally classified as ordinary citizens whose legal rights were intact, even though their capacity to seek redress for harms done to them—always fragile in Indonesia—was severely degraded. Since corporate presence was justified with reference to the public good, not only did land and labor laws favor corporations, local-level legal arrangements required government officials to help smooth their work, leaving villagers with scant protection. For workers at Natco who had formal labor rights, idioms of family loyalty both protected them and kept them in line. In every corner of the plantation zone, corporate occupation shaped possibilities for social action in profound and disturbing ways.

For Natco, remaking forms of life was integral to its mandate: the plantation was designed as an exemplary site to demonstrate the virtues of New Order development. Within its borders, hierarchy and workplace discipline were embedded in the organization of time, space, bodies, and material goods, and enacted in events like cleanliness competitions. Managers and workers saw themselves as modeling a kind of modernity rendered more striking by its contrast with the backwardness of the Kalimantan interior, as they saw it. Natco's practices created a sharp social boundary that separated workers from Malay and Dayak villagers, whom they saw as utterly different and inferior. Natco's logistical arrangements cut off the flow of money into the surrounding area as trade routes were reoriented toward distant sites, and workers developed few connections with local families. For local villagers these hierarchies and separations heightened their sense that Natco, its managers, and its workers were not neighbors but an alien, occupying force.

Twenty years into Indonesia's post-Suharto reformasi, Natco was formally absolved of any obligation to relieve poverty in surrounding villages. Its directors and managers were free to create prosperity for their cronies and abandon everyone else. Priva paid out envelopes left and right but took no responsibility for the fate of former landholders and limited responsibility for its out-growers, as chapter 3 showed. Villagers in Muara Tangkos had no means to access the modern lifestyles modeled at Natco; they were simply the audience. Without land and or steady jobs, they could not afford to educate their children for prosperous and modern futures. They struggled to survive, but neither the corporations nor government authorities acknowledged that they had suffered a loss. They were indeed made into new subjects—manusia konyol, people who were induced or coerced to make a sacrifice then abandoned and tossed aside.

5

Corporate Presence

In this chapter we ask: Why are corporate plantations still present and expanding across Indonesia? Since 2000 multiple critics have exposed the damage that oil palm plantations cause to forests, ecosystems, customary communities, and people's livelihoods. Problems with land acquisition, labor standards, out-grower schemes, co-ops, and credit have been reported with monotonous consistency. Yet every year more plantation licenses are issued, and government and industry proponents announce ambitious targets for further expansion. Experts have declared that 26 million hectares (double the current area) is suitable for oil palm cultivation.[1] This chapter tracks three elements that enable this expansion: the limited scope of critiques that stop short of calling the corporate mandate into question; reform efforts that protect oil palm corporations by promising to turn bad oil into good; and the nexus of powers that defend the corporate mandate and preclude serious consideration of smallholder-based alternatives.

Decades of Critique

In previous chapters we examined critical discourses and practices that emerged among workers, out-growers, and villagers who lived in Tanjung's plantation zone and were directly affected by the presence of plantation corporations. Pak Ibrahim, a former company man, hoped the mill would burn down; Tina said she hated the company; Iksan seethed with fury at manipulations of his pay; Pak Luwar was so worried about the future of his grandchildren he had panic attacks. Most critiques focused on specific grievances and the goal of collective protests was to shift the balance so that the companies extracted less and gave more. Villagers in 1999 demanded the return of some of their land, not all of it; out-growers sought a better deal; workers who staged wildcat strikes wanted fair compensation for their labor and the risks they bore. Some Dayaks in Tapang Dacin wanted to end the occupation, but most accepted that it would continue. The plantations' massive presence shaped their landscapes and livelihoods, and their sense of what they could achieve. Circa 2015 critics who were situated at a greater distance from plantation zones framed their concerns differently, but they too took corporate presence for granted. Here we review the principle critiques and their limitations, beginning at the district level.

District Critics—Social Impact and Sustainability

In Sanggau in 2010–12, oil palm was booming. In a lecture he gave to open our seminar in 2012, the district head focused on his plan to require corporations to give more generous shares to members of "one-roof" partnership schemes, and he mentioned the need to improve water management and soil fertility. These improvements aside, he expressed continued support for plantation corporations, noting that only corporations had the technical capacity to grow oil palm efficiently; rubber, he said, could be left to the people. He pointed out the prosperity that oil palm had brought to out-growers he had visited: "Look at their houses, they are better than my house, it makes me proud and happy to see them. They are making IDR12–14 million (USD1,200–1,400) per month or at least IDR3 million (USD300)." Responding to these words, Dayak leader Pak Jaelani questioned the prosperity narrative. For decades he had been trying to persuade the district government to do some serious fact-finding: Did oil palm really bring prosperity to ordinary people? Could it support their livelihoods into the future? Would it cause social conflicts that endangered national unity? Was there any evidence to back up corporate claims? Sustainability was of particular concern to him because he was thinking ahead to the end of the boom, when residents of a district like Sanggau whose livelihoods were so heavily dependent on oil palm would face extraordinary suffering. He was unsure whether it would be possible to repurpose the land or how many decades it would take.

Reliable data on livelihood impacts of the kind Dayak critic Pak Jaelani was seeking are remarkably scarce. Most reports of prosperity are anecdotal and focus on out-growers who have done well, like the ones the district head encountered during his field trip. No doubt some out-growers prosper, and numerous survey-based studies from Kalimantan, Sumatra, and Papua confirm this. Independent smallholders also prosper if they have access to infrastructure and investment funds.[2] But many out-growers struggle and stagnate, as we showed in chapter 3, and they risk ruin when infrastructure fails or the global price drops. In contrast to the livelihood impacts for out-growers and independent smallholders, which are mixed, there are to our knowledge no studies that show a beneficial outcome to former landholders from the presence of plantations. Local landholders lose their land, obtain few jobs, and they are not guaranteed access to out-grower schemes. The only local benefits, if any, are not from the plantation but from potential access to a mill that is only relevant for farmers who have the desire and capacity to grow oil palm independently. The outcomes are especially dire in remote areas, which are precisely the areas targeted for corporate occupation on the grounds that plantations bring jobs, prosperity, and development.

In Papua a survey-based study of the environmental and social impacts of several oil palm plantations conducted by the Centre for International Forest Research (CIFOR) found that losses to local landholders were catastrophic. One corporation took over 20,000 hectares but did not provide an out-grower scheme and hired few locals. In the survey 86 percent of Papuan respondents reported negative changes to their livelihoods due to the distance they had to travel to access residual farmland and forest resources; they had reduced access to food, and 88 percent of them had lost sources of income. They also reported negative environmental impacts such as water and air pollution and increased incidences of human and crop diseases. Ninety-three percent of respondents regretted the presence of the plantation.[3] Another CIFOR study confirmed that local losses are not offset by development benefits at the provincial level as plantations operate in isolation with few multipliers. Most of the added value stays within the corporate nexus (75 percent) and workers are mostly migrants.[4]

Despite confirming that corporate presence in Papua produced significant harms and brought little or no benefit to the local population or the province, the CIFOR research team did not propose an alternative development path. Instead it proposed a series of technical fixes: "to reduce the negative impacts and trade-offs of oil palm plantations and maximize their economic potential, government decision makers need to restrict the use of forested land for plantation development, enforce existing regulations on concession allocation and environmental management, improve monitoring of labor practices, recognize traditional land use rights, and make land transfer agreements involving customary land more transparent and legally binding."[5] The limit of this critique is that implementing the proposed fixes would not secure benefits for Papuans; at best it would mitigate their losses. Further, implementation assumes that "government decision makers" are dedicated to the public interest—an assumption CIFOR's own studies show to be misplaced. Read in this light, the report is a ritual performance that seeks to conjure a regulatory state into existence by describing its properties. It sets aside its own critique by holding out a promise of improvement to come.

A very large-scale quantitative study on Kalimantan reached the same conclusion as the CIFOR study: corporate plantations brought no benefits to remote areas. The study used the government's village-level statistics (PODES) cross-referenced with spatial data on plantation locations and biophysical conditions to compare 6,600 villages in matched pairs, with and without oil palm plantations. It found that in subsistence-oriented villages that grew their own food with cash crops as a supplement, the arrival of oil palm plantations had a negative effect: there was less progress on all social and economic indicators than in control villages. In more market-oriented villages plantations brought a slight improvement in economic indicators, but environmental damage and social conflicts were more severe. Overall the study concluded that corporate occupation brought more harm than good.[6]

These studies in Kalimantan and Papua confirm the fears of the Dayak elder who attended our seminar: Pak Jaelani's ground-level observations made him skeptical of the narrative that corporate plantations brought prosperity, and he could see the rising level of conflict and environmental destruction. In 2017 the Sanggau District head agreed to stop issuing new plantation location permits due to a shortage of land. During a 2019 seminar attended by officials from Jakarta he said, "It is enough now, we have no more land for oil palm." He pronounced the hope that the many corporations already present in the district would bring some benefits to the people.[7]

It was a remarkable comment: forty years after Project Sanggau opened the door for plantation development, the district head was still hoping for prosperity to arrive. It was proof of prosperity and sustainability the Dayak elder wanted, and it was not forthcoming.

Provincial Critics—Occupation on a Massive Scale

Plantation location permits are issued by district heads who benefit from the toll booths they control while claiming kudos for bringing prosperity to remote areas. The provincial-level planning agency (Bappeda) has an "oversight and coordination" function but limited control over district officials. Its main tools are the 2007 Spatial Planning Law and the 2009 Environmental Law, which are often set aside when they interfere with lucrative investment. The Civil Society Coalition for Fair and Sustainable Spatial Planning in West Kalimantan compiled data to illustrate this problem. It calculated that in 2014, of the province's total land area (14.4 million hectares), 4.8 million hectares had been allocated to 326 oil palm corporations, 1.5 million hectares to 651 mining corporations, 3.7 million hectares to 151 timber corporations, and 3.7 million was protected forest. This left a mere 0.7 million hectares for the farming, residential, and infrastructural needs of 4.3 million people. Ignoring the land squeeze, the provincial government still proposed to allocate a further 1.5 million hectares to plantation corporations.[8]

Throwing fuel on the flames, in 2015, the Department of Transmigration in Jakarta requested more provincial land—a further 3.5 million hectares—for allocation to settlers from other islands. The result was an uproar. A coalition of students and ethnic and religious associations vigorously opposed the plan, and the governor, a Dayak, sided with them. Protestors noted the shortage of land for local people, land conflict, forest loss, and unfair bias that favored transmigrants over locals. Protestors also pointed out that transmigration is supposed to bring prosperity to backward areas, but its purported benefits have not been evaluated.[9] The planned expansion was put on hold, but in 2017 a new version was launched, this time to place 1 million transmigrant households on the border with Malaysia in "partnership" with oil palm corporations.[10] The plan was strongly promoted by a representative of the Indonesian Oil Palm Producers Association (GAPKI), who argued that the cooperation between plantation corporations and the Transmigration Department had brought benefits to remote areas.[11] His enthusiasm for transmigration was no surprise. Since the transmigration program adopted the one-roof approach the standard 2 hectare plot allocated to

MAP 5.1 Plantation Concessions and Location Permits, West Kalimantan Province, 2011

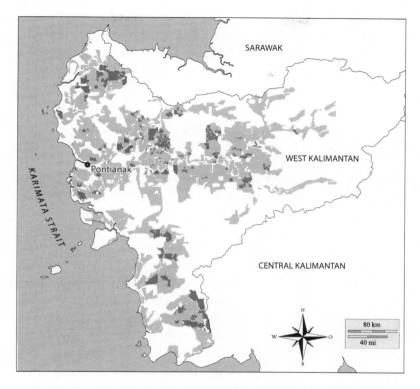

This map presents corporate occupation visually at a provincial scale. The dark blocks are plantations with legal concessions (HGU). Light blocks represent location permits or concessions-in-progress, which may be held speculatively, sold to another corporation, or reserved as a "land-bank" for future expansion. By 2011, concessions and permits blanketed most of the best farmland in more densely populated parts of the province along the Kapuas River and in the northwest along the coast. Transmigrants were also concentrated in these areas. White areas were mainly protected forest or peat. A great many new permits were issued in the decade after the map was made, hence corporate occupation is ever more complete. A 2017 moratorium on new permits in primary forest peatland did not affect permits already issued, nor did it extend to rubber groves and other village land that corporations acquire. In 2020 we searched in vain for an updated map. NGOs in Pontianak City argue that lack of transparency about the size, location, and ownership of corporate concessions makes it difficult for them to monitor developments or help defend villagers' rights. Government agencies also lack data. Presidential Instruction No. 8/2018 attempts to address this problem by requiring district heads to conduct an inventory of all corporate and individual oil palm holdings and confirm their legal status, an onerous request with which they may not comply. SOURCE: BADAN PERTANAHAN NASIONAL, KALIMANTAN BARAT. REDRAWN BY D. L. GUMELAR transmigrants has been integrated with the core plantation. Transmigrants with no plots of their own end up providing cheap day labor for the plantation, a government-subsidized gift to GAPKI members.[12] Transmigration is a high-profile program that attracts public scrutiny, hence provincial critics were able to mobilize against it; they are less successful in mobilizing against plantation expansion because it is controlled by district heads and occurs one location permit at a time (map 5.1).

Policy Critics—Environment, Human Rights, and Corruption

After the year 2000, national advocacy groups that previously focused on the negative environmental and human rights impacts of timber extraction began to draw attention to similar problems with expanding oil palm plantations.[13] The Indonesian Forum for Environment (Wahana Lingkungan Hidup [WALHI]) was joined by Sawit Watch, an advocacy group focused on oil palm that conducts research in collaboration with transnational research and funding agencies.[14] Their main focus has been legal and institutional reform. They are aware of many deficiencies in the state apparatus (bad laws, bad actors, bad practices) but hold out the hope that these can be rectified. Hence their reports and campaigns highlighting environmental damage and human rights abuse routinely conclude with calls to government and industry to take corrective action.

The problems identified by advocacy researchers are recurrent. Pollution of rivers and streams by runoff of agricultural chemicals and mill effluent is widely reported. Researchers note that forest loss and water pollution are more damaging for poorer people who depend directly on these resources and cannot afford to buy food in town or dig private wells. The degradation of customary institutions as a result of the recruitment of customary leaders to land release teams, and their positioning as company men, is frequently noted. The fragility of livelihoods for out-growers who are bonded to corporations and stuck with delinquent co-ops features in many reports, together with the unfairness of one-roof schemes. Limited access to plantation jobs, unemployment among former landholders, low wages, the prevalence of casual and subcontract work, and hazardous work conditions are reported to be widespread.[15]

Environmental concerns and land conflicts are the most prominent issues raised in the policy-oriented academic and advocacy literature on oil palm. Environmental groups focus on the loss of forests and biodiversity, although the extent of clearing in primary forest is debated.[16] Land conflict is a huge problem since most plantations occupy forest and farmland previously used by customary landholders. The problem of coerced land release and the lack of formal written commitments from plantation corporations regarding out-grower schemes is very common. Many studies report that land conflicts between villagers and plantation corporations, and the discord sown among villagers, are enduring. Even if conflicts appear to be settled they are prone to reignite, since the underlying problems of land rights, access to shares of plantation wealth, and the challenge of survival for newly landless people are unresolved.[17]

The extent and severity of land conflicts is monitored by the Consortium for Agrarian Reform (KPA). In its 2018 annual report KPA recorded 410 new land conflicts across Indonesia of which 35 percent of the cases and 73 percent of the land area involved plantations.[18] From 2014 (the year President Joko Widodo took office) to 2018 land conflicts tracked by KPA resulted in 41 deaths, 546 assaults, and 940 people charged with criminal offenses.[19] KPA and the Indigenous People's Alliance (AMAN) have drawn special attention to the vulnerability of customary communities, so far without much result. A comprehensive four-volume report by Indonesia's Human Rights Commission published in 2015 detailed human rights violations concerning indigenous people (customary communities) in the forest zone, but business continued as usual.[20]

As we explained in the introduction, even if they do not belong to customary communities, most rural people hold their land on the basis of customary rights, and they are exposed to land seizure. According to the constitution, the government decides which land uses provide "the maximum benefit of the people" (clause 33:3), words that ruling regimes since 1966 have used to justify corporate concessions. KPA, AMAN, and other activist groups that demand a moratorium on concessions and the redistribution of concession land to the original landholders and/or to the tillers have little traction in the national arena. Pragmatically, most critics assume that corporate expansion will continue unabated and focus their efforts on making corporations obey the law, respect human rights, and engage with indigenous or customary communities following UN standards for "free, prior and informed consent." Some critics place their hope in a World Bank–supported project to create a single national map showing the boundaries of the state-claimed forest, state-granted concessions, and customary territories. The idea is that transparent information will reduce overlaps, but the fate of this attempted spatial fix is telling: as of 2018 the "one map" did not include customary territories and only the president and a few senior officials in Jakarta were authorized to see the map.[21] In an order of impunity, obscurity is a tool; too much clarity could upset crony-corporate relations.

Reform on the corruption front has been official policy since the beginning of reformasi in 1998. The National Anti-Corruption Commission (KPK) has specifically targeted corruption in the oil palm sector, with an initial focus on tax avoidance. A 2017 KPK report found that only 10 percent of individuals and corporations eligible to pay income tax on their oil palm holdings made the obligatory self-report. Overall, KPK estimated that tax collection in the oil palm sector was only 40–45 percent of the legislated amounts.[22] The corruption focus did not address an even deeper problem identified in a study commissioned by the Climate Policy Initiative: the very low rate of taxation applied to oil palm corporations. The tax-to-GDP ratio for oil palm is around 3.4 percent, much lower than the 12–13 percent ratio for manufacturing, electricity, and gas. The oil palm industry contributed only around USD1 billion to national tax revenues in 2012–13, 64 percent from export tax, 15 percent from land and building tax, 15 percent from income tax on individuals and corporations, and 6 percent value added tax. The land and building tax, the only revenue stream that flows from plantation corporations to district governments, was just USD100 million nationwide.

The land and building tax furnished only 2.3 percent of tax revenue in Sanggau, hence the district head's insistence that corporations should pay for their own roads. The tax is based on an artificially low land value that keeps costs low for corporations. Low taxes encourage corporations to secure big concessions, even when they cannot fully develop them, as big concessions enable them to leverage big bank loans.[23] It is a tax structure highly favorable to plantation corporations and unfavorable to the districts and villages where plantations are installed. These findings confirm that corporate plantations are not lucrative sources of tax revenue, as industry proponents suggest; if they bring prosperity and development, it is not via taxes. The findings also show the limits of an anticorruption agenda that attempts to make corporations obey the law but leaves the procorporate bias of the law unchallenged.

Transnational Critics — Biodiversity, Climate Change, and Human Rights

The transnational Center for International Forest Research (CIFOR) has played a leading role in research on forest and biodiversity loss, fires, and carbon emissions.[24] After 2010 it stepped up its monitoring of oil palm expansion to support initiatives to mitigate climate change. Its research on social impacts has been more limited, and the CIFOR studies we quoted earlier discovered catastrophic damage and negligible benefit but proposed only modest good governance–style reforms. CIFOR's base is in Indonesia and it needs to sustain collegial relations with Indonesian government ministries, a position that curtails its critique.

Transnational research and advocacy groups such as the World Rainforest Alliance, Greenpeace, and Amnesty International have some autonomy. Their work is oriented toward a global public and uses media campaigns to generate action, at the cost of some simplification. To highlight the problem of forest loss, campaigns focus on the oil palm industry's impact on charismatic species such as orangutans and Sumatran tigers.[25] To highlight corporate neglect, campaigns focus on indigenous people or child and bonded labor, which are clear human rights violations.[26] The broader context that makes all Indonesian workers vulnerable—the absence of unions, the massive labor reserve, the exclusion of casual workers from the protection of labor law—requires more explanation.

Advocacy strategies include public awareness campaigns, product boycotts, lobbying parliaments, and putting major corporations and the banks that fund them under the spotlight to oblige them to live up to their corporate promises. As with the other initiatives we have discussed in this section their critical intervention is limited by an assumption that plantation corporations will continue their occupation of rural Indonesia. Hence their goal is to reform corporations, so they do less harm. It is an approach that aligns with attempts by the oil palm industry to reform its image, adopt improved practices, and convince critics that bad oil can be made good. Industry-driven reform is the topic to which we now turn.

Good Oil, Bad Oil

Oil palm corporations and their government supporters (hereafter, industry proponents) often repeat the narrative that oil palm is intrinsically good. It provides a greener oil to the world than its competitors due to its high productivity per hectare: it is said to be up to eight times more productive per hectare than soy, so if less oil palm was grown more hectares of Amazonian rainforests and grasslands would need to be converted.[27] Proponents also argue that the oil palm industry is good for Indonesia as corporations bring prosperity to remote areas, provide jobs, and furnish the nation with tax revenues and foreign exchange. They push back against the narrative painting palm oil black, the "black campaign" as they call it, which they consider unfair as it emphasizes only bad effects and ignores the good.[28] The industry association GAPKI, which represents Indonesia's corporate oil palm producers, has an entire section of its website under the title "Myths and Facts" dedicated to correcting information it regards as inaccurate.[29] Proponents suggest that the black campaign was launched by environmental and human rights NGOs based mainly in Europe and masks a self-serving agenda: to protect oils and biofuels produced in rich countries (soy, olive, corn, canola, rapeseed) from competition. Proponents also point out that a European Union ban or boycott would not hurt Indonesia too much since only 15 percent of Indonesia's crude palm oil is sent to Europe; 61 percent heads to India where the black campaign lacks traction.[30]

Despite their defensive stance industry proponents acknowledge that some plantation corporations act badly and should be encouraged to reform their practices and conform to the law. As with reform efforts in other harm-producing industries (mining, tobacco), the outcome of reform and the deployment of what Marina Welker calls the "ameliorative disciplines" is to sustain corporate presence, with some adjustments.[31] With oil palm, reform narratives suggest that problems can be addressed through technical measures such as the introduction of standards, monitoring, providing face masks and gloves for women exposed to toxic chemicals, and so on. They do not bring the rationale for corporate presence into question. Instead they focus efforts on isolating bad corporations and their delinquent practices so that good corporations and good palm oil prevail. Here we examine two reform initiatives and track their effects at the site of Pak Wakijan's new plantation.

The Roundtable on Sustainable Palm Oil

The Roundtable on Sustainable Palm Oil (RSPO) was founded in 2004 to provide a forum in which multiple stakeholders could identify problems collaboratively and implement solutions voluntarily over time. It was an industry-driven response to rising criticism and adverse media coverage over forest loss. The three founding parties were Unilever (the Anglo-Dutch processed-food and detergent corporation), Golden Hope Plantations, and the World Wildlife Fund (WWF).[32] The involvement of WWF was a pragmatic bargain. Since conservation agencies recognized that they had no political means to prevent the advancing tide of oil palm, their best bet was to secure industry commitments to conserve selected spaces. These include nationally designated protected areas and what came to be called "high conservation value"

(HCV) areas—enclaves within concession boundaries that corporations agree to set aside as habitat for species other than oil palm (but not for human use).

An important goal of RSPO is to counter the industry's negative image with media campaigns. One such campaign ran under the title "Good Oil, Bad Oil," adopting a strategy that acknowledges bad palm oil upfront. According to the campaign website, "The production of 'bad' palm oil is rapidly destroying virgin rainforests and ecosystems, causing greenhouse gas emissions to rise and putting many species at risk of extinction. If grown sustainably, 'good' palm oil can benefit local communities with fair working conditions while also helping protect our invaluable species and forests." Animated short films featured on the campaign website show popular consumer items like cookies and ice cream that contain palm oil and ask the viewer: Is it good or bad palm oil? The animation answers the question by filling a box with a check mark or a cross. As the campaign strategists announce, "With support from bloggers in the United States and Europe and a big push on social media we're asking everyone to become better informed about the palm oil debate and help raise awareness of good palm oil."[33]

Good palm oil, for RSPO, is palm oil that has been certified to meet RSPO standards. In 2015 this was around 20 percent of global production and 12 percent of palm oil produced in Indonesia.[34] Corporations seeking to have their plantations certified "sustainable" must commit to seven principles: (1) behave ethically and transparently; (2) operate legally and respect rights; (3) optimize productivity, efficiency, positive impacts, and resilience; (4) respect community and human rights and deliver benefits; (5) support smallholder inclusion; (6) respect workers' rights and conditions; and (7) protect, conserve, and enhance ecosystems and the environment. The seven principles are linked to specific practices and technical requirements, each of which must be measured for certification to be awarded and sustained.

The ultimate goal for RSPO is to "improve the quality of life of oil palm farmers, create a more prosperous palm oil industry, and enable us to better conserve our planet and its resources" and deliver "change where it matters most—on the ground."[35] RSPO's mode of engagement with palm oil producers is based on what it calls its "theory of change." The theory is that "good oil" does not emerge overnight: it is the product of incremental changes in individuals, communities, and corporations. As managers and workers learn about RSPO principles and start to adopt the prescribed techniques they will experience a transformation that leads them to reject the bad and select the good. Visitors to a plantation (figure 5.1) or to a campaign website (figure 5.2) will be similarly transformed.

FIGURE 5.1 RSPO Invites Visitors to Check Out a Plantation

An animated video on the good oil/bad oil campaign website presents the "theory of change" by featuring a vehicle with a driver and three white passengers driving through a plantation. One of the passengers says, "Wow, what an amazing view." The driver/guide replies, "It is. This is what a plantation looks like when sustainable palm oil is the norm." The "amazing view" shows a row of palms with workers wearing boots and hard hats and a cluster of neat houses with red roofs. Since the visitors ask to know more, the guide proceeds to explain RSPO's vision of "a space where oil palm, the environment, and local communities can coexist in harmony." The idea of the video's staging is that visitors who see something new and impressive will be inspired to learn more about it; from new knowledge will come support for RSPO's goal to make sustainable palm oil the norm. SOURCE: *THEORY OF CHANGE–RSPO'S ROADMAP TOWARDS SUSTAINABLE PALM OIL*. https://www.youtube.com/watch?v=nPMLpEHhHTU.

FIGURE 5.2 RSPO's Theory of Change

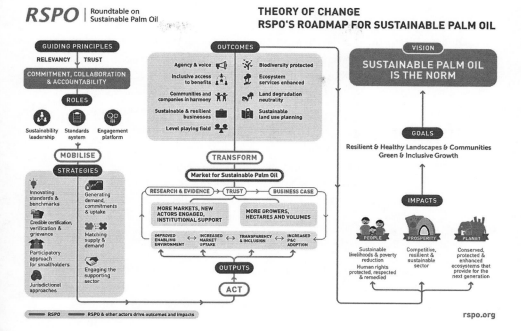

In this diagram change is rendered technical in the form of a road map with arrows passing through nodes and moving steadily forward. The expected reader of the diagram is a Euro-American consumer concerned about oil palm's social and environmental impacts; its purpose is to convince the reader that RSPO has a plan to address those concerns. The critical node is in the center: the market for sustainable palm oil. It is from an increase in market demand for "good" palm oil that a beneficial transformation will flow; hence demand must be created, and the reader/consumer is invited to join in. SOURCE: https://rspo.org/impact/theory-of-change.

The RSPO certification program is voluntary. In 2011 only 4 percent of corporations registered as members of Indonesia's oil palm industry association (GAPKI) had sought RSPO certification for their plantations (16 out of 435).[36] GAPKI members found the standards high, the certification process cumbersome, and they rejected the regulation of their activities by what they saw as a foreign institution. As an alternative GAPKI promoted the development of a national certification program, Indonesia Sustainable Palm Oil (ISPO), which has been compulsory for all growers since 2017. A transnational advocacy group, the Forest Peoples Programme, assessed different certification program requirements for land acquisition, treatment of smallholders, social and environmental safeguards, labor standards, gender and ethnic discrimination, quality assurance, and access to remedy. By these measures RSPO scored 102 out of 117 while ISPO scored 34 out of 117.[37] It should be noted that ISPO does little more than require plantation corporations to obey Indonesian law. But, as shown in previous chapters, Indonesian land and labor laws provide little protection for villagers or workers, so even if they were implemented, they would not transform bad oil into good.

For Indonesia the limited reach of the RSPO, the low standards set by ISPO and Indonesian law, and the prevalence of the mafia system present formidable obstacles to reform. ISPO standards enable companies to check boxes that disguise or "greenwash" problematic practices, and they create opportunities for new actors (certification companies, consultants, watch-dogs) to erect new toll booths. The ISPO requirement to certify all planta-tions ensures that verification is perfunctory and implementation lax.

No Deforestation, No Peat, No Exploitation

Still under attack from critics, some transnational corporations attempted to step up the reform agenda by using the leverage of their dominance in the supply chain. Around 2012 Wilmar, Musim Mas, and Golden Agri Resources, three corporations that refine about half the crude palm oil produced in Indonesia and Malaysia, adopted No Deforestation, No Peat, No Exploitation (NDPE) sourcing policies. This means they committed themselves to fol-low high standards for forest protection, avoid any plantation development on peat, and ensure that their treatment of communities and workers met both national and transnational human rights standards. They would also use their market leverage to encourage other corporations to follow suit: all their own subsidiaries and third-party plantations supplying crude palm oil to their refineries had to comply with NDPE standards.[38]

The strengths of the NDPE strategy are notable: many corporations im-proved their practices as a result. For example, Amnesty International's campaign to highlight problematic labor practices induced an Indone-sian subsidiary of Wilmar to eliminate casual employment, previously at 50 percent; increase wages; and reduce some of the heavy production tar-gets that forced workers to do unpaid overtime and rely on help from family.[39] The NDPE strategy has three important limitations: first, plan-tations that do not meet NDPE standards can still find refineries that will buy their product; second, monitoring supply chains that involve hun-dreds of plantations creates a fertile environment for the mafia system and box-ticking modes of compliance; third, and most seriously, the idea that corporations can be made good suspends critical scrutiny of their expansion.

Many studies have demonstrated the challenge of regulating oil palm plantations through standards in a context of decentralized powers, entrenched corruption, and weak rule of law.[40] To deepen the debate we turn to an examination of Pak Wakijan's new plantation where RSPO and ISPO standards were faithfully applied, yet the outcome was still business as usual.

Pak Wakijan's New Plantation

In 2017 Pak Wakijan was not finished with oil palm. He bought a concession in a neighboring district from a Malaysian corporation, Genting Plantations.[41] The concession cost him USD3.2 million and covered 17,000 hectares. Genting is a member of the RSPO. It had completed the RSPO's required High Conservation Value and Socio-Environmental Impact Assessments and applied for RSPO certification for the concession in 2014. According to the RSPO assessor's report, the concession was lightly populated with only 2,497 residents (around six hundred households) located in two villages. The report noted that residents were reluctant to lose their rubber fields but concluded that they would be satisfied with the money the company planned to spend on them through its program for Corporate Social Responsibility.[42] At a "stakeholder consultation" meeting held in the subdistrict office in 2013 and attended by twenty-seven participants (eight from government, seven from the company, twelve from the two villages), the invited villagers confirmed that they supported the proposed plantation in principle. They expressed concerns over access to plantation jobs, future land access, and river pollution. Genting affirmed that it would protect 1,455 hectares of High Conservation Value area and plant 12,000 hectares of oil palm, 9,600 as the plantation core and 2,400 for out-growers. It promised to follow RSPO's process of "free prior informed consent" for land acquisition and to involve community members in participatory mapping and land inventory.[43]

Based on the documents submitted to RSPO it appeared that everything concerning Pak Wakijan's new concession was done correctly: there was popular consent, a commitment to environmental protection, and a promise that land would be acquired without coercion. But there was another story. According to the environmental watchdog Chain Reaction Research, 10,000 hectares of the concession was high-carbon forest and orangutan habitat.[44] Cutting high-carbon forest meets RSPO and ISPO standards and is legal in Indonesia so long as the forest is not classified as protected, but it violates the big refineries' NDPE commitment. Hence Genting could not sell to the big refineries and its oil would fetch a lower price. There was also a problem of coercion. Villagers had been resisting corporate occupation since 1998. Two corporations had tried and failed to get a foothold. Villagers had lobbied to get 14,000 hectares of village land officially recognized as "village and customary forest," a classification that would protect it from plantation use, but they were only partly successful. In 2008 they received a ministerial decree protecting 2,400 hectares of old-growth forest, but the secondary forest they used for rice cultivation and their extensive rubber groves were still exposed to corporate designs.[45]

In discussion with journalists following the story, the headman of one of the affected villages insisted that villagers were satisfied with their existing livelihoods. "When oil palm companies first tried to come in around 1998, we all agreed to reject them. That is because our rubber gardens are enough to support us. Rubber guarantees our livelihoods. We have enough money to send our children to school in the district capital and meet our daily needs. We even have enough to buy motorbikes and install satellite TV."[46] The headman's statement confirmed that villagers were already prosperous, and they were fully open to the wider world (children away in high school, motorbikes, satellite TV). Hence, they could not be classified as backward people who suffered from a "low demand for necessities," the diagnosis used by Project Sanggau to justify its presence in the 1980s. Moreover, they successfully met their own needs without corporate help. They had, in short, no need for the kinds of development that plantation corporations promised to deliver. Plantations would bring them only losses, not gains.

Although many villagers roundly rejected corporate occupation, they could not prevent it.[47] Predictably, allies of the corporation started to fracture villagers' opposition using the standard technique: they converted customary and village leaders into company men who collaborated with the corporation.[48] Our scrutiny of the list of participant names at the crucial "stakeholder consultation" meeting held in the subdistrict in 2013 showed that the headman of the most affected village who led the opposition did not attend.[49]

The stakeholder consultation report had some striking gaps. It noted that villagers were concerned that they would be squeezed for land, but it did not provide any discussion of this point.[50] The report said nothing about the sociopolitical impacts villagers would experience when 17,000 hectares of their land was occupied by the corporation. Nor did it quantify the economic losses they would sustain when their rubber gardens were bulldozed and replaced by 12,000 hectares of monocrop palm owned by a corporation. While the 2014 "Summary of HCV and SEIA Report" had several mentions of rubber as the foundation of the local economy, the "Summary Report of Planning and Management"—the key report that outlined the company's plans for a consensual and participatory process—did not mention rubber at all. The omission followed the script of the "denial of denial"; rather than acknowledge that villagers' rubber trees would be destroyed, it overlooked the fact that they were ever there.

Perhaps the assessors looked at the village land area and thought villagers had more than enough for their needs. If so, their calculations were mistaken. On average they had 20 hectares per household, which is only enough to maintain some rice and rubber, some protected forest, and a modest reserve for the next generation.[51] Based on the size of the proposed plantation and information given on the planning map, it appears that Pak Wakijan's new plantation would take up all the land suitable for farming, leaving villagers with none. Newly landless villagers could not retreat to nearby forests or neighboring villages because all the surrounding land was already allocated to three different plantation corporations or classified as protected forest.[52] How then would villagers live? In the best-case scenario, the 673 households would receive a monthly payment from the promised one-roof out-grower scheme (2,400 hectares) if it materialized and if it were allocated fairly at 4 hectares per household. The payments might be enough to buy food and other necessities, but their livelihood would be fragile: they would have no safety net if the price of palm oil dropped or they had health emergencies, nor would they be able to provide land or education for their children. Plantation life would be a dead end for them, hence their protracted twenty-year resistance.

An analysis by Greenpeace suggested that Genting was aware the forest clearing would contravene its NDPE commitment, hence its decision to sell the license to Pak Wakijan's corporation.[53] Advocacy groups investigated this transaction as an example of the strategy used by high profile RSPO members like Genting to hide or transfer assets that exposed them to reputational risk.[54] Pak Wakijan's corporation was unlisted and he was not a public figure, so he did not face the same reputational risk. Nevertheless, he took steps to confirm his environmental commitments by enrolling his corporation as a member of the Friends Forum for Gunung Palung National Park.[55] He still proceeded with the plan to bulldoze villagers' rubber trees and reserve forests because the plan complied with Indonesian law and RSPO standards, for which the value of village rubber gardens is severely discounted.

The district head welcomed the arrival of Pak Wakijan's new plantation, repeating the narrative that corporations bring prosperity and development. In his 2017 speech at the ceremony to declare the new plantation open he noted that the government could not provide jobs or roads for its people, hence it had opened the door "as widely as possible" for corporations to develop natural resources for the people's benefit. He applauded the area that Pak Wakijan's company had set aside for its high conservation value, stating, "We don't need to worry about the company's environmental commitments anymore."[56] He did not acknowledge the losses that villagers would suffer under corporate occupation, or the extreme fragility this form of development imposed.

RSPO's theory of change suggests that new practices make new subjects. When corporations follow RSPO's prescribed procedures they will establish "a space where oil palm, the environment, and local communities can co-exist in harmony." But Pak Wakijan's new plantation did not establish conditions for harmonious coexistence, and it was not unique. The RSPO complaints system is burdened by hundreds of reports of land disputes involving RSPO members. It is far easier to write a report than it is to deliver the kind of change to which RSPO aspires: "change where it matters most—on the ground." The RSPO consultation process green-washed corporate occupation at the expense of villagers' livelihoods. It enabled the district head to congratulate Pak Wakijan on his corporation's conservation commitment and confirmed its bona fides. With RSPO certification in hand, nothing else needed to be discussed. The villagers' rejection of the argument that they needed a corporation to bring them prosperity was set aside, and business proceeded pretty much as usual.

Alternatives Foreclosed

Industry-driven reform efforts, like human rights and environmental campaigns, sustain corporate expansion by rendering problems technical and proposing fixes such as improved laws and regulations, certification, and "good governance." The focus on making bad corporations good deflects attention from two crucial questions: Is growing oil palm in massive corporate plantations efficient? And is the plantation model an effective means to bring jobs and development to rural areas? Here we develop the argument that support for smallholders would be more efficient on both counts and discuss the measures deployed to sustain plantation corporations despite their serious failings.

Corporations versus Smallholders

Oil palm industry proponents emphasize the active role of smallholders in their public campaigns to tap into (and co-opt) positive images that associate smallholders with self-sufficiency and prosperity earned through hard work. In Indonesia's popular discourse farmers are seen as "small people" who are modest and honest in contrast with "big people" (and corporations) who cannot be trusted. The smallholder who is technically advanced is the ideal; hence corporations that support such farmers acquire a share of the farmers' positive image. The word "farmer" appears far more prominently on the RSPO website than plantation or corporation; Indonesia's Ministry of Agriculture sponsored the formation of an oil palm smallholder organization, APKASINDO, as part of its response to the black campaign;[57] and Indonesia's Oil Palm Producers Association, GAPKI, proudly states that 40 percent of Indonesia's oil palm area is managed by smallholders.

On closer examination, pronouncements of corporate support for smallholders are misleading. Many smallholders are debt-bound and barely holding on to fragile out-grower plots; many so-called smallholdings are unlicensed plantations of 25–500 hectares owned by government officials, politicians, and entrepreneurs; and the distribution of smallholdings is highly uneven. In Kalimantan's three main oil palm provinces, smallholders control only 23 percent of the cultivated area. Corporations are unwilling to provide out-grower schemes, and managers do not want to deal with village smallholders, whom they view as "the source of problems." One manager from a private plantation in Sanggau put the matter thus:

> If we could just buy the land without any partnership agreement, we would be happier: if we could establish just our own plantation, without sharing the land and so losing productivity, for us that would be amazing. The main problem nowadays in the field is the social issue, so if we could just buy their land without any other relations with them it would be better. We could plant faster, manage the land better, optimize productivity, and so on. . . . And mostly we would have no problem from them. The government does not let that happen because people need jobs, you see![58]

Although they were deeply flawed, government-supported out-grower schemes like the PIR-BUN-Trans scheme implemented by Priva envisaged an important role for smallholders in modern agroindustry. This role was reflected in the prescribed land allocation ratio: 30 percent for the plantation core, 70 percent for out-growers. After 2013 the government reset the ratio to favor corporations: they could cultivate 100 percent of the concession area and develop an additional 20 percent for out-growers on villagers' own residual land, a requirement that is not enforced.[59] Even the 20 percent is nominal as most companies prefer to place the "out-grower" land under direct plantation management using the one-roof approach.[60] The one-roof approach also dominates replanting schemes. A 2017 government program that offered replanting credit to out-growers made the funds contingent on smallholders submitting their plots to corporate management; it offered no help for smallholders like those at Priva who longed to break free from the corporation and recover their autonomy.[61] GAPKI argued that one-roof schemes facilitate ISPO certification, which is too challenging for independent farmers to handle on their own.[62]

Industry proponents state that professional management is necessary for high productivity, but the evidence is mixed. Average plantation yields in Malaysia are 23 tons of fresh fruit bunches per hectare, in Sumatra 18 tons, and in Kalimantan 15 tons.[63] Smallholder yields are also highly variable, but under good conditions smallholders can outcompete plantations.[64] At Priva some out-growers obtained yields that were far higher than the plantation core, much to the embarrassment of company managers. In the period 2005–10, the average on the Priva core was 14.4 tons, while 1,000 hectares of out-grower plots produced 16.1 tons. From 2011 to 2014, 5,000 hectare out-grower plots outperformed the plantation core. Unsurprisingly, high out-grower productivity was concentrated in blocks with good roads to the mill.[65] Infrastructure was the limitation, not smallholder capacity. As we noted in the introduction there are no significant economies of scale in the cultivation of oil palm; smallholder oil palm cultivation conforms to the "inverse relation" in which small farms are more efficient per unit of land because of closer supervision.[66] Recall Ekay and Efi from Tapang Dacin, who spread fertilizers and other agricultural chemicals themselves to eliminate waste and theft and monitored closely to ensure that fruit was not harvested too early or too late. Even out-growers with low yields were more efficient per unit of labor than Priva as they did not need to hire managers, foremen, clerks, and guards.

In addition to efficiency, smallholders have other virtues. They are less hierarchical than plantations, and they distribute wealth more evenly. When they have firm control of sufficient land, diverse crops, no crushing debt, and access to some off-farm income, independent smallholders hold on tightly to their land.[67] The land selling among out-growers we described in chapter 3 was the consequence of fragilities built into the out-grower scheme that left many farmers without emergency reserves. Successful out-growers managed to accumulate; they also distributed and diversified. Ekay and Efi could manage only 20 hectares before the challenges of supervision overwhelmed them, limiting concentration. They had to treat loyal workers well to hold on to them and they paid their workers double what they could earn on plantations. Johan, Jikin, Omar, and Ekay transferred land to their children through inheritance and supported their education so some of them could enter different employment sectors. In contrast, the two corporations sought to expand and concentrate: Natco planned to renew its concession and absorb more village land under one roof; and Pak Wakijan bought a new plantation, putting 38,000 plus 17,000 hectares under his control.

Smallholdings are more flexible than plantations in responding to ecological and market dynamics. These features were clearly demonstrated by farmers up the Tangkos River who still had control of their land. They developed their farming enterprises at their own pace and balanced the attractions of oil palm with the need to keep future pathways open. So long as they maintained their mixed livelihoods and ample land they were somewhat protected from adverse prices or ecological collapse. Responding to the high price of rice in 2008 many reverted to planting their own rice in 2009, a practice they had set aside for some years; they converted land near roads to independent oil palm; and they retained extensive rubber fields that were both a source of income and a land reserve for their descendants. They did not intercrop their oil palm because of the roads: they thought land near a road should be monocropped with palm to maximize their return, while less-accessible land could be used for other crops. It was a diversification strategy that worked well so long as no corporation occupied their reserved land. When the price of rubber crashed in 2015 some family members left to seek wage work in other districts, returning when they had enough cash. Some had their motorbikes seized when they could not make their monthly payments, but they did not lose their land, nor did they lack food during this difficult period.

All the villagers in our research area aspired to plant oil palm independently because they recognized oil palm as a lucrative crop that produces a good income from a compact plot of land, with little need for labor. They struggled to retain family land when the plantations arrived and borrowed and saved to buy new land where they could establish farms and futures for their children. They were held back by the corporate monopoly over land in their own villages and in the subdistrict. They were also held back by a lack of access to mills that treated them fairly. The challenges they encountered in developing their farms and generating prosperity on their own terms were not incidental. They were the outcome of policies that consistently favor corporations that we recap in the form of a list:

- a corporate mandate that permits corporations to externalize social and environmental costs
- favorable laws and regulations, including land and labor law
- non-enforcement of costly obligations such as the provision of outgrower schemes
- cheap labor underwritten by the lack of unionization and the transmigration program
- access to cheap credit using the concession license as collateral
- corporate bailouts when bankruptcy looms
- support of government officials and politicians through legal mechanisms (coordination teams) and public performances (e.g., the district head's welcome to Pak Wakijan's new plantation)
- deployments of army and police to break up protests and blockades
- routine use of payoffs to officials and politicians to secure licenses, weak or complicit oversight, protection from public challenge, and immunity from prosecution.

Can Plantation Corporations Fail?

Everything was forever, until it was no more. The title of Alexie Yurchak's book reminds us to consider multiple forms of fragility as well as apparent stasis. Ecological collapse is always a possibility with monocrop cultivation, but a century after intensive production began oil palms are still growing in Indonesia and Malaysia, albeit with chemical life support. So far, pests have been managed and fertilizers keep palms producing until they are replaced every twenty-five years like worn-out parts of an industrial machine.[68]

A drop in the market price could cause corporations to fail, but it would have to be steep and protracted. From 2010 to 2020 market analysts found that corporate plantations were "money-pumps" netting investors very high returns. Even in 2015 (a year of low market price) industry analysts found that efficient plantation corporations netted gross margins around 27 percent and inefficient plantations still broke even.[69] Far from heralding an imminent collapse, market analysts projected that lower prices would invite a wave of consolidation as big corporations eager to expand their production quickly bought out smaller corporations that had already completed the time-consuming processes of land acquisition and land clearing.[70]

A collapse of political support could cause plantation corporations to fail, but support through the nexus of powers summarized in the list has been solid since 1966 when the New Order began. Despite ongoing demands by land rights activists to stop issuing corporate concessions, the political conditions for a nationwide change in the corporate-crony nexus do not exist at present. Efforts by peasant groups to reclaim land from plantation corporations are small in scale and the overwhelming trend is heading in the opposite direction as more and more land is taken from "small people" and allocated to corporations.[71]

Political support for particular plantations can waiver. At Natco so much wealth was siphoned away that in 2015 it was close to bankruptcy. Although the effects upon workers and out-growers were dire, this situation was not unusual: Indonesia's state-owned enterprises are repeatedly drained to the point of bankruptcy by the officials who run them and politicians who treat them as cash-cows, then revived.[72] In this case the Ministry of State-Owned Enterprises mobilized political powers to protect all the failing state plantations by merging them into a single national state plantation holding corporation and injecting new funds from the state budget. The nexus of powers supporting Priva was more fragile and in the 2000s the corporation entered a downward spiral. Internal and external theft led to underfertilized palms, low yields, poor road maintenance, and a reduced capacity to buy local support or protection. Pak Wakijan's decision to fire his managers in 2011 and hire a more professional management team was an attempt to control the leakage and restore the company to profit. The outcomes were mixed: some toll booths were closed, but skilled harvesters left for other plantations; the new managers' rules provoked the withdrawal of workers' effort and an expensive out-grower blockade. Despite these troubles Pak Wakijan's corporation must have had sufficient profits, assets, or political support for a bank to advance the funds he used to buy his USD3.2 million new plantation.

The political and financial rescue of struggling oil palm plantations contrasts with the fate of many rubber and tea plantations in Java and Sumatra in the period 1930–57. These plantations were invaded by squatters when prices were low and state security was weak. Some disappeared permanently; others reemerged when market conditions were favorable and corporations had enough political support to evict squatters and secure fresh funds. Corporate concessions tend to have a palimpsestic effect: once issued, the land does not fully revert to its customary owners even if they repossess it for a while.[73] The colonial-era rubber plantation in Tanjung was a prime example of this pattern. The seventy-five-year plantation concession passed between a

series of corporate owners from 1899 to 1974, and there were several bank-
ruptcies; only 600 hectares of the 12,000 hectare concession were ever
planted with rubber, and in the 1970s even the 600 hectares were repos-
sessed by locals. Yet in 1980 most of the original 12,000 hectare concession
was assigned to Natco and in 1990 the remainder was allocated to Priva.

Conclusion

In this chapter we posed the question: Why are corporate oil palm plantations still present and expanding across Indonesia? For two decades scores
of concerned observers have identified many serious harms associated with
corporate oil palm but during the same period concessions have massively
expanded. It is well known that plantation corporations dispossess villagers, clear forests, and pollute rivers; that jobs created by plantations are
relatively few and increasingly precarious; that out-grower schemes trap
farmers in an unfair situation; and that for villagers robbed of their means
of livelihood the situation is dire. Remarkably, industry proponents have
not found it necessary to demonstrate that any of the purported benefits of
plantation-based oil palm are actually delivered. So why have critics made
no headway at all?

A key part of our answer is that plantation corporations are granted concessions so they can carry out beneficial functions on the state's behalf. They
are tasked with growing export crops to generate foreign exchange and
expected to bring jobs and prosperity to remote areas. In return for these
purported benefits they are permitted to reap profits for owners and shareholders. Some level of harm is understood to be part of the package. Until
this fundamental paradox is addressed, corporate presence is quite secure.
National and transnational efforts to reform plantations take note of harms
but stop short of challenging the necessity for corporate presence. Efforts
focus instead on the reduction of harm through technical fixes and certification. These efforts have encouraged corporations to adopt some new practices (sustainability protocols and protective masks), but it was business as
usual on Pak Wakijan's new plantation.

By creating a distinction between good and bad corporations and holding
out the possibility that bad corporations can become good, initiatives like
RSPO, ISPO, and NDPE set questions about the necessity for corporate presence aside. Child labor is bad, but adult labor can be employed with "no exploitation"; cutting "high conservation value" or "high carbon" forest is bad,
but bulldozing villagers' rubber trees and replacing their mixed farms with

monocropped palm can be certified "sustainable." Harms are not eliminated, but they are repositioned outside the arena of debate.

Corporate presence is further enabled by the dismissal of smallholder alternatives. A vigorous independent smallholder sector would stand in the way of plantation expansion. It would take up land, compete for labor, drive up wages, and undermine the argument that only plantations can grow oil palm efficiently. It would also cut off a key channel of extraction since independent smallholders firmly in control of their own land and able to trade freely are subject to fewer tolls and are less vulnerable to extortion.

Most critics are policy-oriented and attempt to bring the practices of plantation corporations into line with transnational standards of environmental protection and human rights. The policy approach assumes that the state operates in the public interest and problems such as corruption and rights abuse can be remedied by governance reform. Only a few studies take the actually existing form of the state as their starting point, notably work by Australian scholars Rob Cramb and John McCarthy. These scholars are skeptical that reform agendas can interrupt the pro-corporate bias that is written into the law, or the crony-corporate cabals that profit from the status quo.[74] But their critiques—like ours—generally lack traction because they cannot be readily translated into technically prescribed reform.

Although we could join the well-established chorus of critics calling for a complete and permanent end to plantation concessions, the call is futile because at the time of writing the counterforces necessary for such a reversal are not in place.[75] Efforts to document instances where state agencies have experimented with smallholder-friendly models or independent farmers have prospered in the interstices of corporate dominance have not changed the tide.[76] Worker action, out-grower protests, villagers' demands, and international standards make very little headway; plantation corporations and the cronies who support them operate with impunity most of the time. Corporate plantations are politically favored and protected. Even poorly run plantations that approach bankruptcy are bailed out and injected with fresh capital. They are not permitted to fail because they generate profits for banks and corporations and distribute benefits to an extended network of actors. It is not one element but multiple complicities and diverse modes of material and discursive consolidation that keep plantation corporations intact and their presence expanding despite decades of well-established environmental and social critique. They have some fragilities—arguably, they are emperors without clothes—but it is not apparent what set of forces can unsettle them. Everything is forever, so far.

Conclusion

Plantation life is life under corporate occupation. This is the principal finding of our ethnographic research, which aimed to explore the forms of life that emerge in Indonesia's contemporary plantation zone and generate insights on the always-situated workings of global capitalism today. Since money only becomes capital when it can be brought into relation with "dense constellations of flesh and earth," ethnographic inquiry is a crucial resource. We embraced the grounded specificity of the plantation zone we studied to ask a series of questions. What were the prior conditions that made it possible for Natco and Priva to become established in Sanggau District, and what novel sets of relations did their presence generate? Who worked for these two plantations and why? What did it mean for farmers to be bound to a corporation? What were the forms of life that emerged in the plantation zone? And finally, why are corporate plantations still present and expanding across Indonesia?

Our questions were framed by an approach that combined attention to political economy with its focus on how land, labor, and capital are assembled to produce profit; and political technology with its focus on how discourses and practices form subjects and set conditions for particular forms of life. Twinning concepts drawn from political economy and political technology enabled us to conduct a theoretically driven ethnographic analysis while embracing the contradictions we encountered. Our attempt to make sense of the plantation zone led us to a novel theorization of corporate occupation as a political technology that generated practices that both jangled and aligned. Like other occupying forces (military, colonial), the plantation corporations we studied took over huge areas of land that they secured by a combination of law and force; they degraded citizenship by turning village leaders into collaborators; and they conscripted people to forms of life with terms they could not control.

Recapping our analysis from the perspective of political economy, we showed that plantation corporations are rendered profitable by the significant government-orchestrated subsidies they receive. The corporations we studied did not pay market price for the land they acquired (chapter 1); their state-supplied concession licenses gave them access to credit at very low interest; and they were furnished with cheap labor by excluding casual workers from the protection of the labor law (chapter 2) and by out-grower schemes that bound farmers through the mechanism of debt (chapter 3). The extent of these subsidies is not unique to our study site or to plantation corporations: a great many contemporary corporations would collapse if they had to survive the harsh winds of competition without state-orchestrated protection; they may well be outcompeted by smaller firms and farms that are more efficient. Corporations are also subsidized by being permitted to externalize the costs of water pollution, species reduction, and the livelihoods they displace. Both the profitability and putative efficiency of plantation corporations are produced through a nexus where political economy and political technology combine.

Recapping from the perspective of political technology, we noted that Indonesia's plantation corporations bear a state-sanctioned mandate to bring prosperity to remote regions and are licensed to reorganize economies and ecologies on a massive scale. Their occupation is also grounded in imperial debris, notably in the residues of colonial racial rule that are embedded in Indonesia's land law and in the positioning of villagers as social inferiors incapable of modern production. In the plantation zone we studied the educative technologies of the family state, formed in the shadow of the massacres of 1965–66, produced subjects who knew better than to launch a frontal challenge to the status quo.

Political economy and political technology did not line up neatly. Regimes of extraction were multiple, and the order of impunity that underwrote them had mixed results. The privileges accorded to corporations enabled profit but interfered with it as well. Paying tolls secured permits but weakened recourse to law and exposed corporations to ongoing predation. Undermining village government was helpful to corporations engaged in land acquisition, but it left them in a fragile position: blockades and theft became routine. Eliminating unions and treating workers like children generated a kind of stability, but it entrenched a mafia system that brought Natco close to bankruptcy and reduced yields at Priva to a level that was embarrassingly low. Villagers who came to desire modern lives yet were denied access to a "rightful share" of plantation wealth responded by stealing palm fruit, setting fires, building barricades, and refusing the position of manusia konyol, people whose sacrifice benefits other people but not themselves.

The order of impunity that sets the conditions of life in Indonesia's plantation zone calls into question the description of corporate capitalism as a system of production underwritten by "free" markets and the rule of law. Writing about the 1950s, historian Alec Gordon argued that the end of colonial rule in Asia marked an irreversible political shift. Henceforward, Asia's plantation formats would be quite different from those of the colonial period because they would lack the "immense and impressive array of coercion that must be deployed to ensure plantation survival."[1] Plantations would be reduced to what he called "ordinary capitalist estates." They would have to pay market prices for land and labor as workers formed unions and public opinion turned against land grabbing and indenture. He imagined, that is, a world in which there would be just one regime of extraction and it would be based in law, democratically secured rights, and legitimate profit.

Our study has shown that an "immense and impressive array of coercion" reemerged with the New Order and it still exists, dispersed in diverse networks and practices. Maybe today land cannot be grabbed outright, but a legally constituted land release team usually gets the job done; maybe workers cannot be beaten with sticks, but a system of incentives can induce them to work beyond the point of exhaustion; maybe citizens have legal rights, but they lack the means to claim those rights. The criminal code can still be used to punish them for "actions that cause loss to another party," and direct coercion still operates as well, when farmers seeking to hold on to their land or protesters at a mill are met by thugs or police paid by corporations.[2]

Corporate presence is protected both by law and by corporate-crony cabals intent on extracting wealth. Whatever harms plantation corporations cause, so long as they continue to funnel funds to people of power, it is unlikely that their political supporters will desert them. Indonesian intellectuals Pramoedya Ananta Toer and Mochtar Lubis argued that army officers led the way in establishing regimes of extraction backed by impunity in the post-independence period when they claimed a position as heroes of the liberation war and interpreted that position as a license to grab property and kick "small people" around.[3] Villagers in Tanjung witnessed this form of extraction firsthand. The army officers who took control of the colonial rubber plantation after it was nationalized in 1958 soon started to strip its assets. By the 1970s there was almost nothing left. The army-managers sold off the generator, electric cables, machinery, and the buildings themselves, including the timber and the metal roofs. Only the old colonial manager's house set atop a small hill still stood in 1980 when Natco arrived. Like the managers of the tea plantation Pujo studied in Java, these army-managers were men of strength (*wong rosa*, in Javanese), strong enough to carry everything away. In fact they were stronger: they could act with impunity because they had the protection of their office and their military-corporate-crony networks.

The networks supporting the order of impunity today include a wider set of actors than in colonial times. Plantation managers in colonial Sumatra had to negotiate with indigenous rulers for access to land, and with the colonial bureaucracy for plantation licenses and the supply of contract workers. But they did not pay much attention to colonial officials and treated them as servants or irritants if they attempted to restrict corporate expansion or enforce even minimal worker protections. Contemporary plantation corporations must negotiate with politicians, military, police, and bureaucrats at multiple levels and in many different ministries. Hence, they pay more tolls, but they also enroll a great many more people who gain a pecuniary interest in supporting corporations.

The networks that secure corporate presence provide one form of impunity. Corporations have another form of impunity that is integral to their mandate. This is the "corporate paradox" Barkan exposed: even a completely virtuous corporation that obeyed every law, met every standard, and refused to pay any tolls at all would still be licensed to occupy massive areas of land and produce serious harms. As we explained in the introduction, Indonesia's constitution and numerous laws invite both state-owned and private corporations to help meet state objectives of generating prosperity and creating jobs. Corporations are adjuncts of state power and instruments through which the state attempts to fulfill its mandate.

The open door for plantation corporations is imperial debris. It is grounded in the racialized argument that neither the government nor Indonesia's small-scale farmers can create prosperity on their own. Returning to the words of the district head who opened Pak Wakijan's new plantation: "The government can build some infrastructure but to develop the people's economy investment and the private sector is needed; we can't hire everyone as government officials, military or police; that is why the state has opened its doors as wide as possible to the private sector." According to this narrative, development of the "people's economy" is the task of corporations that are licensed to destroy the people's economy, a paradox indeed. Development is also equated with the provision of salaried jobs like those of government officials, military, and police, radically discounting the value of farm-based livelihoods and discounting the social value of the farming families who pursue such livelihoods, even when they make good money.[4]

A government or corporation that assumed small-scale farmers were capable of generating their own prosperity, that acted to increase their capability to the point of independence, or that recognized they had already achieved prosperity and independence without corporate intervention would eliminate the rationale for installing plantations. Hence the prosperity of the "people's economy" prior to the arrival of Pak Wakijan's new plantation could not be acknowledged in the company's planning documents or in the district head's welcome speech: recognition of their achievements would render corporate occupation unnecessary. Occupation cannot be recognized as an alien presence that causes a loss; the denial of rights, of access to land, water, and future possibilities must be denied or somehow overlooked. Indeed, for some industry proponents and plantation managers, an earnest belief in a mission to help develop the nation and bring prosperity to remote areas continues to be important. It has elements of both personal and professional commitment. In a 2019 conference presentation Tania attended, a representative of Indonesia's oil palm association (GAPKI) described the extreme pressure the industry was facing to meet transnational environmental and social standards, but he passionately restated the industry's benevolent role: "We can't forget our brothers in Papua," he said. "They still need us."

What are the corporate harms? Many of the harms that follow from corporate presence have been identified by the critics we have cited throughout this book. An unexpected harm we identified was the degradation of everyday citizenship in the plantation zone as government officials were officially required to smooth the path of corporations (both private and state-owned) at the expense of workers and villagers, who lost protection and means of redress. Another harm was to oblige Natco and Priva managers, workers, outgrowers, and villagers to become thieves or to live among thieves as a means of survival or modest advance—a form of life many found quite appalling.

Harms in Tanjung were magnified because five adjacent corporations saturated the subdistrict, robbing villagers of access to farmland while offering them few jobs. Even a single large plantation in a remote area can devastate livelihoods, as CIFOR found in Papua, where villagers had no way to reach their remaining forest resources. Scale matters; so does impunity.

According to villagers' accounts the colonial rubber plantation in Tanjung was not too harmful because it was small and weak: it did not dominate people or territory and lacked political support, so it had to be a good neighbor and adapt to the locality.

Abandonment is a further harm: plantation corporations routinely abandon people who do not meet their calculus of value. These are people who are too old, too sick, too unruly, too unskilled, or who simply stand in the way of corporate advance. Many Indonesians are effectively abandoned by the state, but people who have experienced a specific, material harm readily name the contradiction: You say the plantation is here to bring us prosperity, but where is the proof? In Tanjung abandoned people insisted that their lives did have value: they should not simply be thrown away like old rags. They asserted a place inside a national moral and legal order in which their sacrifice should be rewarded, but they struggled in vain for recognition, and they had no means to make the state or corporations take responsibility for the damage they had caused.

Industry proponents could argue that undermining villagers' livelihoods is necessary to achieve national export targets; if so, villagers would want their sacrifice to be acknowledged and compensated. They would insist on a rightful share so that they and their descendants can also live well. In Tanjung, villagers believed in national development and they wanted to achieve prosperity for their families. They had very low expectations about what the government or corporations would do to make their lives better. But they rejected a mode of development that subjected them to land seizure, damaged bodies, and catastrophic loss of their means of livelihood. Insult was added to injury when they saw plantation corporations, their favored workers, and allies prosper while they were consigned to the position of an audience. Whatever share of plantation wealth they received, it was far less than their due.

Tragically, there is no need for any harm at all. With access to infrastructure Indonesian villagers have repeatedly shown their willingness to produce global market crops on their own. They do not need corporations to enable or encourage this path. Corporate presence in Indonesian agriculture has never been technically necessary. For three centuries independent farmers have grown global market crops efficiently and with enthusiasm whenever markets beckoned. They were absent only when their cash crop farming was suppressed to protect corporate monopolies, a move sometimes dressed up with patronizing advice to concentrate on subsistence pursuits.[5] Villagers whose land has been occupied have no opportunity to demonstrate the prosperity they could have generated or the paths they may have chosen to follow. Diverse and flexible farming futures foreclosed is perhaps the biggest corporate harm of all.

A challenge that could be made to our analysis is that we happened to study two unusually troubled, inefficient, and corrupt plantations. Anticipating this challenge we would respond as follows. While our analysis stayed close to our ethnographic data, it was not simply descriptive. We constantly posed and attempted to answer "why" questions. Why is it so? What practices and processes produced the forms of life we encountered? Our findings are situated but they are not random. They invite rather than foreclose critically informed comparison. If researchers with data from other places and times find that plantation life takes quite different forms, which elements produce the difference? Is it a different crop? Or political system? Or legal system? Or labor regime? Or site of insertion? Is land more abundant and less contested? If there is no mafia system, how is the creation of toll booths prevented or controlled? Is the premise that enables plantation presence something other than underutilized land and smallholder incapacity? If corporations do not become an occupying force, how is their power limited and contained? If "small people" are treated as full citizens who cannot be kicked around with impunity, how is their citizenship framed and secured? If villagers and workers are satisfied that they have received a rightful share of plantation wealth, what conditions enable this outcome?

"Contemporary globalization," writes Barkan, "radically expands the argument that corporate privileges and the concomitant abandonment of populations are necessary for public welfare."[6] Promoting corporate occupation of vast areas of land on the grounds that plantations are the best way to produce global market crops and bring prosperity to remote regions is a striking iteration of this much broader argument. Abandonment is condoned as the necessary counterpart to productivity and profit. Occupation and abandonment were at the core of the novel forms of life generated by the plantation corporations we studied. They are both the conditions for and the product of global capitalism, one form of which we have examined ethnographically through the lens of a particular place.

Appendix

Collaborative Practices

Solo research and writing is still the norm in our home discipline, sociocultural anthropology, although collaboration is becoming more established.[1] By working closely together from initial planning through to a fully coauthored text and including a large number of students in our research, we have perhaps pushed the genre a bit farther than most. Here we outline the practices we engaged in and reflect on the insights we were able to generate by taking a collaborative approach.

We met in 2002 at a conference on social forestry organized by NGOs with funding from international donors. During one of the small group sessions Pujo started a conversation: "You must be an anthropologist." "How did you know?" "Because you are taking notes, and it is the badge of our tribe: when everyone talks, we just take notes." We discovered common interests and some years later obtained funds from Canada's Social Science and Humanities Research Council for a project titled, "Producing Wealth and Poverty in Indonesia's New Rural Economies." When we began joint research in Kalimantan's oil palm zone in 2010, we combined our expertise on plantations, crop booms, land, and agrarian relations, but we decided to start fieldwork afresh in a site that was new to both of us; hence neither of us was the guide.

At both of the plantations we studied, managers were watchful, anxious that we might expose corporate secrets, but many were willing to share their experiences and perspectives. We obtained a permit to conduct research in the state plantation (Natco), but not for the private plantation (Priva). Nevertheless, some Priva managers and workers talked to us in the privacy of their homes, and residents in surrounding villages were free to host us. During our first month together in the research area we visited plantation and village offices, hamlets, and labor barracks in and around the two plantations to get an overview of different places, people, and issues. From there we selected twenty research sites that represented a cross section of the entire "plantation zone": the two plantation cores, out-grower areas, and peripheries where there was some oil palm, but most of the local Malay and Dayak population continued to depend on tapping rubber trees and growing swidden rice.

The spatial spread and distinct ways of life in different corners of the plantation zone made our field site not one but many, and it enabled us to make good use of a team research approach. Our team comprised the two of us and about sixty mainly undergraduate students per year for three years, 2010–12. The students were from our two universities, Toronto (ten per year) and Gadjah Mada (fifty). We assigned three team members to each of the twenty sites where the students spent one to two months conducting research using techniques such as participant observation, semistructured interviews, and rapid appraisal–style surveys. Students selected their own research topics which they wrote up in individual research papers and bachelor's theses. Some returned for subsequent research, and those pursuing MA and PhD degrees stayed for longer periods.

All team members, including ourselves, kept and shared daily field notes. Team members' age, gender, and linguistic competence gave them access to particular sectors of the plantation population. Javanese-speaking students readily formed bonds with Javanese workers and transmigrants. Male students could easily spend time with young male plantation workers both on the job and after hours, when they engaged in drinking, gambling, and other kinds of entertainment. One male student, for example, rode around for a month in a truck that picked up palm fruit, taking note of bad roads, frustrated drivers, and long waits to off-load fruit at the mill. A female student spent her time with female office workers and learned about their everyday struggles to improve their family status. Students from Canada with limited skills in Indonesian made good use of their capacities for observation, keeping notes on the food they ate, daily routines in the homes and farms of their host families, and social events like festivals and weddings. Not all of the students' data were of the same quality, but they greatly extended and deepened our understanding of different dimensions of plantation life. We have cited just a few of the student reports that were directly relevant to our argument, but the thousand pages they wrote helped to shape our analysis.

In addition to supervising the students, a significant commitment, we spent our time in the plantation zone both together and apart. We spent enough time together that we both knew all the people and places that appeared in our respective field notes, generating a shared data pool that we could both make sense of. We also spent time apart as we each focused our attention on a different part of the zone: Tania was more often in the plantation cores and Pujo more often among out-growers and in upriver areas. Tania spent a total of four months in the zone over the period 2010–15 and Pujo spent six months. When combined with the students' field notes the total pool of data we had to draw on was enormous; our challenge was to select the most reliable reports and draw upon our knowledge of the context to interpret them.

We had different approaches to our fieldwork that were linked to our distinct styles of anthropology. For Pujo, following Stanley Diamond, the strength of anthropology is storytelling; hence he uses idiosyncratic people, events, and observations to drive his analysis.[2] He attributes his approach to the position of a "native anthropologist" studying his own culture, in which everything is normal, hence the idiosyncratic offers a useful way to "make the familiar strange" and open it up for questioning. Tania avoids the idiosyncratic for fear of reproducing a colonial exotic. She starts from the assumption that her interlocutors are potential collaborators who may have an analysis of their own they are willing to share. Our interlocutors readily spotted the difference, commenting to Pujo that Tania asked difficult questions and gave them headaches. This was not a complaint but an affectionate observation. Pujo's approach involved more casual observation, participation, and conversation, as he sat around drinking coffee or rice wine, opened up a topic of conversation, and waited for the stories to emerge.

Our different fieldwork styles were also generated by our interlocutors. They expected Tania, a foreigner far from home, to have a serious purpose in her visit and they were generous in helping her to complete her task. Sometimes this meant explaining things, digging into their memories, and reflecting on their situation, practices that depart from the normal cadence of casual conversation. They expected conversations with Pujo to follow more familiar styles. In addition to his role as a scholar they saw him as a possible node in their networks—someone who might help their children if they were able to go and study in Java. Hence the forging of a potentially enduring social relationship was a bigger part of the conversational dynamic. The differences in our fieldwork practices and styles of anthropology were not absolute; they were more like poles of a common continuum. When we were together we could use our different approaches or sometimes we just took turns—when one ran out of energy or ideas, the other took over. The same was true of our writing process where our approaches and styles were complementary.

The joint writing process was guided by a commitment we made to avoid recreating a colonial relationship in which foreign researchers rely on Indonesian researchers as field assistants and native informants, but not as full partners in the analysis and writing. For Pujo it was crucial that Indonesian students in the team had the opportunity to learn research skills, conduct research on topics of their choice, and write up their results. The two of us agreed that we would each publish our research findings separately in the form of articles on different topics, but we would write this book together.

In our first attempt at joint writing we divided up the chapters with Tania writing in English and Pujo in Indonesian. Pujo wanted Tania to produce a full manuscript in which she would translate and integrate his chapter drafts, but neither of us was happy with the result: it was becoming Tania's text, reproducing the colonial dynamic we set out to avoid. Our second attempt took a different approach. We sat side by side for four solid months surrounded by a mountain of field notes, reviewing our data, discussing what sense to make of it, organizing our ideas and arguments, and writing together line by line on a shared screen. We followed up for many more months long-distance using Skype for talk and a shared Google doc for text. Our discussions often took this format. One would ask: So what is really going on here? Or, what are we really trying to say here? Or, do we have evidence for that? The other would respond with an example, "from what I saw. . . ." Then one of us would suggest taking a step back: "Can we analyze this some more?"

Analysis followed the anthropological tradition of working iteratively between theory and data. Political economy was common ground for us, but we did not start out with a theory about corporate occupation, or a sense of how important political technology would become in our analysis. We came to these conceptualizations as we read and reread our field notes alongside books and articles, seeking resources to help us make sense of what we had found. Our exchanges helped us to pull out implicit ideas to see whether they held up. Tania usually held the keyboard because we were writing in English, but Pujo was always anticipating translation: if he could not fully grasp the meaning of a sentence Tania composed, he would not be able to translate it properly. A challenge in translation often meant that a concept we had introduced was not working well, so we discussed the ideas again and searched for better terms to express them.

....

Another form of collaboration entered our writing process when we presented our preliminary findings at seminars in Indonesia, including one at the district head's office and another with a mixed group of activists, scholars, and industry representatives in the provincial capital Pontianak. These seminars generated important data and reflections. We also circulated the first full draft of our manuscript to more than a dozen colleagues and graduate students, who read it carefully and gave us very thoughtful feedback, prompting a major reframing of our analysis. We would like to thank these collaborators by name, as they made fundamental contributions to our analysis. Firat Bozcali, Stephen Campbell, Rob Cramb, Girish Daswani, Michael Eilenberg, Andrew Gilbert, Derek Hall, John McCarthy, Donald Moore, Hollis Moore, Andrea Muehlebach, Birgit Müller, Shozab Raza, Laksmi Savitri, and Ben White provided written comments on all or part of the draft. Ben and Donald read two versions with extraordinary insight and care. Bianca Dahl, Aaron Kappeler, Jacob Nerenberg, and Gavin Smith contributed ideas through a book workshop in Toronto, and David Gilbert, Maira Hayat, Zahra Hayat, Bridget Martin, Julia Sizek, and Ailen Vega offered valuable feedback in Berkeley. We have both been inspired by the Southeast Asia geographer Rodolphe De Koninck and by dedicated scholars of Indonesia's agrarian milieu, especially Jan Breman, Michael Dove, Ben White, and the late Frans Hüsken.

The funding agencies that support academic work are not exactly collaborators, but our generous referees and the unnamed scholars who volunteered time to adjudicate grant and fellowship proposals enabled crucial inputs. In addition to funds from Canada's Social Sciences and Humanities Research Council we received funding from our two universities to support the student participation. We had the privilege of a month together for intensive uninterrupted writing as fellows of the Bellagio Center of the Rockefeller Foundation. Tania was also supported by a fellowship at the Asian Research Institute, National University of Singapore, and a writing fellowship from University of Toronto's Jackman Humanities Institute. We would like to thank Ken Wissoker, Lisa Lawley, and the professional team at Duke University Press for their fine work. As always, we thank our loving and patient families for tolerating our long absences and writers' obsessions.

Notes

Preface

1 Rendra, *Potret Pembangunan Dalam Puisi;* Mangunwijaya, *Durga/Umayi.*
2 Indonesian has one word, *perusahaan,* for corporation and company. We use the term *corporation* for the formal legal entity and *company* for everyday references to the embodied presence of a plantation: its infrastructure, activities and staff.
3 For the history of the pipe, see van Schendel, *Djolotigo.* Leaky pipes that transport oil, fuel insurgencies, and damage ecologies in the Niger Delta are discussed in Watts, "A Tale of Two Gulfs."

Introduction

For purposes of comparison, 1 hectare = approximately 2.5 acres.

1 See C. L. R James, *Black Jacobins;* Gilroy, *Black Atlantic.*
2 On high modernism see J. Scott, *Seeing Like a State.*
3 On the global transformations plantations wrought see Mintz, *Sweetness and Power;* Wolf, *Europe.*
4 See Daniel, Bernstein, and Brass, *Plantations, Proletarians and Peasants.*
5 For an excellent overview of the oil palm industry in Indonesia and Malaysia see Cramb and McCarthy, *Oil Palm Complex.*
6 Tania watched a French TV show in which two environmentally conscious families went to buy the same list of groceries. The family who deliberately avoided products containing palm oil was able to find substitutes, but their basket of groceries cost twice as much.

7   Badan Pusat Statistik (BPS), *Indonesia Foreign Trade Statistics*, 13. After petro-
    leum exports declined in the 1980s palm oil became the biggest contributor to
    Indonesia's foreign exports at 16 percent with an annual value of around USD20
    billion.

8   Our estimate of 15 million includes people who work on plantations and live
    nearby. Oil palm cultivation employs around 3.2 million people, supporting 12.8
    million household members. See Hawkins, Chen, and Wigglesworth, *Indonesian
    Palm Oil Production Sector*, 8. This calculation assumes one worker per 4 hectares;
    labor ratios are discussed in Cramb and McCarthy, "Characterising Oil Palm
    Production," 66n9.

9   Byerlee, "Fall and Rise Again."

10 Deninger et al., *Rising Global Interest in Farmland*. For critiques of this report see De
    Schutter, "How Not to Think"; Li, "Centering Labour" and "What Is Land?"

11 See "Hasil Studi IUCN, Pencerahan Untuk Kampanye Hitam Kelapa
    Sawit." *Kompas*, February 4, 2019; for a critique see Colchester, "Indonesian
    Government."

12 Hawkins, Chen, and Wigglesworth, *Indonesian Palm Oil Production Sector*, 8.

13 For an overview of the extensive literature on landgrabs see B. White et al.,
    "New Enclosures." On corporate incentives to acquire farmland see Fairbairn,
    Fields of Gold.

14 The names of the two plantation corporations, personal names, and place
    names below district level are pseudonyms.

15 See Ferguson, *Expectations of Modernity*; Dinius and Vergara, *Company Towns in
    the Americas*; Grandin, *Fordlandia*.

16 Mintz and Wolf argue that on modern plantations bureaucracy replaced
    paternalism, which was more characteristic of haciendas; but paternalism and
    "delegated despotism" are important themes in studies of plantation labor in
    Africa. See Addison, *Chiefs of the Plantation*; Du Toit, "Micro-Politics of Paternal-
    ism"; Rutherford, *Farm Worker Labor Struggles*.

17 Mezzadra and Neilson, *Politics of Operations*, 3. Sandro Mezzadra and Brett
    Neilson stress the imaginative dimension of capitalist projects and the work it
    takes to implement them. See also the feminist agenda for grounding studies of
    capitalism in the specificities of place, race, culture, kinship, and the multispe-
    cies affordances of particular milieu in Bear et al., "Gens." Much research in the
    fields of political ecology, environmental anthropology, and human geography
    is deeply attentive to space, materiality, and meaningful practices.

18 Marx, *Capital*.

19 On land appropriation, primitive accumulation, and "accumulation by dispos-
    session" see Harvey, *New Imperialism*. For studies of land-grabbing in Southeast
    Asia see Baird, "Problems for the Plantations"; Kenney-Lazar, "Relations of
    Sovereignty"; Hall, "Land Grabs, Land Control" and "Primitive Accumulation,
    Accumulation by Dispossession"; Schoenberger, Hall, and Vandergeest, "What

Happened." On labor regimes see Arnold and Campbell, "Labour Regime Transformation in Myanmar"; Li, "Price of Un/Freedom."

20 Foucault, *Power/Knowledge*, 194.

21 Foucault, "Govermentality."

22 See, among others, Cooper and Stoler, *Tensions of Empire*; D. Scott, *Conscripts of
Modernity*; Mbembe, *On the Postcolony*; Li, *Will to Improve*; Moore, *Suffering for Ter-
ritory*; Bridge, "Material Worlds"; Watts, "Tale of Two Gulfs"; Peluso and Lund,
"New Frontiers of Land Control"; Eilenberg and Cons, *Frontier Assemblages*;
Robbins, *Political Ecology*.

23 For discussion of the dual mandate for colonial rule in Africa enunciated by
Lord Lugard, see Moore, *Suffering for Territory*, 13.

24 Barkan, *Corporate Sovereignty*, 161.

25 See Oxfam, *Towards a More Equal Indonesia*, 8; World Bank, *Indonesia's Rising
Divide*, 18.

26 On corporate welfare see Hall, "Rethinking Primitive Accumulation," 1197;
Harvey, "Neoliberalism as Creative Destruction." Laws, policies, and develop-
ment narratives that favor plantations are discussed in Susanti and Maryudi,
"Development Narratives"; Cramb and McCarthy, *Oil Palm Complex*; Byerlee,
"Fall and Rise Again"; Dove, *Banana Tree at the Gate*; Pichler, "Legal Disposses-
sion"; Paoli et al., *Oil Palm in Indonesia*.

27 See Appel, *Licit Life of Capitalism*.

28 On challenges to regulation, see Barkan, *Corporate Sovereignty*.

29 Barkan, *Corporate Sovereignty*, 7.

30 See Weizman, *Hollow Land*; Makdisi, "Architecture of Erasure." On oil and
uneven topographies of extraction and rule in the Niger Delta, see Watts, "Tale
of Two Gulfs."

31 Wolf and Mintz, "Haciendas and Plantations." See Krupa, "State by Proxy," on
private indirect government in Latin America; on Africa, see Mbembe, *On the
Postcolony*.

32 The role of concessions in diverse projects of state territorialization is explored
in Hardin, "Concessionary Politics"; Vandergeest and Peluso, "Territorialization
and State Power."

33 Makdisi, "Architecture of Erasure," 555.

34 Everyday citizenship is discussed in Berenschot, Nordholt, and Bakker, introduction to *Citizenship and Democratization in Southeast Asia*.

35 On state familism see Bourchier, *Illiberal Democracy in Indonesia*.

36 On moral evaluations see Ferguson, *Give a Man a Fish*. On moral economies
and peasant insurgency see J. Scott, *Moral Economy* and *Weapons of the Weak*.
On illicit versus illegal, see Roitman, "Ethics of Illegality"; Harriss-White and
Michelutti, introduction to *The Wild East*; Gupta, "Blurred Boundaries"; Appel,
Licit Life of Capitalism.

37 D. Scott, "Colonial Governmentality," 193.

38 D. Scott, *Conscripts of Modernity*; Asad, "Conscripts of Western Civilization."

39 On the concept of a "rightful share" see Ferguson, *Give a Man a Fish*.

40 See Povinelli, *Economies of Abandonment*, 77.

41 Stoler, "Imperial Debris"; see also Stoler, *Duress*.

42 Robinson, *Black Marxism*, 2.

43 Robinson, *Black Marxism*, 4.

44 Alatas, *Myth of the Lazy Native*.

45 *Bhinneka Tunggal Ika* (Diverse but one) is the national motto. The association between a culture (*budaya*) and an ethnic group (*suku*) is everyday talk in Indonesia. Indonesian anthropology was shaped by concepts of "culture and personality" via the prominent scholar Koentjaraningrat, who trained in the United States in the 1950s. See Koentjaraningrat, *Masyarakat Terasing Di Indonesia*.

46 Bhandar, *Colonial Lives of Property*.

47 On narratives of native backwardness used to justify plantation expansion see McCarthy and Cramb, "Policy Narratives, Landholder Engagement"; Dove, *Banana Tree at the Gate*.

48 Activists devised the term *masyarakat adat* (customary community) to align with the global category Indigenous People, although the question of who is indigenous in Indonesia is subject to debate. See Li, "Articulating Indigenous Identity in Indonesia" and "Epilogue"; Willem van der Muur et al., "Changing Indigeneity Politics in Indonesia."

49 On Indonesia's land regime see McCarthy and Robinson, *Land and Development in Indonesia*. On the limited coverage of land titles, see World Bank, *Towards Indonesian Land Reforms*, xxxvii.

50 Gray zones and partial recognition of property rights are discussed in Sikor and Lund, "Access and Property"; Lund, *Nine-Tenths of the Law*.

51 Lund, *Nine-Tenths of the Law*, 14.

52 Brazil and Vietnam have similar internal-colonization programs to settle "frontier" areas; see De Koninck, "Geopolitics of Land"; Slater, "Justice for Whom?"

53 Geertz, *Agricultural Involution*. See also Li, "Involution's Dynamic Others," "Price of Un/Freedom," and sources therein. On market proclivities in rural Southeast Asia more broadly, see Hall, "Rethinking Primitive Accumulation" and "Land Grabs, Land Control."

54 On the use of quotas to coerce the cultivation of coffee, see Breman, *Mobilizing Labour*; Li, Pelletier, and Sangadji, "Unfree Labour and Extractive Regimes."

55 Li, "Price of Un/Freedom."

56 Dove, *Banana Tree at the Gate*.

57 Furnivall, *Netherlands India*, 216, 223–25.

58 Netherlands Indies Government, *Landbouwatlas Van Java En Madoera*.

59 See Pelzer, *Planter and Peasant*; Stoler, *Capitalism and Confrontation*; Breman, *Taming the Coolie Beast*; Houben, "Profit versus Ethics."

60 See B. White, "Remembering the Indonesian Peasants' Front"; Stoler, *Capitalism and Confrontation*. There were 553 reported labor strikes in foreign-owned plantations in the period 1951–55; see de Groot Heupner, "Palm Oil Plantation," 12.

61 On military rule in plantations in the 1950s see Mackie, "Indonesia's Government Estates."

62 G. B. Robinson, *Killing Season*, 301. Geoffrey B. Robinson notes that estimates of the number of people killed range from 78,500 to 3 million, but among scholars 500,000 is the broad consensus (315n1).

63 See B. R. O'G. Anderson, "Indonesian Nationalism Today"; Eickhoff, van Klinken, and Robinson, "1965 Today"; Cribb, "System of Exemptions"; G. B. Robinson, *Killing Season*; Stoler, *Capitalism and Confrontation*; Hadiz, "Capitalism, Primitive Accumulation"; Hadiz and Robison, "Political Economy of Oligarchy"; Aspinall and Gerry van Klinken, *State and Illegality in Indonesia*.

64 See N. J. White, "Surviving Sukarno"; Toussaint, *World Bank and the IMF*.

65 Bullard, Bello, and Mallhotra, "Taming the Tigers."

66 Silver, "Do the Donors Have It Right?"

67 Robison and Hadiz, *Reorganising Power in Indonesia*, 234; see also Casson and Obidzinski, "From New Order." Investment in the recovery of manufacturing remained stalled; see Wie, "Impact of the Economic Crisis."

68 Mbembe, *On the Postcolony*.

69 Baker and Milne, "Dirty Money States."

70 J. Scott, *Seeing Like a State*; Mitchell, *Rule of Experts*, 114–19.

71 For New Order damage to principles of public service and the creation of "floating politicians" without a constituency see Bourchier, *Illiberal Democracy*, 242; G. B. Robinson, *Killing Season*; Dick and Mulholland, "Politics of Corruption in Indonesia."

72 Predatory political-bureaucratic practices, oligarchy, and illegality are discussed in two excellent collections: Aspinall and van Klinken, *State and Illegality*, and van Klinken and Barker, *State of Authority*. See also Hadiz and Robison, "Political Economy of Oligarchy." On the distinction between the *pays légal* and *pays réel*, see Jean-Bayart and Ellis, "Africa in the World." For comparable crony-corporate cabals in India, see Harriss-White and Michelutti, introduction to *The Wild East*; in Pakistan, see Akhtar, *Politics of Common Sense*.

73 Apriliyanti and Kristiansen, "Logics of Political Business."

74 On mafia as an emic term, see Aspinall and van Klinken, "State and Illegality," 26–27; "Amien Rais Sebut Indonesia Dikuasai Mafia, TKN: Dia Hanya Suudzon." *Tempo.co*, January 29, 2019, https://nasional.tempo.co/read/1170129/amien-rais -sebut-indonesia-dikuasai-mafia-tkn-dia-hanya-suudzon/full&view=ok. For similar uses of the term *mafia* in India, see Harriss-White and Michelutti, introduction to *The Wild East*.

75 Butt and Lindsey, "Judicial Mafia."

76 For "informal costs" in Central Kalimantan, see Setiawan et al., "Opposing Interests," 477; for West Kalimantan, see Prabowo et al., "Conversion of Forests." See also McCarthy and Zen, "Regulating the Oil Palm Boom," 558; McCarthy, Vel, and Afiff, "Trajectories of Land Acquisition."

77 Gecko Project, *Indonesia for Sale*; on election finance and plantation expansion in West Kalimantan, see Tim Liputan Mendalam, "Kelapa Sawit, Antara Kepentingan Politik"; in Aceh, see Lund, "Predatory Peace"; see also Varkkey, "Patronage Politics as a Driver."

78 Hawkins, Chen, and Wigglesworth, *Indonesian Palm Oil Production Sector*, 32.

79 Average calculated from Indexmundi.com.

80 Calculation based on Hawkins, Chen, and Wigglesworth, *Indonesian Palm Oil Production Sector*, 27.

81 Hawkins, Chen, and Wigglesworth, *Indonesian Palm Oil Production Sector*, 3–4.

82 Hawkins, Chen, and Wigglesworth, *Indonesian Palm Oil Production Sector*, 27–28.

83 On sources of capital for plantation corporations see Cramb and McCarthy, "Characterising Oil Palm Production," 36, 46–48; TuK Indonesia, "Banks behind Indonesian Palm Oil."

84 Feintrenie, Chong, and Levang, "Why Do Farmers Prefer Oil Palm?," 394. See also Cramb and McCarthy, "Characterising Oil Palm," 32; Byerlee, "Fall and Rise Again." Cramb and Ferraro, "Custom and Capital," compare rewards to corporations, government, and villagers under different production arrangements.

85 Cramb and McCarthy, "Characterising Oil Palm Production," 32; on farm size and productivity see Carter, "Inverse Relationship"; see also Bissonnette and De Koninck, "Return of the Plantation?"

86 On mill size regulations, see Cramb and McCarthy, "Characterising Oil Palm Production," 34–36.

87 Indonesia's richest tycoons hold major shares in transnational oil palm corporations listed on stock exchanges in Singapore, Malaysia, and London, so "transnational" does not necessarily mean "non-Indonesian." See TuK Indonesia, *Tycoons*. On land banks and "virtual" land grabs, see McCarthy, Vel, and Afiff, "Trajectories of Land Acquisition." Newspapers report millions of hectares of unlicensed plantations. See Butler, "Half of Riau's Oil Palm"; "Hasil Studi IUCN, Pencerahan Untuk Kampanye Hitam Kelapa Sawit," *Kompas*, February 4, 2019; "Perkebunan Sawit Tanpa Ijin Marak," *Kompas*, February 22, 2010. Despite official moratoriums on new plantations in primary forest or peatland, expansion continues; see "Effectiveness of Indonesian Palm Oil Moratorium Disputed," *Bangkok Post*, October 1, 2018.

88 Hawkins, Chen, and Wigglesworth, *Indonesian Palm Oil Production Sector*, 10, 23; TuK Indonesia, *Tycoons*; see also Pichler, "Legal Dispossession," 522; Dwyer, *Trying to Follow the Money*, 15.

89 Data computed from Statistik Kelapa Sawit Indonesia show that in 2017 the four main oil palm producing provinces in Sumatra (Riau, Jambi, North Sumatra,

South Sumatra) had a total of 7 million hectares of oil palm, 53 percent in plantations, 47 percent in smallholdings. Three Kalimantan provinces (West, Central, East) had a total of 3.9 million hectares, of which 77 percent were in plantations and 23 percent in smallholdings. The province with the highest percentage of smallholdings (69 percent) is Riau.

90 A range of out-grower schemes is described in Cramb and McCarthy, "Characterising Oil Palm Production."

91 For smallholder typologies, see Zen, Barlow, and Gondowarsito, *Oil Palm*; McCarthy, "Processes of Inclusion"; McCarthy, Gillespie, and Zen, "Swimming Upstream"; Molenaar, *Diagnostic Study*; Jelsma et al., "Unpacking"; Potter, "How Can the People's Sovereignty"; Daemeter Consulting, *Overview of Indonesian Oil Palm*; Rist, Feintrenie, and Levang, "Livelihood Impacts of Oil Palm"; Feintrenie, Chong, and Levang, "Why Do Farmers Prefer Oil Palm?"; Serikat Petani Kelapa Sawit, *Karakteristik Dan Definisi*. Holdings over 25 hectares are legally defined as plantations and require a plantation license.

92 Ferguson, "Proletarian Politics," 4.

93 On conjunctures and relational comparisons see Hart, *Disabling Globalization*.

94 Welker, *Enacting the Corporation*, 131. On different spatial arrangements in extractive zones, see Ferguson, "Seeing Like an Oil Company"; Côte and Benedikt Korf, "Making Concessions"; Watts, "Tale of Two Gulfs"; Appel, *Licit Life of Capitalism*.

95 Differences between the national context for oil palm in Malaysia and Indonesia are explored in Cramb and McCarthy, "Characterising Oil Palm Production."

96 Watts, "Tale of Two Gulfs"; see also Hall, Hirsch, and Li, *Powers of Exclusion*, 88. For a sample of ethnographies of contemporary plantations producing different crops, see the following: on tobacco in the United States, see Benson, *Tobacco Capitalism*; on tea in India, see Besky, *Darjeeling Distinction*; and on bananas in Ecuador, see Striffler, *In the Shadows*. For seminal comparative research on colonial plantations in Asia, see Daniel, Bernstein, and Brass, *Plantations, Proletarians and Peasants*.

97 Beckford, *Persistent Poverty*.

98 Steward et al., *People of Puerto Rico*; Mintz, "Rural Proletariat and the Problem" and *Worker in the Cane*; Trouillot, *Peasants and Capital*.

99 Edgar Tristram Thompson, *Plantation*.

100 Mintz, *Sweetness and Power*. Mintz wrote a preface to Thompson's book.

101 See McKittrick, "Plantation Futures"; Crichlow and Northover, *Globalization and Creole Identities*; Thomas, *Political Life in the Wake*.

102 Tsing, *Mushroom at the End*, 39; see also Haraway and Tsing, "Reflections on the Plantationocene"; Davis et al., "Anthropocene, Capitalocene."

103 Yurchak, *Everything Was Forever*, 282. Thanks to Andrea Muehlebach for suggesting this resonance.

104 Moore, *Suffering for Territory*, 22–24.

105 Navaro-Yashin, *Make-Believe Space*, 20, 75, 174.

106 McKittrick, "Plantation Futures," 11; Wynter, "Novel and History"; see also Hawthorne, "Black Matters Are Spatial Matters."

107 Jong, "Study Puts a Figure." Military forces and armed police are deployed in land conflicts and linked to the death, injury, and imprisonment of protestors. See Sri Palupi et al., *Industri Perkebunan Sawit*; Komnas HAM, *National Inquiry*; Konsorsium Pembaruan Agraria (KPA), *Catatan Ahir Tahun 2018*.

108 On oil palm as a source of development benefit, see the Palm Scribe at https:// thepalmscribe.id/about/ and the Indonesian industry association GAPKI at https://gapki.id/. For critical perspectives, see Sawit Watch at https:// sawitwatch.or.id/; WALHI at https://walhi.or.id/; Mongabay at https://www .mongabay.co.id/; the Forest Peoples Programme at https://www.forestpeoples .org/en/about; and Down to Earth at http://www.downtoearth-indonesia.org/.

Chapter One—Establishing Plantations

1 Managers' perceptions of native backwardness are well described in Dove, *Banana Tree at the Gate* and "Representations of the 'Other.'"

2 Perusahaan Negara Perkebunan 7, "Pertama Di Kalimantan Barat," 17–18.

3 Project Sanggau, PTPN's contentious land acquisition, and local resistance to the transmigration scheme are discussed in Dove, "Plantation Development in West Kalimantan II" and "Plantation Development in West Kalimantan I"; Potter, "Oil Palm and Resistance"; Colchester et al., *Promised Land*; Forest Peoples Programme, *Dayak Leaders' Memories and Dreams*. Dove reports that the government's original plan was to require 3,308 locals to vacate 31,500 hectares and move elsewhere. At the time Dayaks were also being coerced to abandon their longhouses in favor of single-family dwellings. See Marti, *Losing Ground*; Forest Peoples Programme, *Dayak Leaders' Memories and Dreams*.

4 Brinkgreve, *Nota over Den Landbouw*, 9; Semedi, "Palm Oil Wealth and Rumour," 5.

5 For discussion of indigenous concepts of property and their morphings see Li, *Land's End*.

6 "Uang Ganti Rugi Banyak Tidak Sampai Ke Rakyat," *Kompas,* April 7, 1980; "Harus Ditindak Tegas Oknum Pemda Sanggau Yang Terlibat Dalam Manipulasi Ganti Rugi Tanah Adat," *Kompas*, April 8, 1980.

7 "Manipulasi Ganti Rugi Tanah Rakyat Diduga Didiamkan," *Kompas*, February 18, 1985; "Mengecewakan, Proses Manipulasi Uang Rakyat Di Sanggau," *Kompas*, April 7, 1985.

8 See Dove, "Plantation Development in West Kalimantan II," 10.

9 See Forest Peoples Programme and Sawit Watch, *Ghosts on Our Own Land*.

10 See van Klinken, "Blood, Timber, and the State"; Peluso, "Political Ecology of Violence"; Davidson, *From Rebellion to Riots*. Madurese were evacuated from Tanjung without injury but they did not return.

11 "Sawit Milik PTPN XIII Dijarah," *Kompas*, November 14, 1998. Theft and blockades emerged throughout West Kalimantan after 1998. See Potter, "Oil Palm and Resistance." On land struggles and reformasi, see Peluso, Afiff, and Rachman, "Claiming the Grounds for Reform"; Lucas and Warren, "The State, the People."

12 Delay resulting in sale to brokers is a recurrent problem for out-grower schemes. See McCarthy, "Processes of Inclusion."

13 On the concept of a rightful share, see Ferguson, *Give a Man a Fish*. On intergenerational exclusion see Oetami, "Reconciling Development"; Li, "Intergenerational Displacement." Villagers near Newmont's mine have a similar "sense of moral entitlement to a better life based on the presence of Newmont on their territory and the assistance they had extended to it over the years." Welker, *Enacting the Corporation*, 87.

14 An official registration document from 1991 showed an equity investment of 24 percent, with the balance as a bank loan (BPS, *Direktori Perusahaan*). Lack of public access to annual reports is common for Indonesia's private corporations (Hawkins, Chen, and Wigglesworth, *Indonesian Palm Oil Production Sector*, 14). Since 2017 a Sanggau-based NGO has been making plantation data publicly available. See E-Sawit Kabupaten Sanggau: http://esawit.sanggau .go.id.

15 Land release teams are well described in Sirait, *Indigenous Peoples and Oil Palm*. See also Marti, *Losing Ground*, 32–34. Land release at this site is discussed in more detail in Semedi and Bakker, "Between Land Grabbing."

16 The mill had a capacity of 1,440 tons of fresh fruit bunches per twenty-four hours, but in 2012 it processed only 350–650 tons because bad roads and low productivity limited supply.

17 "Sengketa Lahan Priva Berlanjut Sidang Lapangan," *Berita Borneo*, April 28, 2017.

18 Badan Pusat Statistik (BPS), *Kalimantan Barat Dalam Angka* (various years).

19 The devastating impact of the transmigration program on customary communities in Papua is described in Aditjondro, "Transmigration in Irian Jaya."

20 "Petani Plasma Sawit Jual Lahan Sebelum Lunas," *Kompas*, December 31, 1998; "230 Kk Transmigran Kalbar Tagih Janji Lewat LBH Yogya," *Kompas*, January 21, 1995; "Kami Tidak Punya Masa Depan Lagi," *Kompas*, March 30, 2001.

21 Palupi et al., *Privatisasi Transmigrasi Dan Kemitraan Plasma*, 224.

22 Mezzadra and Neilson, *Politics of Operations*, 67.

23 Budiawan, "Perang Ngakal." For recent cases of land release that involved legal confusion, violence, coercion, company tactics, secret meetings, fractured communities, doubled identities, false promises, and absent or forged documents, see de Vos, Köhne, and Roth, "We'll Turn Your Water"; Lund, "Predatory Peace"; Rietberg and Hospes, "Unpacking Land Acquisition"; Institute for Policy Analysis of Conflict, *Anatomy*.

1 As Arnold and Campbell stress, the term "labor regime," which highlights "the interconnected ways in which workers, labor processes and employment are organized and regulated in particular spaces," can be deployed at multiple scales. See Arnold and Campbell, "Labour Regime Transformation," 804. Here we focus on the plantations themselves, while exploring shifting political technologies that brought workers and their employers into fraught alignments.

2 Stoler, *Capitalism and Confrontation*.

3 Low wages and poor conditions are described in Wakker, *Greasy Palms*; Marti, *Losing Ground*; Obidzinski et al., "Environmental and Social Impacts"; Sinaga, "Employment and Income of Workers"; Situmorang, "Strengthening the Peasant;" Accenture, *Exploitative Labor Practices*; Amnesty International, *Great Palm Oil Scandal*.

4 *Buruh* was the term used by Communist-affiliated unions. The pro-planter union SOKSI (a founding element of the New Order party Golkar) introduced the term *karyawan* to obliterate "the necessity for class struggle." See Stoler, *Capitalism and Confrontation*, 159.

5 Stoler, *Capitalism and Confrontation*, 175–76. Thanks to Ann Stoler and Ben White for clarifying this point.

6 "PTPN XIII Berhenti Beroperasi Untuk Sementara," *Kompas*, July 26, 2018.

7 In Sumatra nascent unions provide education to encourage workers to become more critical of exploitation and inequality, which they tend to accept as "just the way it is." See de Groot Heupner, "Palm Oil Plantation," 33–34.

8 On challenges faced by state plantation workers and retirees, see "Mantan Karyawan PTPN XIII Tuntut Pembagian Santunan Hari Tua." *JPNN.com*, March 2, 2019. https://www.jpnn.com/news/mantan-karyawan-ptpn-xiii-tuntut-pembagian -santunan-hari-tua; Barral, "Paternalistic Supervision of Labour." PTPN's glossy annual reports reveal nothing of the turbulence: see http://www.ptpn13.com/.

9 Stoler, *Capitalism and Confrontation*, 198.

10 "Karyawan Panen PT PSA Tertimpa Tandan Buah Sawit Hingga Tewas Di Tempat," *RiauNews*, October 25, 2016, http://www.riaubook.com/berita/21706 /karyawan-panen-pt-psa-tertimpa-tandan-buah-sawit-hingga-tewas-di-tempat.

11 On migrant workers as entrepreneurs see Lindquist, Ziang, and Yeoh, "Opening the Black Box"; McKeown, "How the Box Became Black"; Pye, "Transnational Space and Workers."

12 Lindquist, "Labour Recruitment."

13 Natco reported its productivity in 2001 as 19.3 tons; see PTPN XIII, *Annual Report 2002*, 14. Figures for Priva were provided to out-grower co-ops and shared with the research team.

14 On landless women who remain in enclaves while men migrate out, see Sirait, *Indigenous Peoples and Oil Palm*, 65; Marti, *Losing Ground*, 92–93; Julia and B. White, "Gendered Experience," 1004.

15 Lung damage is caused by the chemical paraquat, which is banned in many countries but still used in Kalimantan. See Kita and Pesticide Action Network, *Poisoned and Silenced*; Julia and B. White, "Gendered Experience." Companies providing milk as a detox agent were reported in Yan, "'I've Never Been Normal Again.'"

16 Similar expressive forms of female worker self-preservation are reported in Semedi, "Struggle for Dignity."

17 See B. Anderson, "Exit Suharto." The accusation of Communist affiliation is still used to license repression, arrest, and attack of protestors. See Harsono, *Indonesia's "Anti-Communism" Law*; G. B. Robinson, *Killing Season*.

18 Tambun, *Seperempat Abad*.

19 http://www.fspbun.org.

20 For a powerful analysis of Indonesia's state familism see Bourchier, *Illiberal Democracy*.

21 Stoler, "Perceptions of Protest."

22 De Groot Heupner, "Palm Oil Plantation," 49. On severe repression of attempts to unionize plantation workers in Riau see IUF, UITA, and IUL, *Marketing Sustainability*; in Sumatra see Siagian et al., *Loss of Reason*.

23 From 1945 Indonesia's Communist Party was legal and from 1949 it was unarmed. It took the "parliamentary road" and won 16 percent of the vote in the 1955 national elections. In 1963 it claimed to have 3.5 million card-carrying members and twenty million in affiliated unions. See Robinson, *Killing Season*, 43.

24 The tolerance of theft and illicit earnings by staff of the VOC is discussed in Adams, "Principals and Agents."

Chapter Three—Fragile Plots

1 The fragility of local farmers in out-grower schemes in Sumatra is well described in McCarthy, "Processes of Inclusion."

2 Indonesia's "contract farmers" seldom hold written contracts; see B. White, "Nucleus and Plasma." On contract farming more broadly, see Little and Watts, *Living under Contract*.

3 Waged and bonded work disguised as entrepreneurial "freedom" is discussed in Harriss-White, "Labour and Petty Production"; Tsing, "Supply Chains"; Mercuri, "Beyond the Self-Entrepreneurial Myth."

4 Priva reportedly paid IDR27 million (USD2,700) per kilometer for the initial road construction instead of the recommended sum of IDR42 million, so the roads may have been poor quality from the outset.

5 See Du Toit, "Without the Blanket," 1093.

6 Problems with out-grower co-ops are reported in Rist, Feintrenie, and Levang, "Livelihood Impacts of Oil Palm"; Potter, "Oil Palm and Resistance"; Forest

Peoples Programme and Sawit Watch, *Ghosts on Our Own Land*; Marti, *Losing Ground*; McCarthy, "Where Is Justice?"; Colchester et al., *Promised Land*; Sirait, *Indigenous Peoples and Oil Palm*.

7 The troubled history of co-ops in Indonesia is discussed in Henley, "Custom and Koperasi"; B. White, "Nucleus and Plasma." Organicist concepts of Indonesian society are examined in Bourchier, *Illiberal Democracy*.

8 The Oil Palm Smallholders' Association (Serikat Petani Kelapa Sawit) is attempting to build an independent farmer-based movement; see https://www.spks.or.id/. At the time of our research in 2010–12 the Sanggau branch was inactive.

9 Hirschman, *Exit, Voice, and Loyalty*, identified these three options for responding to the decline in firms, organizations, and states.

10 On processes and mechanisms of differentiation, see B. White, "Problems in the Empirical Analysis"; for class differentiation linked to oil palm, see McCarthy, "Processes of Inclusion."

11 Potter, "New Transmigration."

12 Several sources note that 2 hectares is insufficient and propose a 6 hectare minimum. See Zen, Barlow, and Gondowarsito, *Oil Palm in Indonesian Socio-Economic Improvement*; Marti, *Losing Ground*; Colchester and Chao, *Conflict or Consent*; Sirait, *Indigenous Peoples*.

13 See Elmhirst et al., "Gender and Generation"; Julia and B. White, "Gendered Experience of Dispossesion"; Li, *Social Impacts of Oil Palm*.

14 Managers at Newmont's mine also called their discretionary cash the "Panadol fund" (Welker, *Enacting the Corporation*, 106.) Recurrent protests and ad hoc fixes are common in Indonesia's plantations (Colchester and Chao, *Conflict or Consent*; Marti, *Losing Ground*), mines (Welker, *Enacting the Corporation*), and timber concessions (McCarthy, "Where Is Justice?"). See also Rosser and Edwin, "Politics of Corporate Social Responsibility."

15 On predatory doubling see Roitman, "Ethics of Illegality"; Mbembe, *On the Postcolony*; Bakker, "Illegality for the General Good"; Baker, "Rhizome State."

16 "Warga Segel Priva Sanggau," *Tribun Pontianak*, January 13, 2013.

Chapter Four—Forms of Life

1 D. Scott, *Conscripts of Modernity*, 119.

2 On everyday citizenship in Indonesia see Berenschot, Schulte Nordholt, and Bakker, introduction to *Citizenship and Democratization in Southeast Asia*.

3 Chamim et al., *Raja Limbung*, 105.

4 On brokers and land syndicates working for regional elites, see Purnomo et al., "Jaringan Aktor Dan Regulasi Kebakaran"; Gilbert and Afrizal, "Land Exclusion Dilemma."

5 "PTPN XIII Perlu Ubah Visi Dan Misi," *Kompas*, April 29, 2000.

6 "Pemda Sanggau Minta 30% Laba PTPN XIII," *Kompas*, April 22, 2010.

7 The rackets of politicians and bureaucrats are public secrets and their pronouncements popularly understood as theater. See Aspinall and van Klinken, "State and Illegality," 2; van Klinken and Barker, *State of Authority*.

8 Plantation managers complain that local strongmen are "like kings who can make your life miserable if you do not have a good relationship with them"; see Varkkey, "Patronage Politics as a Driver," 319. In some provinces, corporations rely heavily on militias and gangs. See Bakker, "Militias, Security and Citizenship" and "Illegality for the General Good?"; Gilbert and Afrizal, "Land Exclusion Dilemma"; Lund, "Predatory Peace."

9 Everyday policing is described in Baker, "Parman Economy" and "Rhizome State."

10 Even formal workers are weakly protected as inspectors visit only 1 percent of firms each year. See World Bank, *Indonesia Jobs Report*, 56–61; International Labour Organization, *Labour and Social Trends*, 49.

11 "Pontianak," *Kompas*, September 9, 1998. Corporations have the legal right to make revealing company secrets a punishable offense; see Barkan, *Corporate Sovereignty*, 32.

12 "Dugaan Korupsi. Dirut PTPN III-Medan Ditahan Kejati Kalbar," *Kompas*, February 25, 2006; Government of Indonesia, *Keputusan Mahkamah Agung*.

13 "PTPN XIII Berhenti Beroperasi Untuk Sementara," *Kompas*, July 26, 2018; "PTPN XIII Kritis," *Tribun Pontianak*, July 21, 2018; "Bos Holding Perkebunan Angkat Suara Soal PTPN XIII 'Bangkrut,'" *CNN Indonesia*, August 7, 2018.

14 "Petani Plasma Berunjuk Rasa Di Kantor PTPN XIII," *Kompas*, November 24, 2015.

15 https://www.holding-perkebunan.com.

16 Similar practices on state plantations in Sumatra are reported in de Groot Heupner, "Palm Oil Plantation"; Barral, "Paternalistic Supervision of Labour."

17 Dyah Oktafianti, field notes, Emplasmen, Muara Tangkos, Indonesia, April 30–July 28, 2010.

18 Oktafianti, field notes.

19 Barral reports that workers on state plantations in Sumatra were grateful if managers greeted them. One director made an annual Ramadan safari to worker housing blocks in multiple plantations to demonstrate paternal care; see Barral, "Paternalistic Supervision of Labour."

20 Purwasari, "Budaya Hutang Di Kalangan Karyawati."

21 Perusahaan Negara Perkebunan 7, *Pertama Di Kalimantan Barat*, 17–18.

22 Sudibyo, "Konon Kita Saudara," 42.

23 Sudibyo, "Konon Kita Saudara."

24 In Sanggau District only 2 percent of the labor force is employed in manufacturing; 82 percent are men. See Li, *Social Impacts of Oil Palm*.

25 Zhuo, "Past, Present and Future."

26 On lack of transparency and low monthly payments in one-roof schemes, see Colchester and Chao, *Conflict or Consent?*; Li, "Centering Labour"; McCarthy, Gillespie, and Zen, "Swimming Upstream"; Palupi et al., *Privatisasi Transmigrasi*.

27 See Rosser and Edwin, "Politics of Corporate Social Responsibility."

28 See Welker, *Enacting the Corporation*, 62. On state evasion of inconvenient data see Barak and van Schendel, "Introduction."

29 Makdisi, "Architecture of Erasure," 555.

Chapter Five—Corporate Presence

1 Hawkins, Chen, and Wigglesworth, *Indonesian Palm Oil Production Sector*, 9.

2 See Budidarsono et al., *Socioeconomic Impact Assessment*; Rist, Feintrenie, and Levang, "Livelihood Impacts of Oil Palm."

3 See Obidzinski et al., "Environmental and Social Impacts."

4 Obidzinski, Dermawan, and Hadianto, "Oil Palm Plantation Investments."

5 Obidzinski et al., "Environmental and Social Impacts," 1.

6 Santika et al., "Does Oil Palm Agriculture Help?"

7 "Bupati Sanggau Ajak Investasi Di Sektor Pertanian," *Antara Kalbar*, April 1, 2017; "Paolus Hadi: Sudah Cukuplah, Lahan Kita Sudah Habis," *Equator.co.id*, March 1, 2019.

8 Lembaga Gemawan, *Public Review*.

9 "Ratusan Mahasiswa Demo Tolak Program Transmigrasi Di Kalbar," *Tribun Pontianak*, May 18, 2015; Damianus, *Tolak Tegas Program*.

10 Palupi et al., *Privatisasi Transmigrasi*, 75–77.

11 Palupi et al., *Privatisasi Transmigrasi*, 110, 47.

12 Palupi et al., *Privatisasi Transmigrasi*; Li, "Situating Transmigration."

13 Peluso, Afiff, and Rachman, "Claiming the Grounds for Reform"; Lucas and Warren, "State, the People."

14 See Sawit Watch at https://sawitwatch.or.id/; WALHI at https://walhi.or.id/; Mongabay at https://www.mongabay.co.id/; the Forest Peoples Programme at https://www.forestpeoples.org/en/about; Down to Earth at http://www.downtoearth-indonesia.org/.

15 A list of recurrent themes and sources is provided in Cramb and McCarthy, introduction to *Oil Palm Complex*. Sources we consulted include Obidzinski et al., "Environmental and Social Impacts"; Marti, *Losing Ground*; Colchester et al., *Promised Land*; Colchester and Chao, *Conflict or Consent?*; McCarthy, "Where Is Justice?"; McCarthy and Zen, "Regulating"; McCarthy, Gillespie, and Zen, "Swimming Upstream"; Sirait, *Indigenous Peoples*; Rist, Feintrenie, and Levang, "Livelihood Impacts of Oil Palm"; Zen, Barlow, and Gondowarsito, *Oil Palm*; Potter, "Oil Palm and Resistance"; Wakker, *Greasy Palms*; Sinaga, "Employment and Income of Workers"; Amnesty International, *Great Palm Oil Scandal*; Accenture, *Exploitative Labor Practices*; Sheil et al., *Impacts and Opportunities*; Feintrenie, Chong, and Levang, "Why Do Farmers Prefer?"

16 Obidzinski et al., "Environmental and Social Impacts."

17 On the land squeeze caused by plantation presence, see McCarthy, "Where Is Justice?"; Stoler, *Capitalism and Confrontation*; Li, "Centering Labour"; Dove, "Plantation Development II"; Potter, "New Transmigration 'Paradigm' in Indonesia." For colonial Sumatra, see Pelzer, *Planter and Peasant*.

18 Konsorsium Pembaruan Agraria (KPA), *Catatan Ahir Tahun*, 16, 25. The report names the corporations involved; it also discusses "latent" conflicts that can re-erupt at any time.

19 Konsorsium Pembaruan Agraria (KPA), *Catatan Ahir Tahun*, 41.

20 Komnas HAM, *National Inquiry*.

21 Aliansi Masyarakat Adat Nusantara (AMAN), *Geoportal Kebijakan*.

22 "KPK Temukan 63 Ribu Wajib Pajak Industri Sawit Kemplang Pajak," *CNN Indonesia*, April 5, 2017, https://www.cnnindonesia.com/nasional /20170503174824-12-212023/kpk-temukan-63-ribu-wajib-pajak-industri-sawit -kemplang-pajak. Corruption Watch quantified the loss of state revenues from unlicensed plantations; see Wasef and Ilyas, *Merampok Hutan Dan Uang Negara*.

23 Obidzinski et al., "Environmental and Social Impacts," 25; these authors report that half the concession area in Kalimantan and Sumatra is unplanted.

24 See reports available at cifor.org.

25 See Rainforest Action Network, *Conflict Palm Oil*; Human Rights Watch, *"When We Lost the Forest."*

26 See Accenture, *Exploitative Labor*; E. Benjamin Skinner, "Indonesia's Palm Oil Industry Rife with Human-Rights Abuses," *Bloomberg Businessweek*, July 20, 2013, http://www.bloomberg.com/bw/articles/2013-07-18/indonesias-palm-oil -industry-rife-with-human-rights-abuses; Finnwatch, *Law of the Jungle*; Sawit Watch and International Labor Rights Forum, *Empty Assurances*; Amnesty International, *Great Palm Oil Scandal*.

27 For reasons of productivity, the International Union for the Conservation of Nature (IUCN) argues that palm oil should be made sustainable but not replaced; see IUCN, *Palm Oil and Biodiversity*. For a critical perspective, see Colchester, "Indonesian Government."

28 Industry attempts to counter the "black campaign" are summarized in Choiruzzad, "Save Palm Oil."

29 https://gapki.id/.

30 Badan Pusat Statistik (BPS), *Statistik Kelapa Sawit Indonesia*, 13. After India, at 61 percent, is the Netherlands at 10 percent, Malaysia and Singapore at 13 percent, and Italy at 6 percent. China is not among the top five export destinations. Growing competition from soy is discussed in Hawkins, Chen, and Wigglesworth, *Indonesian Palm Oil Production Sector*.

31 Welker, *Enacting the Corporation*. See Benson and Kirsch, "Capitalism and the Politics," for an account of tobacco and mining industry strategies to evade responsibility for harm and the "politics of resignation" among critics who

see no prospect of significant change; see also Welker, Partridge, and Hardin, "Corporate Lives."

32 Harisons and Crosfield sold Golden Hope (its plantation group) to Malaysian government interests in 1982; in 2007 it was merged with Guthrie and Sime Darby to form Sime Darby. Thanks to Rob Cramb for this information.

33 https://rspo.org/about/goodbadpalmoil; https://goodbadpalmoil.org/.

34 For global certification numbers, see https://rspo.org/about/goodbadpalmoil; for Indonesia see Santika et al., "Does Oil Palm Agriculture Help?," 108.

35 https://goodbadpalmoil.org/; https://rspo.org/impact/theory-of-change.

36 McCarthy, "Certifying in Contested Spaces," 1876. The RSPO complaints system is burdened by hundreds of reports of land disputes involving RSPO members; see Silva-Castañeda, "Forest of Evidence."

37 Forest Peoples Programme, *Comparison*.

38 Mighty Earth, *Over 60 NGOs Call*. See the comprehensive commitments stated in Wilmar, "No Deforestation, No Peat."

39 Amnesty International, *Great Palm Oil Scandal*. Wilmar's sustainability progress reports are available at wilmar-international.com.

40 Colchester and Chao, *Conflict or Consent?*; McCarthy, Gillespie, and Zen, "Swimming Upstream"; McCarthy, "Certifying in Contested Spaces"; McCarthy and Zen, "Regulating the Oil Palm Boom"; Obidzinski et al., "Environmental and Social Impacts"; Varkkey, "Patronage Politics"; McCarthy, "Where Is Justice?" For a broader discussion of attempts at "global environmental governance" in contexts of illegality or a "shadow state," see Duffy, "Global Environmental Governance."

41 Greenpeace, *Final Countdown*. 78.

42 Genting Plantations, *Pt Permata Sawit Mandiri Summary*.

43 Genting Plantations, *Summary Report of Planning*.

44 Chain Reaction Research, *Shadow Companies*, 6.

45 Aseanty Pahlevi, "Hutan Desa Sebadak Raya, Tegar Bertahan Di Tengah Kepungan Kebun Sawit Perusahaan"; Genting Plantations, *Summary Report of Planning*.

46 Aseanty Pahlevi, "A Dayak Village Campaigns for Rights to Its Forests."

47 Initial rejection is quite common in Kalimantan and Sumatra; the challenge is to sustain it over the long haul.

48 Wijatnika Ika, "Menjaga Hutan Ala Masyarakat."

49 Genting Plantations, *Summary Report of Planning*; Aseanty Pahlevi, "A Dayak Village Campaigns for Rights to Its Forests."

50 Genting Plantations, *Summary Report of Planning*, 7.

51 For debates about native land needs in the context of plantation expansion, see Pelzer, *Planter and Peasant*; Dove, "Plantation Development I."

52 See map in Genting Plantations, *Summary Report of Planning*, 3.

53 Greenpeace, *Final Countdown*, 78.

54 Chain Reaction Research, *Shadow Companies*.

55   IJ-REDD+ Project, "Sagupa Forum."

56   "Bupati Resmikan Lokasi Pt PSM," *Ketapang News*, June 5, 2017, http:// ketapangnews.com/2017/06/bupati-resmikan-lokasi-pt-psm/.

57   https://www.dpp-apkasindo.com/tentang.html.

58   Quoted in Mercuri, "Beyond the Self-Entrepreneurial Myth," 32.

59   Out-grower schemes are well described in Cramb and McCarthy, "Characterising Oil Palm Production," 49–64. Corporate reluctance to work with out-growers is discussed in McCarthy and Cramb, "Policy Narratives, Landholder Objectives"; McCarthy, Gillespie, and Zen, "Swimming Upstream"; Colchester and Chao, *Conflict or Consent?*; Marti, *Losing Ground*; Potter, "New Transmigration 'Paradigm' in Indonesia." For publicly listed corporations' compliance with out-grower requirement see Hawkins, Chen, and Wigglesworth, *Indonesian Palm Oil Production Sector*, 13.

60   Palupi et al., *Privatisasi Transmigrasi*; Potter, "New Transmigration 'Paradigm' in Indonesia"; Li, "Situating Transmigration."

61   "PSR: Replanting Sawit Dan Replanting Tata Kelola," *Perkebunannews*, October 29, 2018, https://perkebunannews.com/psr-replanting-sawit-dan-replanting -tata-kelola/; Palupi et al., *Privatisasi Transmigrasi*, 233.

62   Gabungan Pengusaha Kelapa Sawit Indonesia (GAPKI), *"Replanting" Kemitraan* and *Kemitraan Sawit*.

63   Cramb and McCarthy, "Characterising Oil Palm Production," 67n14. Productivity for publicly listed plantation corporations in Indonesia in 2015 ranged from 14 tons to 26 tons; see Hawkins, Chen, and Wigglesworth, *Indonesian Palm Oil Production Sector*, 31.

64   Smallholder productivity is discussed in Cramb and Sujang, "Mouse Deer and the Crocodile"; Cramb and McCarthy, "Characterising Oil Palm Production"; Molenaar, *Diagnostic Study*; Zen, Barlow, and Gondowarsito, *Oil Palm*; World Bank and International Finance Corporation, *World Bank Group Framework*.

65   Data issued to out-grower co-ops and shared with the research team.

66   See Carter, "Identification of the Inverse Relationship."

67   Some researchers argue that oil palm is a "rich man's crop" in which farmers with small plots and low productivity tend to be outcompeted. See McCarthy, "Processes of Inclusion"; Sheil et al., *Impacts and Opportunities of Oil Palm*; McCarthy, Gillespie, and Zen, "Swimming Upstream." Our findings confirm that schemes that allocate 2 hectare plots expose out-growers to a spiral of debt and land loss, but farmers in control of their own land added oil palm to mixed livelihoods with good results. See also Cramb and Sujang, "Mouse Deer and the Crocodile"; Feintrenie, Chong, and Levang, "Why Do Farmers Prefer?"

68   Some Malaysian plantations have replanted three times on the same spot; see Sheil et al., *Impacts and Opportunities of Oil Palm*, 7.

69   Hawkins, Chen, and Wigglesworth, *Indonesian Palm Oil Production Sector*, 30; see also Cramb and McCarthy, "Characterising Oil Palm Production," 36–37.

70   Hawkins, Chen, and Wigglesworth, *Indonesian Palm Oil Production Sector*.

71 On "reverse land reform" that takes poor people's land and redistributes it to corporations see Cramb and McCarthy, "Characterising Oil Palm Production," 41; on attempts to reclaim land from corporations, see Lund and Rachman, "Occupied!"; Gilbert and Afrizal, "Land Exclusion Dilemma."

72 See Apriliyanti and Kristiansen, "Logics of Political Business."

73 The palimpsest effect of corporate concessions and failed projects is discussed in McCarthy, Vel, and Afiff, "Trajectories of Land Acquisition."

74 Cramb, "Political Economy"; McCarthy, Gillespie, and Zen, "Swimming Upstream"; McCarthy, "Certifying in Contested Spaces"; McCarthy and Cramb, "Policy Narratives"; McCarthy, "Limits of Legality"; see also Pichler, "Legal Dispossession."

75 A moratorium on new plantations that would leave smallholders to grow the palms while corporations focus on milling and processing has been recommended consistently by activists, scholars, and development agencies. See Feintrenie, Chong, and Levang, "Why Do Farmers Prefer?," 394; Cramb and Sujang, "Mouse Deer and the Crocodile"; Rist, Feintrenie, and Levang, "Livelihood Impacts of Oil Palm," 1019; Zen, Barlow, and Gondowarsito, *Oil Palm*; World Bank and International Finance Corporation, *World Bank Group Framework*, 25; Konsorsium Pembaruan Agraria (KPA), *Catatan Ahir Tahun*. The independent smallholder association SPKS proposes financial support for farmers with 4 hectares or fewer to enable them to plant this lucrative crop; see Serikat Petani Kelapa Sawit, *Karakteristik Dan Definisi*.

76 Cramb and Sujang, "Mouse Deer and the Crocodile"; McCarthy, Gillespie, and Zen, "Swimming Upstream."

Conclusion

1 Gordon, "Plantation Colonialism, Capitalism, and Critics," 480. Alec Gordon later proposed the category of "neo-plantations" for cases where independent governments mimic colonial-era coercion; see Gordon, "Towards a Model," 326.

2 A clause in the 2004 Plantation Law criminalizing actions that cause corporate losses was removed in the 2014 version, but arrests continued. In the period 2014–18 KPA recorded 940 arrests linked to land disputes. Konsorsium Pembaruan Agraria (KPA), *Catatan Ahir Tahun*.

3 Lubis, *Twilight in Jakarta*; Pramoedya Ananta Toer, *Tjerita Dari Djakarta*. See also B. R. O'G. Anderson, "Indonesian Nationalism"; Eickhoff, van Klinken, and Robinson, "1965 Today"; Cribb, "System of Exemptions"; Robinson, *Killing Season*.

4 "Bupati Resmikan Lokasi Pt PSM," *Ketapang News*, June 5, 2017, http://ketapangnews.com/2017/06/bupati-resmikan-lokasi-pt-psm/. The equation of formal government jobs with "development" fails to note that most Indonesians gain their livelihoods from self-employment or paid work in small firms, farms,

and other "nonstandard" kinds of work. See the discussion in Ferguson and Li, *Beyond the "Proper Job."*

5 Colonial and contemporary attempts to consign Indonesia's farmers to non-market niches are discussed in Li, "Involution's Dynamic Others," "Indigeneity, Capitalism," and "Fixing Non-Market Subjects"; Geertz, *Agricultural Involution*; Dove, *Banana Tree at the Gate.*

6 Barkan, *Corporate Sovereignty*, 38.

Appendix

1 For thoughtful discussion of the challenges and rewards of collaboration in ethnographic research, see Choy et al., "A New Form of Collaboration," and Shah et al., *Ground Down by Growth.*

2 See Diamond, "Anthropology in Question."

Bibliography

Accenture and Humanity United. *Exploitative Labor Practices in the Global Palm Oil Industry*. 2012. http://humanityunited.org/pdfs/Modern_Slavery_in_the_Palm _Oil_Industry.pdf.

Adams, Julia. "Principals and Agents, Colonialists and Company Men: The Decay of Colonial Control in the Dutch East Indies." *American Sociological Review* 61, no. 1 (1996): 12–28.

Addison, Lincoln. *Chiefs of the Plantation: Authority and Contestation on the South Africa-Zimbabwe Border*. Montreal: McGill-Queen's University Press, 2019.

Aditjondro, G. J. "Transmigration in Irian Jaya: Issues, Targets and Alternative Approaches." *Prisma* 41 (1986): 67–82.

Akhtar, Aasim Sajjad. *The Politics of Common Sense: State, Society and Culture in Pakistan*. Cambridge: Cambridge University Press, 2017.

Alatas, Syed Hussein. *The Myth of the Lazy Native: A Study of the Image of the Malays, Filipinos and Javanese from the 16th to the 20th Century and Its Function in the Ideology of Colonial Capitalism*. London: Routledge, 1977.

Aliansi Masyarakat Adat Nusantara (AMAN). *Geoportal Kebijakan Satu Peta Diluncurkan Untuk Siapa?* 2018. http://www.aman.or.id/2018/12/geoportal-kebijakan-satu -peta-diluncurkan-untuk-siapa/.

Amnesty International. *The Great Palm Oil Scandal: Labour Abuses behind the Big Brand Names*. 2016. https://www.amnesty.org/en/documents/asa21/5184/2016/en/.

Anderson, B. R. O'G. "Indonesian Nationalism Today and in the Future." *Indonesia*, no. 67 (April 1999): 1–11.

Anderson, Benedict. "Exit Suharto: Obituary for a Mediocre Tyrant." *New Left Review* 50 (March–April 2008).

Appel, Hannah. *The Licit Life of Capitalism: US Oil in Equatorial Guinea*. Durham, NC: Duke University Press, 2019.

Apriliyanti, Indri Dwi, and Stein Oluf Kristiansen. "The Logics of Political Business in State-Owned Enterprises: The Case of Indonesia." *International Journal of Emerging Markets* 14, no. 5 (2019): 709–30.

Arnold, Dennis, and Stephen Campbell. "Labour Regime Transformation in Myanmar: Constitutive Processes of Contestation." *Development and Change* 48, no. 4 (2017): 801–24.

Asad, Talal. "Conscripts of Western Civilization." In *Civilization in Crisis*, vol. 1, edited by Christina Ward Gailey, 333–51. Gainesville: University of Florida Press, 1992.

Aseanty Pahlevi. "A Dayak Village Campaigns for Rights to Its Forests." Mongabay, October 8, 2015. https://news.mongabay.com/2015/10/149997/.

Aseanty Pahlevi. "Hutan Desa Sebadak Raya, Tegar Bertahan Di Tengah Kepungan Kebun Sawit Perusahaan." Mongabay, May 3, 2015. https://www.mongabay.co .id/2015/05/03/hutan-desa-sebadak-raya-tegar-bertahan-di-tengah-kepungan -kebun-sawit-perusahaan/.

Aspinall, Edward, and Gerry van Klinken, eds. *The State and Illegality in Indonesia*. Leiden: KITLV Press, 2011.

Aspinall, Edward, and Gerry van Klinken. "The State and Illegality in Indonesia." In Aspinall and van Klinken, *The State and Illegality in Indonesia*, 1–30.

Badan Pusat Statistik (BPS). *Direktori Perusahaan Perkebunan Kelapa Sawit 2017*, 2018.

Badan Pusat Statistik (BPS). *Indonesia Foreign Trade Statistics 2017*, 2018.

Badan Pusat Statistik (BPS). *Kalimantan Barat Dalam Angka*. Various years.

Badan Pusat Statistik (BPS). *Statistik Kelapa Sawit Indonesia*. 2019.

Baird, Ian G. "Problems for the Plantations: Challenges for Large-Scale Land Concessions in Laos and Cambodia." *Journal of Agrarian Change* 20, no. 3 (2020): 387–407.

Baker, Jacqui. "The Parman Economy: Post-Authoritarian Shifts in the Off-Budget Economy of Indonesia's Security Institutions." *Indonesia*, no. 96 (2013): 123–50.

Baker, Jacqui. "The Rhizome State: Democratizing Indonesia's Off-Budget Economy." *Critical Asian Studies* 47, no. 2 (2015): 309–36.

Baker, Jacqui, and Sarah Milne. "Dirty Money States: Illicit Economies and the State in Southeast Asia." *Critical Asian Studies* 47, no. 2 (2015): 151–76.

Bakker, Laurens. "Illegality for the General Good? Vigilantism and Social Responsibility in Contemporary Indonesia." *Critique of Anthropology* 35, no. 1 (2015): 78–93.

Bakker, Laurens. "Militias, Security and Citizenship in Indonesia." In Berenschot, Nordholt, and Bakker, *Citizenship and Democratization in Southeast Asia*, 125–54.

Barak, Kalir, and Willem van Schendel. "Introduction: Nonrecording States between Legibility and Looking Away." *Focaal* 2017, no. 77 (2017): 1–7.

Barkan, Joshua. *Corporate Sovereignty: Law and Government under Capitalism*. Minneapolis: University of Minnesota Press, 2013.

Barral, Stephanie. "Paternalistic Supervision of Labour in Indonesian Plantations: Between Dependence and Autonomy." *Journal of Agrarian Change* 14, no. 2 (2014): 240–59.

Bayart, Jean-François, and Stephen Ellis. "Africa in the World: A History of Extraversion." *African Affairs* 99, no. 395 (2000): 217–67.

Bear, Laura, Karen Ho, Anna Lowenhaupt Tsing, and Sylvia Yanagisako. "Gens: A Feminist Manifesto for the Study of Capitalism." Theorizing the Contemporary. *Fieldsights*, March 30, 2015. http://culanth.org/fieldsights/652-gens-a -feminist-manifesto-for-the-study-of-capitalism.

Beckford, George. *Persistent Poverty: Underdevelopment in Plantation Economies of the Third World.* New York: Oxford University Press, 1972.

Benson, Peter. *Tobacco Capitalism: Growers, Migrant Workers, and the Changing Face of a Global Industry.* Princeton, NJ: Princeton University Press, 2012.

Benson, Peter, and Stuart Kirsch. "Capitalism and the Politics of Resignation." *Current Anthropology* 51, no. 4 (2010): 459–86.

Berenschot, Ward, Henk Schulte Nordholt, and Laurens Bakker, eds. *Citizenship and Democratization in Southeast Asia.* Leiden: Brill online, 2016.

Berenschot, Ward, Henk Schulte Nordholt, and Laurens Bakker. "Introduction: Citizenship and Democratization in Postcolonial Southeast Asia." In Berenschot, Nordholt, and Bakker, *Citizenship and Democratization in Southeast Asia*, 1–38.

Besky, Sarah. *The Darjeeling Distinction: Labor and Justice on Fair-Trade Tea Plantations in India.* Berkeley: University of California Press, 2013.

Bhandar, Brenna. *Colonial Lives of Property: Law, Land, and Racial Regimes of Ownership.* Durham, NC: Duke University Press, 2018.

Bissonnette, Jean-Francois, and Rodolphe De Koninck. "The Return of the Plantation? Historical and Contemporary Trends in the Relation between Plantations and Smallholdings in Southeast Asia." *Journal of Peasant Studies* 44, no. 4 (2015): 918–38.

Bourchier, David. *Illiberal Democracy in Indonesia: The Ideology of the Family State.* London: Routledge, 2015.

Breman, Jan. *Mobilizing Labour for the Global Coffee Market: Profits from an Unfree Work Regime in Colonial Java.* Amsterdam: Amsterdam University Press, 2015.

Breman, Jan. *Taming the Coolie Beast: Plantation Society and the Colonial Order in Southeast Asia.* Delhi: Oxford University Press, 1989.

Bridge, Gavin. "Material Worlds: Natural Resources, Resource Geography and the Material Economy." *Geography Compass* 3, no. 3 (2009): 1217–44.

Brinkgreve, J. H. *Nota over Den Landbouw in West Borneo.* Pontianak: Djabatan Penerangan Pertanian Kalimantan Barat, 1947.

Budiawan, Odit. "Perang Ngakal: Transaksi Tanah Dan Goncangan Sosial Dalam Introduksi Kelapa Sawit Di Wilayah Pedesaan Kalimantan Barat." Master's thesis, Universitas Gadjah Mada, 2013.

Budidarsono, S. M. Sofiyuddin, A. Rahmanulloh, and S. Dewi. *Socioeconomic Impact Assessment of Palm Oil Production.* Technical Brief 27. Bogor: World Agroforestry Centre, 2012.

Bullard, Nicola, Walden Bello, and Kamal Mallhotra. "Taming the Tigers: The IMF and the Asian Crisis." *Third World Quarterly* 19, no. 3 (1998): 505–55.

Butler, Rhett A. "Half of Riau's Oil Palm Plantations Are Illegal." Mongabay. August 12, 2014. https://news.mongabay.com/2014/08/half-of-riaus-oil-palm -plantations-are-illegal/.

Butt, Simon, and Tim Lindsey. "Judicial Mafia: The Courts and State Illegality in Indonesia." In Aspinall and van Klinken, *The State and Illegality in Indonesia,* 189–213.

Byerlee, Derek. "The Fall and Rise Again of Plantations in Tropical Asia: History Repeated?" *Land* 3, no. 3 (2014): 574–97.

Carter, Michael. "Identification of the Inverse Relationship between Farm Size and Productivity: An Empirical Analysis of Peasant Agricultural Production." *Oxford Economic Papers* 36, no. 1 (1984): 131–45.

Casson, Anne, and Krystof Obidzinski. "From New Order to Regional Autonomy: Shifting Dynamics of 'Illegal' Logging in Kalimantan, Indonesia." *World Development* 30, no. 12 (2002): 2133–51.

Chain Reaction Research. *Shadow Companies Present Palm Oil Investor Risks and Undermine NDPE Efforts.* June 21, 2018. https://chainreactionresearch.com/wp-content /uploads/2018/06/Shadow-Company-June-22-2018-Final-for-sharepoint.pdf.

Chamim, Mardiyah, Dwi Setyo Irawanto, Yusi Avianto Pareanom, Hae Zen, and Irfan Budiman. *Raja Limbung: Seabad Perjalanan Sawit Di Indonesia.* Bogor, Indonesia: Sawit Watch, Tempo Institute, Insist, 2012.

Choiruzzad, Shofwan Al Banna. "Save Palm Oil, Save the Nation: Palm Oil Companies and the Shaping of Indonesia's National Interest." *Asian Politics and Policy* 11, no. 1 (2019): 8–26.

Choy, Timothy K., Lieba Faier, Michael J. Hathaway, Miyako Inoue, Shiho Satsuka, and Anna Tsing. "A New Form of Collaboration in Cultural Anthropology: Matsutake Worlds." *American Ethnologist* 36, no. 2 (2009): 380–403.

Colchester, Marcus. "Indonesian Government May Be Pinning False Hopes on IUCN Oil Palm Report." Forest Peoples Programme, February 12, 2019. https:// www.forestpeoples.org/en/lands-forests-territories-iucn-palm-oil-rspo/news -article/2019/indonesian-government-may-be-pinning.

Colchester, Marcus, and Sophie Chao. *Conflict or Consent? The Oil Palm Sector at a Crossroads.* Moreton-in-Marsh, UK: Forest Peoples Programme, Sawit Watch, and Transformasi untuk Keadilan Indonesia, 2013. https://www.forestpeoples .org/en/topics/palm-oil-rspo/publication/2013/conflict-or-consent-oil-palm -sector-crossroads.

Colchester, Marcus, Norman Jiwan, Andiko, Martua Sirait, Asep Yunan Firdaus, A Surambo, and Herbert Pane. *Promised Land: Palm Oil and Land Acquisition in Indonesia: Implications for Local Communities and Indigenous Peoples.* Forest Peoples Programme and Perkumpulan Sawit Watch, 2006. https://www.forestpeoples .org/en/topics/palm-oil-rspo/publication/2010/promised-land-palm-oil-and -land-acquisition-indonesia-implicat.

Cooper, Frederick, and Ann Laura Stoler, eds. *Tensions of Empire: Colonial Cultures in a Bourgeois World.* Berkeley: University of California Press, 1997.

Côte, Muriel, and Benedikt Korf. "Making Concessions: Extractive Enclaves, Entangled Capitalism and Regulative Pluralism at the Gold Mining Frontier in Burkina Faso." *World Development* 101 (2018): 466–76.

Cramb, Rob. "The Political Economy of Large-Scale Oil Palm Development in Sarawak." In Cramb and McCarthy, *The Oil Palm Complex: Smallholders, Agribusiness and the State in Indonesia and Malaysia,* 189–246.

Cramb, Rob, and John McCarthy. "Characterising Oil Palm Production in Indonesia and Malaysia." In Cramb and McCarthy, *The Oil Palm Complex: Smallholders, Agribusiness and the State in Indonesia and Malaysia,* 27–77.

Cramb, Rob, and John McCarthy. "Introduction." In Cramb and McCarthy, *The Oil Palm Complex: Smallholders, Agribusiness and the State in Indonesia and Malaysia,* 1–26.

Cramb, Rob, and John McCarthy, eds. *The Oil Palm Complex: Smallholders, Agribusiness and the State in Indonesia and Malaysia.* Singapore: NUS Press, 2016.

Cramb, Rob, and Patrick S. Sujang. "The Mouse Deer and the Crocodile: Oil Palm Smallholders and Livelihood Strategies in Sarawak, Malaysia." *Journal of Peasant Studies* 40, no. 1 (2013): 129–54.

Cramb, Robert A., and Deanna Ferraro. "Custom and Capital: A Financial Appraisal of Alternative Arrangements for Large-Scale Oil Palm Development on Customary Land in Sarawak, Malaysia." *Malaysian Journal of Economic Studies* 49, no. 1 (2012): 49–69.

Cribb, Robert. "A System of Exemptions: Historicizing State Illegality in Indonesia." In Aspinall and van Klinken, *The State and Illegality in Indonesia,* 31–44.

Crichlow, Michaeline A., and Patricia Northover. *Globalization and Creole Identities: The Shaping of Power in Post-Plantation Spaces.* Durham, NC: Duke University Press, 2009.

Daemeter Consulting. *Overview of Indonesian Oil Palm Smallholder Farmers: A Typology of Organizational Models, Needs, and Investment Opportunities.* 2015. http://daemeter.org/new/uploads/20160105233051.Smallholders_Book_050116_web.pdf.

Damianus, Siyok. *Tolak Tegas Program Transmigrasi Baru Di Kalimantan.* Change.org, 2015. https://www.change.org/p/presiden-republik-indonesia-kementerian-transmigrasi-tolak-program-transmigrasi-baru-di-kalimantan.

Daniel, Valentine, Henry Bernstein, and Tom Brass, eds. *Plantations, Proletarians and Peasants in Colonial Asia.* London: Frank Cass, 1992.

Davidson, Jamie S. *From Rebellion to Riots: Collective Violence on Indonesian Borneo.* Madison: University of Wisconsin Press, 2008.

Davis, Janae, Alex A. Moulton, Levi van Sant, and Brian Williams. "Anthropocene, Capitalocene, . . . Plantationocene?: A Manifesto for Ecological Justice in an Age of Global Crises." *Geography Compass* 13, no. 5 (2019): e12438.

de Groot Heupner, Susan. "The Palm Oil Plantation of North Sumatra: A System of Repression and Structural Violence: A Case Study on the Independent Trade Union and Its Efforts to Organize and Mobilize Plantation Workers." Bachelor's honors thesis, Murdoch University, 2016.

De Koninck, Rodolphe. "On the Geopolitics of Land Colonization: Order and Disorder on the Frontiers of Vietnam and Indonesia." *Moussons* 9 (2006): 35–59.

De Schutter, Olivier. "How Not to Think of Land-Grabbing: Three Critiques of Large-Scale Investments in Farmland." *Journal of Peasant Studies* 38, no. 2 (2011): 249–79.

de Vos, Rosanne, Michiel Köhne, and Dik Roth. "'We'll Turn Your Water into Coca-Cola': The Atomizing Practices of Oil Palm Plantation Development in Indonesia." *Journal of Agrarian Change* 18, no. 2 (2018): 385–405.

Deninger, Klaus, Derek Byerlee, Jonathan Lindsay, Andrew Norton, Harris Selod, and Mercedes Stickler. *Rising Global Interest in Farmland: Can It Yield Sustainable and Equitable Benefits?* Washington, DC: World Bank, 2011.

Diamond, Stanley. "Anthropology in Question." *Dialectical Anthropology* 28, no. 1 (2004): 11–32.

Dick, Howard, and Jeremy Mulholland. "The Politics of Corruption in Indonesia." *Georgetown Journal of International Affairs* 17, no. 1 (2016): 43–49.

Dinius, Oliver J., and Angela Vergara, eds. *Company Towns in the Americas: Landscape, Power, and Working-Class Communities.* Athens: University of Georgia Press, 2011.

Dove, Michael. *The Banana Tree at the Gate.* New Haven, CT: Yale University Press, 2011.

Dove, Michael. "Plantation Development in West Kalimantan I: Extant Population/Lab Balances." *Borneo Research Bulletin* 17, no. 2 (1985): 95–105.

Dove, Michael. "Plantation Development in West Kalimantan II: The Perceptions of the Indigenous Population." *Borneo Research Bulletin* 18, no. 1 (1985): 3–27.

Dove, Michael. "Representations of the 'Other' by Others: The Ethnographic Challenge Posed by Planters' Views of Peasants in Indonesia." In Li, *Transforming the Indonesian Uplands: Marginality, Power and Production*, 203–29.

Du Toit, Andries. "The Micro-Politics of Paternalism: The Discourses of Management and Resistance on South African Fruit and Wine Farms." *Journal of Southern African Studies* 19, no. 2 (1993): 314–36.

Du Toit, Andries. "Without the Blanket of the Land: Agrarian Change and Biopolitics in Post-Apartheid South Africa." *The Journal of Peasant Studies* 45, no. 5–6 (2018): 1086–107.

Duffy, Rosaleen. "Global Environmental Governance and the Challenge of Shadow States: The Impact of Illicit Sapphire Mining in Madagascar." *Development and Change* 36, no. 5 (2005): 825–43.

Dwyer, Michael B. *Trying to Follow the Money: Possibilities and Limits of Investor Transparency in Southeast Asia's Rush for "Available" Land.* Bogor, Indonesia: CIFOR, 2015.

Eickhoff, Martijn, Gerry van Klinken, and Geoffrey Robinson. "1965 Today: Living with the Indonesian Massacres." *Journal of Genocide Research* 19, no. 4 (2017): 449–64.

Eilenberg, Michael, and Jason Cons, eds. *Frontier Assemblages: The Emergent Politics of Resource Frontiers in Asia:* Oxford: Wiley-Blackwell, 2019.

Elmhirst, Rebecca, Mia Siscawati, Bimbika Sijapati Basnett, and Dian Ekowati. "Gender and Generation in Engagements with Oil Palm in East Kalimantan, Indonesia: Insights from Feminist Political Ecology." *Journal of Peasant Studies* 44, no. 6 (2017): 1135–57.

Fairbairn, Madeleine. *Fields of Gold: Financing the Global Land Rush.* Ithaca, NY: Cornell University Press, 2020.

Feintrenie, Laurène, Wan Kian Chong, and Patrice Levang. "Why Do Farmers Prefer Oil Palm? Lessons Learnt from Bungo District, Indonesia." *Small-Scale Forestry* 9 (2010): 379–96.

Ferguson, James. *Expectations of Modernity.* Berkeley: University of California Press, 1999.

Ferguson, James. *Give a Man a Fish.* Durham, NC: Duke University Press, 2015.

Ferguson, James. "Proletarian Politics Today: On the Perils and Possibilities of Historical Analogy." *Comparative Studies in Society and History* 61, no. 1 (2019): 4–22.

Ferguson, James. "Seeing Like an Oil Company: Space, Security, and Global Capital in Neoliberal Africa." *American Anthropologist* 107, no. 3 (2005): 377–82.

Ferguson, James, and Tania Murray Li. *Beyond the "Proper Job": Political-Economic Analysis after the Century of Labouring Man.* Working Paper 51. Cape Town: Institute for Poverty, Land and Agrarian Studies (PLAAS), University of Western Cape, 2018.

Finnwatch. *The Law of the Jungle: Corporate Responsibility of Finnish Palm Oil Purchases.* May 2014. https://www.finnwatch.org/images/palmoil.pdf.

Forest Peoples Programme. *A Comparison of Leading Palm Oil Certification Standards.* Jakarta: Forest Peoples Programme, 2017. https://www.forestpeoples.org/en/responsible-finance-palm-oil-rspo/report/2017/comparison-leading-palm-oil-certification-standards.

Forest Peoples Programme. *Dayak Leaders' Memories and Dreams: Report on a Survey of Oil Palm Plantations and Indigenous Peoples in West Kalimantan.* Jakarta: Forest Peoples Programme, 2005. http://www.forestpeoples.org/sites/default/files/publication/2010/08/dayaksurvoilpalmjul05eng.pdf.

Forest Peoples Programme and Sawit Watch. *Ghosts on Our Own Land: Indonesian Oil Palm Smallholders and the Roundtable on Sustainable Palm Oil.* Jakarta: Forest Peoples Programme and Sawit Watch, 2006. https://www.forestpeoples.org/sites/default/files/publication/2011/02/ghostsonourownlandtxt06eng.pdf.

Foucault, Michel. "Governmentality." In *The Foucault Effect: Studies in Governmentality,* edited by Graham Burchell, Colin Gordon, and Peter Miller, 87–104. Chicago: University of Chicago Press, 1991.

Foucault, Michel. *Power/Knowledge: Selected Interviews and Other Writings 1972–1977.* Brighton, UK: Harvester Press, 1980.

Furnivall, J. S. *Netherlands India: A Study of Plural Economy.* Cambridge: Cambridge University Press, [1939] 1967.

Gabungan Pengusaha Kelapa Sawit Indonesia (GAPKI). *"Replanting" Kemitraan, Replanting Kebun Sawit Berkelanjutan.* 2018. https://gapki.id/news/3444/replanting
-kemitraan-replanting-kebun-sawit-berkelanjutan.

GAPKI. *Kemitraan Sawit Lahirkan Revolusi Sawit Dunia.* 2017. https://gapki.id/news/3115
/kemitraan-sawit-lahirkan-revolusi-sawit-dunia.

The Gecko Project. "Indonesia for Sale: The Making of a Palm Oil Fiefdom." October 11, 2017. https://thegeckoproject.org/indonesiaforsale/home.

Geertz, Clifford. *Agricultural Involution: The Processes of Ecological Change in Indonesia.* Berkeley: University of California Press, 1963.

Genting Plantations. *Pt Permata Sawit Mandiri Summary of HCV and SEIA Reports.* 2014. https://www.rspo.org/file/Summary%20of%20HCV%20&%20SEIA%20PT%20
PSM_1.pdf.

Genting Plantations. *Summary Report of Planning and Management of Pt Permata Sawit Mandiri.* 2014. https://docplayer.info/47226531-Summary-report-of-planning
-and-management-of-pt-permata-sawit-mandiri-ketapang-district-and-west
-kalimantan-province-indonesia.html.

Gilbert, David E., and Afrizal. "The Land Exclusion Dilemma and Sumatra's Agrarian Reactionaries." *Journal of Peasant Studies* 46, no. 4 (2019): 681–701.

Gilroy, Paul. *The Black Atlantic: Modernity and Double Consciousness.* London: Verso, 1993.

Gordon, Alec. "Plantation Colonialism, Capitalism, and Critics." *Journal of Contemporary Asia* 30, no. 4 (2000): 465–91.

Gordon, Alec. "Towards a Model of Asian Plantation Systems." *Journal of Contemporary Asia* 31, no. 3 (2001): 306–30.

Government of Indonesia. *Keputusan Mahkamah Agung No. 2121 K/Pdt/2013.* 2013. Jakarta: Mahkamah Agung.

Grandin, Greg. *Fordlandia: The Rise and Fall of Henry Ford's Forgotten Jungle City.* New York: Metropolitan Books, 2009.

Greenpeace. *The Final Countdown: Now or Never to Reform the Palm Oil Industry.* 2018. https://www.greenpeace.org/international/publication/18455/the-final
-countdown-forests-indonesia-palm-oil/.

Gupta, Akhil. "Blurred Boundaries: The Discourse of Corruption, the Culture of Politics, and the Imagined State." *American Ethnologist* 22, no. 2 (1995): 375–402.

Hadiz, Vedi. "Capitalism, Primitive Accumulation and the 1960s' Massacres: Revisiting the New Order and Its Violent Genesis." *Inter-Asia Cultural Studies* 16, no. 2 (2015): 306–15.

Hadiz, Vedi, and Richard Robison. "The Political Economy of Oligarchy and the Reorganization of Power in Indonesia." *Indonesia*, no. 96 (2013): 35–57.

Hall, Derek. "Land Grabs, Land Control, and Southeast Asian Crop Booms." *Journal of Peasant Studies* 38, no. 4 (2011): 811–31.

Hall, Derek. "Primitive Accumulation, Accumulation by Dispossession and the Global Land Grab." *Third World Quarterly* 34, no. 9 (2013): 1582–604.

Hall, Derek. "Rethinking Primitive Accumulation: Theoretical Tensions and Rural Southeast Asian Complexities." *Antipode* 44, no. 4 (2012): 1188–208.

Hall, Derek, Philip Hirsch, and Tania Murray Li. *Powers of Exclusion: Land Dilemmas in Southeast Asia*. Singapore: NUS Press, 2011.

Haraway, Donna, and Anna Tsing. "Reflections on the Plantationocene: A Conversation with Donna Haraway and Anna Tsing Moderated by Gregg Mitman." *Edge Effects,* June 18, 2019 (updated October 12, 2019). https://edgeeffects.net/haraway-tsing-plantationocene/.

Hardin, Rebecca. "Concessionary Politics: Property, Patronage, and Political Rivalry in Central African Forest Management." *Current Anthropology* 52, no. S3 (2011): S113–S125.

Harriss-White, Barbara. "Labour and Petty Production." *Development and Change* 45, no. 5 (2014): 981–1000.

Harriss-White, Barbara, and Lucia Michelutti. "Introduction." In *The Wild East: Criminal Political Economies in South Asia,* edited by Barbara Harriss-White and Lucia Michelutti, 1–34. London: UCL Press, 2019.

Harsono, Andreas. *Indonesia's "Anti-Communism" Law Used against Environmental Activist*. Human Rights Watch. 2018. https://www.hrw.org/news/2018/01/12/indonesias-anti-communism-law-used-against-environmental-activist.

Hart, Gillian. *Disabling Globalization: Places of Power in Post-Apartheid South Africa*. Berkeley: University of California Press, 2002.

Harvey, David. "Neoliberalism as Creative Destruction." *Annals of the American Academy of Political and Social Science* 610 (2007): 22–44.

Harvey, David. *The New Imperialism*. Oxford: Oxford University Press, 2003.

Hawkins, Doug, Yingheng Chen, and Thomas Wigglesworth. *Indonesian Palm Oil Production Sector: A Wave of Consolidation to Come*. London: Hardman Agribusiness, 2016.

Hawthorne, Camilla. "Black Matters Are Spatial Matters: Black Geographies for the Twenty-First Century." *Geography Compass* 13, no. 11 (July 25, 2019).

Henley, David. "Custom and Koperasi: The Cooperative Ideal in Indonesia." In *The Revival of Tradition in Indonesian Politics: The Deployment of Adat from Colonialism to Indigenism,* edited by Jamie S. Davidson and David Henley. London: Routledge, 2012.

Hirschman, Albert O. *Exit, Voice, and Loyalty: Responses to Decline in Firms, Organizations, and States*. Cambridge, MA: Harvard University Press, 1970.

Houben, V. J. H. "Profit versus Ethics: Government Enterprises in the Late Colonial State." In *The Late Colonial State in Indonesia: Political and Economic Foundations of the Netherlands Indies 1880–1942,* edited by Robert Cribb, 191–211. Leiden: KITLV Press, 1994.

Human Rights Watch. *"When We Lost the Forest, We Lost Everything": Oil Palm Plantations and Rights Violations in Indonesia*. 2019. https://www.hrw.org/report/2019/09/23/when-we-lost-forest-we-lost-everything/oil-palm-plantations-and-rights-violations.

IJ REDD+ Project. "The Sagupa Forum: Sharing for Strengthening of GPNP Management." *Japan International Cooperation Agency*, June 2018, https://www.jica.go.jp /project/english/indonesia/015/newsletter/c8hovm0000bhgukm-att/policy_06 .pdf.

Institute for Policy Analysis of Conflict. *Anatomy of an Indonesian Oil Palm Conflict.* 2016. http://www.understandingconflict.org/en/conflict/read/54/Anatomy-of -an-Indonesian-Oil-Palm-Conflict.

International Labour Organization. *Labour and Social Trends in Indonesia 2013: Reinforcing the Role of Decent Work in Equitable Growth.* 2013. https://www.ilo.org /jakarta/whatwedo/publications/WCMS_233249/lang—en/index.htm.

International Union for the Conservation of Nature (IUCN). *Palm Oil and Biodiversity.* 2019. https://www.iucn.org/resources/issues-briefs/palm-oil-and-biodiversity.

IUF, UITA, and IUL (International Union of Food, Agricultural, Hotel, Restaurant, Catering, Tobacco and Allied Workers' Associations). "Marketing Sustainability: RSPO Ignores Serious Rights Violations." February 2006. http://docplayer .net/71406198-Marketing-sustainability-rspo-ignores-serious-rights-violations .html.

James, C. L. R. *The Black Jacobins: Toussaint L'Ouverture and the San Domingo Revolution.* London: Vintage, [1938] 1989.

Jelsma, Idsert, G. C. Schoneveld, Annelies Zoomers, and A. C. M. van Westen. "Unpacking Indonesia's Independent Oil Palm Smallholders: An Actor-Disaggregated Approach to Identifying Environmental and Social Performance Challenges." *Land Use Policy* 69 (2017): 281–97.

Jong, Hans Nicholas. "Study Puts a Figure to Hidden Cost of Community–Company Conflict in Palm Oil Industry." *Mongabay.* April 25, 2018. https://news .mongabay.com/2018/04/studies-reveal-gargantuan-costs-of-palm-oil-related -land-conflicts-in-indonesia/.

Julia, and Ben White. "Gendered Experience of Dispossession: Oil Palm Expansion in a Dayak Hibun Community in West Kalimantan." *Journal of Peasant Studies* 39, no. 3–4 (2012): 995–1016.

Kenney-Lazar, Miles. "Relations of Sovereignty: The Uneven Production of Transnational Plantation Territories in Laos." *Transactions of the Institute of British Geographers* 45, no. 2 (2019): 331–44

Koentjaraningrat, ed. *Masyarakat Terasing Di Indonesia.* Jakarta: Gramedia, 1993.

Komnas HAM. *National Inquiry on the Right of Indigenous Peoples on Their Territories in the Forest Zones: Summary of Findings and Recommendations.* Jakarta: Komnas HAM, 2015. http://www.forestpeoples.org/sites/fpp/files/publication/2016/04 /komnas-ham-nationalinquiry-summary-apr2016.pdf.

Konsorsium Pembaruan Agraria (KPA). *Catatan Ahir Tahun: Masa Depan Reforma Agraria Melampaui Tahun Politik.* Jakarta: KPA, 2018. http://kpa.or.id/publikasi /baca/laporan/30/Catahu_2018_Masa_Depan_Reforma_Agraria_Melampaui _Tahun_Politik/.

Krupa, Christopher. "State by Proxy: Privatized Government in the Andes." *Comparative Studies in Society and History* 52, no. 2 (2010): 319–50.

Lembaga Gemawan (Indonesia Corruption Watch). *Public Review: Rancangan Peraturan Daerah Rencana Tata Ruang Wilayah Provinsi Kalimantan Barat*. Pontianak, Indonesia: Lembaga Gemawan, 2013. https://media.neliti.com/media/publications/45365-ID-rancangan-peraturan-daerah-rencana-tata-ruang-wilayah-provinsi-kalimantan-barat.pdf.

Li, Tania Murray. "Articulating Indigenous Identity in Indonesia: Resource Politics and the Tribal Slot." *Comparative Studies in Society and History* 42, no. 1 (2000): 149–79.

Li, Tania Murray. "Centering Labour in the Land Grab Debate." *Journal of Peasant Studies* 38, no. 2 (2011): 281–98.

Li, Tania Murray. "Epilogue: Customary Land Rights and Politics, 25 Years On." *Asia Pacific Journal of Anthropology* 21, no. 1 (2020): 77–84.

Li, Tania Murray. "Fixing Non-Market Subjects: Governing Land and Population in the Global South." *Foucault Studies* 18 (2014): 34–48.

Li, Tania Murray. "Indigeneity, Capitalism, and the Management of Dispossession." *Current Anthropology* 51, no. 3 (2010): 385–414.

Li, Tania Murray. "Intergenerational Displacement in Indonesia's Oil Palm Plantation Zone." *Journal of Peasant Studies* 44, no. 6 (2017): 1158–76.

Li, Tania Murray. "Involution's Dynamic Others." *Journal of the Royal Anthropological Institute* 20, no. 2 (2013): 276–92.

Li, Tania Murray. *Land's End: Capitalist Relations on an Indigenous Frontier*. Durham, NC: Duke University Press, 2014.

Li, Tania Murray. "The Price of Un/Freedom: Indonesia's Colonial and Contemporary Plantation Labour Regimes." *Comparative Studies in Society and History* 59, no. 2 (2017): 245–76.

Li, Tania Murray. "Situating Transmigration in Indonesia's Oil Palm Labour Regime." In Cramb and McCarthy, *The Oil Palm Complex: Smallholders, Agribusiness and the State in Indonesia and Malaysia*, 354–77.

Li, Tania Murray. *Social Impacts of Oil Palm in Indonesia: A Gendered Perspective from West Kalimantan*. Center for International Forestry Research (CIFOR), 2015. https://www.cifor.org/publications/pdf_files/OccPapers/OP-124.pdf.

Li, Tania Murray. *Transforming the Indonesian Uplands: Marginality, Power and Production*. London: Routledge, 1999.

Li, Tania Murray. "What Is Land? Assembling a Resource for Global Investment." *Transactions of the Institute of British Geographers* 39, no. 4 (2014): 589–602.

Li, Tania Murray. *The Will to Improve: Governmentality, Development, and the Practice of Politics*. Durham, NC: Duke University Press, 2007.

Li, Tania Murray, Alexandre Pelletier, and Arianto Sangadji. "Unfree Labour and Extractive Regimes in Colonial Java and Beyond." *Development and Change* 47, no. 3 (2016): 598–611.

Lindquist, Johan. "Labour Recruitment, Circuits of Capital and Gendered Mobility: Reconceptualizing the Indonesian Migration Industry." *Asia Pacific Viewpoint* 83, no. 1 (2010): 115–32.

Lindquist, Johan, Biao Ziang, and Brenda S. A. Yeoh. "Opening the Black Box of Migration: Brokers, the Organization of Transnational Mobility and Changing Political Economy of Asia." *Pacific Affairs* 85, no. 1 (2012): 7–89.

Little, Peter D., and Michael J. Watts, eds. *Living under Contract: Contract Farming and Agrarian Transformation in Sub-Saharan Africa*. Madison: University of Wisconsin Press, 1994.

Lubis, Mochtar. *Twilight in Jakarta*. Translated by Claire Holt and John H. McGlynn. Honolulu: Lontar Foundation and University of Hawai'i Press, [1957] 2013.

Lucas, Anton, and Carol Warren. "The State, the People, and Their Mediators: The Struggle over Agrarian Law Reform in Post–New Order Indonesia." *Indonesia* 76 (2003): 87–126.

Lund, Christian. *Nine-Tenths of the Law: Enduring Dispossession in Indonesua*. New Haven, CT: Yale University Press, 2020.

Lund, Christian. "Predatory Peace: Dispossession at Aceh's Oil Palm Frontier." *Journal of Peasant Studies* 45, no. 2 (2017): 431–52.

Lund, Christian, and Noer Fauzi Rachman. "Occupied! Property, Citizenship and Peasant Movements in Rural Java." *Development and Change* 47, no. 6 (2016): 1316–37.

Mackie, J. A. C. "Indonesia's Government Estates and Their Masters." *Pacific Affairs* 34 (1962): 337–60.

Makdisi, Saree. "The Architecture of Erasure." *Critical Inquiry* 36, no. 3 (2010): 519–59.

Mangunwijaya, Y. B. *Durga/Umayi: A Novel*. Translated by Ward Keeler. Seattle: University of Washington Press, 2004.

Marti, Serge. *Losing Ground: The Human Rights Impacts of Oil Palm Plantation Expansion in Indonesia*. London: Friends of the Earth, LifeMosaic, and Sawit Watch, 2008. https://www.foei.org/wp-content/uploads/2014/08/losingground.pdf.

Marx, Karl. *Capital: A Critique of Political Economy*, vol. 1. Moscow: Progress Publishers, [1867] 1986.

Mbembe, Achille. *On the Postcolony*. Berkeley: University of California Press, 2001.

McCarthy, John. "Certifying in Contested Spaces: Private Regulation in Indonesian Forestry and Oil Palm." *Third World Quarterly* 33, no. 10 (2012): 1871–88.

McCarthy, John. "The Limits of Legality: State, Governance and Resource Control in Indonesia." In Aspinall and van Klinken, *The State and Illegality in Indonesia*, 89–106.

McCarthy, John. "Processes of Inclusion and Adverse Incorporation: Oil Palm and Agrarian Change in Sumatra, Indonesia." *Journal of Peasant Studies* 37, no. 4 (2010): 821–50.

McCarthy, John. "Where Is Justice? Resource Entitlements, Agrarian Transformation and Regional Autonomy in Jambi, Sumatra." In *Community, Environment and Local Governance in Indonesia: Locating the Commonweal*, edited by C. Warren and John F. McCarthy, 167–96. New York: Routledge, 2009.

McCarthy, John, and Rob Cramb. "Policy Narratives, Landholder Engagement, and Oil Palm Expansion on the Malaysian and Indonesian Frontiers." *Geographical Journal* 175, no. 2 (2009): 112–23.

McCarthy, John F., and Kathryn Robinson, eds. *Land and Development in Indonesia: Searching for the People's Sovereignty*. Singapore: ISEAS, 2016.

McCarthy, John, and Zahari Zen. "Regulating the Oil Palm Boom: Assessing the Effectiveness of Environmental Governance Approaches to Agro-Industrial Pollution in Indonesia." *Law and Policy* 32, no. 1 (2010): 153–79.

McCarthy, John, Piers Gillespie, and Zahari Zen. "Swimming Upstream: Local Indonesian Production Networks in 'Globalized' Palm Oil Production." *World Development* 40, no. 3 (2012): 555–69.

McCarthy, John F., Jacqueline A. C. Vel, and Suraya Afiff. "Trajectories of Land Acquisition and Enclosure: Development Schemes, Virtual Land Grabs, and Green Acquisitions in Indonesia's Outer Islands." *Journal of Peasant Studies* 39, no. 2 (2012): 521–50.

McKeown, Adam. "How the Box Became Black: Brokers and the Creation of the Free Migrant." *Pacific Affairs* 85, no. 1 (2012): 21–45.

McKittrick, Katherine. "Plantation Futures." *Small Axe* 17, no. 3 (2013): 1–15.

Mercuri, Marco. "Beyond the Self-Entrepreneurial Myth: Oil Palm Smallholders in Sanggau–West Kalimantan." Master's thesis, Radboud University, 2015.

Mezzadra, Sandro, and Brett Neilson. *The Politics of Operations: Excavating Contemporary Capitalism*. Durham, NC: Duke University Press, 2019.

Mighty Earth. *Over 60 NGOs Call for Stronger Reforms to the Roundtable on Sustainable Palm Oil (RSPO) Standards*. 2018. http://www.mightyearth.org/over-60-ngos -call-for-stronger-reforms-to-the-roundtable-on-sustainable-palm-oil-rspo -standards/.

Mintz, Sidney. "The Rural Proletariat and the Problem of Rural Proletarian Consciousness." *Journal of Peasant Studies* 1, no. 3 (1974): 291–325.

Mintz, Sidney. *Sweetness and Power: The Place of Sugar in Modern History*. New York: Penguin Books, 1986.

Mintz, Sidney. *Worker in the Cane: A Puerto Rican Life History*. New Haven, CT: Yale University Press, 1960.

Mitchell, Timothy. *Rule of Experts: Egypt, Technopolitics, Modernity*. Berkeley: University of California Press, 2002.

Molenaar, Jan Willem. *Diagnostic Study on Indonesian Oil Palm Smallholders: Developing a Better Understanding of Their Performance and Potential*. Washington, DC: International Finance Corporation/World Bank Group, 2013.

Moore, Donald. *Suffering for Territory: Race, Place, and Power in Zimbabwe*. Durham, NC: Duke University Press, 2005.

Navaro-Yashin, Yael. *The Make-Believe Space: Affective Geograpahy in a Postwar Polity*. Durham, NC: Duke University Press, 2012.

Netherlands Indies Government. *Landbouwatlas Van Java En Madoera*. Weltevreden, The Netherlands: Departement van Landbouw, Nijverheid en Handel, 1926.

Obidzinski, Krystof, Rubeta Andriani, Heru Komarudin, and Agus Andrianto. "Environmental and Social Impacts of Oil Palm Plantations and Their Implications for Biofuel Production in Indonesia." *Ecology and Society* 17, no. 1 (2012): 1–19.

Obidzinski, Krystof, Ahmad Dermawan, and Adi Hadianto. "Oil Palm Plantation Investments in Indonesia's Forest Frontiers: Limited Economic Multipliers and Uncertain Benefits for Local Communities." *Environment, Development and Sustainability* 16, no. 6 (2014): 1177–96.

Oetami, Dewi. "Reconciling Development, Conservation, and Social Justice in West Kalimantan." In *The Palm Oil Controversy in Southeast Asia: A Transnational Perspective*, edited by Oliver Pye and Jayati Bhattacharya, 164–78. Singapore: ISEAS, 2013.

Oxfam. *Towards a More Equal Indonesia*. 2017. https://www-cdn.oxfam.org/s3fs-public /bp-towards-more-equal-indonesia-230217-en_0.pdf.

Palupi, Sri, P. Prasetyohadi, Chelluz Pahun, Andriani S. Kusni, Kusni Sulang, Johanes Jenito, and Dudik Warnadi. *Industri Perkebunan Sawit Dan Hak Asasi Manusia: Potret Pelaksanaan Tanggung Jawab Pemerintah Dan Korporasi Terhadap Hak Asasi Manusia Di Kalimantan Tengah*. Jakarta: Institute for Ecosoc Rights, 2015.

Palupi, Sri, Yulia Sri Sukapti, Siti Maemunah, P. Prasetyohadi, and Aksel Tømte. *Privatisasi Transmigrasi Dan Kemitraan Plasma Menopang Industri Sawit: Resiko Hak Asasi Manusia Dalam Kebijakan Transmigrasi Dan Kemitraan Plasma Di Sektor Industri Perkebunan Sawit*. Jakarta: Institute for Ecosoc Rights, and Norwegian Center for Human Rights, 2017.

Paoli, G. D., P. Gillespie, P. L. Wells, L. Hovani, A. E. Sileuw, N. Franklin, and J. Schweithelm. *Oil Palm in Indonesia: Governance, Decision Making and Implications for Sustainable Development*. Jakarta: The Nature Conservancy Indonesia Program. 2013.

Peluso, Nancy. "A Political Ecology of Violence and Territory in West Kalimantan." *Asia Pacific Viewpoint* 49, no. 1 (2008): 48–67.

Peluso, Nancy Lee, and Christian Lund. "New Frontiers of Land Control: An Introduction." *Journal of Peasant Studies* 38, no. 4 (2011): 667–83.

Peluso, Nancy Lee, Suraya Afiff, and Noer Fauzi Rachman. "Claiming the Grounds for Reform: Agrarian and Environmental Movements in Indonesia." *Journal of Agrarian Change* 8, no. 2 (2008): 377–408.

Pelzer, Karl J. *Planter and Peasant: Colonial Policy and the Agrarian Struggle in East Sumatra 1863-1947*. The Hague: Martinus Nijhoff, 1978.

Perusahaan Negara Perkebunan 7. *Pertama Di Kalimantan Barat Pabrik Kelapa Sawit Gunung Meliau*. Pematang Siantar, Indonesia: Perusahaan Negara Perkebunan, 1984.

Pichler, Melanie. "Legal Dispossession: State Strategies and Selectivities in the Expansion of Indonesian Palm Oil and Agrofuel Production." *Development and Change* 46, no. 3 (2015): 508–33.

Potter, Lesley. "How Can the People's Sovereignty Be Achieved in the Oil Palm Sector? Is the Plantation Model Shifting in Favour of Smallholders?" In Mc-

Carthy and Robinson, *Land and Development in Indonesia: Searching for the People's Sovereignty*, 315–42.

Potter, Lesley. "New Transmigration 'Paradigm' in Indonesia: Examples from Kalimantan." *Asia Pacific Viewpoint* 53, no. 3 (2012): 272–87.

Potter, Lesley. "Oil Palm and Resistance in West Kalimantan, Indonesia." In *Agrarian Angst and Rural Resistance in Contemporary Southeast Asia*, edited by Dominique Caouette and Sarah Turner, 105–34. London: Routledge, 2009.

Povinelli, Elizabeth. *Economies of Abandonment: Social Belonging and Endurance in Late Liberalism*. Durham, NC: Duke University Press, 2011.

Prabowo, Doni, Ahmad Maryudi, Senawi Senawi, and Muhammad A. Imron. "Conversion of Forests into Oil Palm Plantations in West Kalimantan, Indonesia: Insights from Actors' Power and Its Dynamics." *Forest Policy and Economics* 78 (2017): 32–39.

Pramoedya Ananta Toer. *Tjerita Dari Djakarta: Sekumpulan Karikatur Keadaan Dan Manusianja*. Jakarta: Grafica, 1957.

PTPN XIII. *Annual Report 2002*. Pontianak: PT Perkebunan Nusantara XIII, 2003.

Purnomo, H., A. A. Dewayani, R. Achdiawan, M. Ali, S. Komar, and B. Okarda. "Jaringan Aktor Dan Regulasi Kebakaran Hutan Dan Lahan." *Lestari Journal* 1, no. 1 (2016): 55–73.

Purwasari, Endang. "Budaya Hutang Di Kalangan Karyawati Emplasmen." Bachelor's thesis, Universitas Gadjah Mada, 2012.

Pye, Oliver. "Transnational Space and Workers' Struggles: Reshaping the Palm Oil Industry in Malaysia." In *The Political Ecology of Agrofuels*, edited by Bettina Engels, Kristina Dietz, Oliver Pye, and Achim Brunnengräber, 186–201. London: Routledge, 2015.

Rainforest Action Network. *Conflict Palm Oil: How U.S. Snack Food Brands Are Contributing to Orangutan Extinction, Climate Change and Human Rights Violations*. 2013. https://www.ran.org/issue/palm_oil/.

Rendra, W. S. *Potret Pembangunan Dalam Puisi*. Jakarta: Pustaka Jaya, 1993.

Rietberg, Petra Irene, and Otto Hospes. "Unpacking Land Acquisition at the Oil Palm Frontier: Obscuring Customary Rights and Local Authority in West Kalimantan, Indonesia." *Asia Pacific Viewpoint* 59, no. 3 (2018): 338–48.

Rist, Lucy, Laurène Feintrenie, and Patrice Levang. "The Livelihood Impacts of Oil Palm: Smallholders in Indonesia." *Biodversity Conservation* 19 (2010): 1009–24.

Robbins, Paul. *Political Ecology: A Critical Introduction*. 3rd ed. Oxford: Wiley-Blackwell, 2019.

Robinson, Cedric. *Black Marxism: The Making of the Black Radical Tradition*. Chapel Hill: University of North Carolina, [1983] 2000.

Robinson, Geoffrey B. *The Killing Season: A History of the Indonesian Massacres, 1965–66*. Princeton, NJ: Princeton University Press, 2018.

Robison, Richard, and Vedi Hadiz. *Reorganising Power in Indonesia: The Politics of Oligarchy in an Age of Markets*. London: RoutledgeCurzon, 2004.

Roitman, Janet. "The Ethics of Illegality in the Chad Basin." In *Law and Disorder in the Postcolony*, edited by John L. Comaroff and Jean Comaroff, 247–72. Chicago: University of Chicago Press, 2006.

Rosser, Andrew, and Donne Edwin. "The Politics of Corporate Social Responsibility in Indonesia." *Pacific Review* 23, no. 1 (2010): 1–22.

Rutherford, Blair. *Farm Worker Labor Struggles in Zimbabwe*. Bloomington: Indiana University Press, 2017.

Santika, Truly, Kerrie A. Wilson, Sugeng Budiharta, Elizabeth A. Law, Tun Min Poh, Marc Ancrenaz, Matthew J. Struebig, and Erik Meijaard. "Does Oil Palm Agriculture Help Alleviate Poverty? A Multidimensional Counterfactual Assessment of Oil Palm Development in Indonesia." *World Development* 120 (2019): 105–17.

Sawit Watch and International Labor Rights Forum. *Empty Assurances: The Human Cost of Oil Palm*. 2013. https://laborrights.org/publications/empty-assurances -human-cost-palm-oil.

Schoenberger, Laura, Derek Hall, and Peter Vandergeest. "What Happened When the Land Grab Came to Southeast Asia?" *Journal of Peasant Studies* 44, no. 4 (2017): 697–725.

Scott, David. "Colonial Governmentality." *Social Text* 43 (1995): 191–220.

Scott, David. *Conscripts of Modernity: The Tragedy of Colonial Enlightenment*. Durham, NC: Duke University Press, 2004.

Scott, James. *The Moral Economy of the Peasant*. New Haven, CT: Yale University Press, 1976.

Scott, James. *Seeing Like a State: How Certain Schemes to Improve the Human Condition Have Failed*. New Haven, CT: Yale University Press, 1998.

Scott, James. *Weapons of the Weak: Everyday Forms of Peasant Resistance*. New Haven, CT: Yale University Press, 1985.

Semedi, Pujo. "Palm Oil Wealth and Rumour Panics in West Kalimantan." *Forum for Development Studies* 41, no. 2 (2014): 233–52.

Semedi, Pujo. "A Struggle for Dignity." In *Labour in Asia*, edited by Huub de Jonge and Toon van Meijl, 61–65. Nijmegen, The Netherlands: De Walvis, 2012.

Semedi, Pujo, and Laurens Bakker. "Between Land Grabbing and Farmers' Benefits: Land Transfers in West Kalimantan, Indonesia." *Asia Pacific Journal of Anthropology* 15, no. 4 (2014): 376–90.

Serikat Petani Kelapa Sawit. *Karakteristik Dan Definisi Petani Kelapa Sawit Swadaya Di Indonesia*. 2017. www.spks-nasional.org.

Setiawan, Eko N., Ahmad Maryudi, Ris H. Purwanto, and Gabriel Lele. "Opposing Interests in the Legalization of Non-Procedural Forest Conversion to Oil Palm in Central Kalimantan, Indonesia." *Land Use Policy* 58 (2016): 472–81.

Shah, Alpa, Jens Lerche, Richard Axelby, Dalel Benbabaali, Brendan Donegan, Jayaseelan Raj, and Vikramaditya Thakur. *Ground Down by Growth: Tribe, Caste, Class and Inequality in Twenty-First-Century India*. London: Pluto Press, 2018.

Sheil, Douglas, Anne Casson, Erik Meijaard, Meine van Noordwijk, Joanne Gaskell, Jacqui Sunderland-Groves, Karah Wertz, and Markku Kanninen. *The Impacts and Opportunities of Oil Palm in Southeast Asia: What Do We Know and What Do We Need to Know?* Occasional Paper No. 51. Bogor, Indonesia: CIFOR, 2009.

Siagian, Saurlin P., Amin Siahaan, Buyung, and Nur Khairani. *The Loss of Reason: Human Rights Violations in the Oil Palm Plantations in Indonesia.* Rantau Selatan, Indonesia: Lentera Rakyat, 2011. https://www.brot-fuer-die-welt.de/fileadmin /mediapool/2_Downloads/Fachinformationen/Aktuell/Aktuell_22_loss-of -reason.pdf.

Sikor, Thomas, and Christian Lund. "Access and Property: A Question of Power and Authority." *Development and Change* 40, no. 1 (2009): 1–22.

Silva-Castañeda, Laura. "A Forest of Evidence: Third-Party Certification and Multiple Forms of Proof—A Case Study of Oil Palm Plantations in Indonesia." *Agriculture and Human Values* 29, no. 3 (2012): 361–70.

Silver, Christopher "Do the Donors Have It Right? Decentralization and Changing Local Governance in Indonesia." *Annals of Regional Science* 37 (2003): 421–34.

Sinaga, Hariati. "Employment and Income of Workers on Indonesian Oil Palm Plantations: Food Crisis at the Micro Level." *Future of Food: Journal on Food, Agriculture and Society* 1, no. 2 (2013): 64–78.

Sirait, Martua. *Indigenous Peoples and Oil Palm Expansion in West Kalimantan, Indonesia.* The Hague: Cordaid, 2009.

Situmorang, Manginar. "Strengthening the Peasant and Plantation Workers' Movement in North Sumatra." *Asia Monitor Resource Centre*, no. 74 (January– March 2010). https://www.amrc.org.hk/content/strengthening-peasant-and -plantation-workers-movement-north-sumatra.

Slater, Candace. "Justice for Whom? Contemporary Images of Amazonia." In *People, Plants and Justice: The Politics of Nature Conservation*, edited by Charles Zerner, 67–82. New York: Columbia University Press, 2000.

Steward, Julian H., Robert A. Manners, Eric R. Wolf, Elena Padilla Seda, Sidney W. Mintz, and Raymond L. Scheele. *The People of Puerto Rico: A Study in Social Anthropology.* Urbana: University of Illinois Press, 1956.

Stoler, Ann Laura. *Capitalism and Confrontation in Sumatra's Plantation Belt, 1870–1979.* Ann Arbor: University of Michigan Press, 1995.

Stoler, Ann Laura. *Duress: Imperial Durabilities in Our Time.* Durham, NC: Duke University Press, 2016.

Stoler, Ann Laura. "Imperial Debris: Reflections on Ruins and Ruination." *Cultural Anthropology* 23, no. 2 (2008): 191–219.

Stoler, Ann Laura. "Perceptions of Protest: Defining the Dangerous in Colonial Sumatra." *American Ethnologist* 12, no. 4 (1985): 642–58.

Striffler, Steve. *In the Shadows of State and Capital: The United Fruit Company, Popular Struggle, and Agrarian Restructuring in Ecuador, 1900–1995.* Durham, NC: Duke University Press, 2001.

Sudibyo, Dian Lintang. "'Konon Kita Saudara': Ketegangan Etnis di Perkebunan Kelapa Sawit Kalimantan Barat." Bachelor's thesis, Universitas Gadjah Mada, 2012.

Susanti, Ari, and Ahmad Maryudi. "Development Narratives, Notions of Forest Crisis, and Boom of Oil Palm Plantations in Indonesia." *Forest Policy and Economics* 73 (2016): 130–39.

Tambun, Eliakim. *Seperempat Abad Pengabdian Korpri, 1971–1996.* Jakarta: Pengurus Pusat Korpri, 1996.

Tenaga Kita and Pesticide Action Network. *Poisoned and Silenced: A Study of Pesticide Poisoning in the Plantations.* 2002. https://www.publiceye.ch/fileadmin/doc /Pestizide/2002_EvB_Poisoned-and-Silenced.pdf.

Thomas, Deborah A. *Political Life in the Wake of the Plantation: Sovereignty, Witnessing, Repair.* Durham, NC: Duke University Press, 2019.

Thompson, Edgar Tristram. *The Plantation.* Edited and with a new introduction by Sidney W. Mintz and George Baca. Columbia: University of South Carolina Press, 2010.

Toussaint, Eric. *The World Bank and the IMF in Indonesia: An Emblematic Interference.* Committee for the Abolition of Illegitmate Debt, 2019. http://www.cadtm.org /The-World-Bank-and-the-IMF-in-Indonesia-an-emblematic-interference.

Trouillot, Michel-Rolphe. *Peasants and Capital: Dominica in the World Economy.* Baltimore, MD: Johns Hopkins University Press, 1988.

Tsing, Anna. "Supply Chains and the Human Condition." *Rethinking Marxism* 21, no. 2 (2009): 148–76.

Tsing, Anna Lowenhaupt. *The Mushroom at the End of the World.* Princeton, NJ: Princeton University Press, 2015.

TuK Indonesia. "Banks behind Indonesian Palm Oil Tycoons Revealed." Banktrack, 2015. https://www.banktrack.org/article/banks_behind_indonesian_palm_oil _tycoons_revealed.

TuK Indonesia. *Tycoons in the Indonesian Palm Oil.* Jakarta: Transformasi untuk Keadilan Indonesia, 2018.

van der Muur, Willem, Jacqueline Vel, Micah R. Fisher, and Kathryn Robinson. "Changing Indigeneity Politics in Indonesia: From Revival to Projects." *Asia Pacific Journal of Anthropology* 20, no. 5 (2019): 379–96.

van Klinken, Gerry. "Blood, Timber, and the State in West Kalimantan, Indonesia." *Asia Pacific Viewpoint* 49, no. 1 (2008): 35–47.

van Klinken, Gerry, and Joshua Barker, eds. *State of Authority: The State in Society in Indonesia.* Ithaca, NY: Cornell Southeast Asia Program Publications, 2009.

van Schendel, Fiona. *Djolotigo: Ontginning En Exploitatie Van Een Particuliere Kofie-Onderneming Op Java, 1875–1898.* Amsterdam: NEHA, 2000.

Vandergeest, Peter, and Nancy Lee Peluso. "Territorialization and State Power in Thailand." *Theory and Society* 24 (1995): 385–426.

Varkkey, Helena. "Patronage Politics as a Driver of Economic Regionalisation: The Indonesian Oil Palm Sector and Transboundary Haze." *Asia Pacific Viewpoint* 53, no. 3 (2012): 314–29.

Wakker, Eric. *Greasy Palms: The Social and Ecological Impacts of Large Scale Oil Palm Plantation in Southeast Asia*. London: Friends of the Earth, 2005.

Wasef, Mouna, and Firdaus Ilyas. *Merampok Hutan Dan Uang Negara*. Jakarta: Indonesia Corruption Watch, 2011. https://antikorupsi.org/id/article/merampok-hutan-dan-uang-negara.

Watts, Michael. "A Tale of Two Gulfs: Life, Death, and Dispossession along Two Oil Frontiers." *American Quarterly* 64, no. 3 (2012): 437–67.

Weizman, Eyal. *Hollow Land: Israel's Architecture of Occupation*. London: Verso, 2007.

Welker, Marina. *Enacting the Corporation: An American Mining Firm in Post-Authoritarian Indonesia*. Berkeley: University of California Press, 2014.

Welker, Marina, Damani J. Partridge, and Rebecca Hardin. "Corporate Lives: New Perspectives on the Social Life of the Corporate Form: An Introduction." *Current Anthropology* 52, no. S3 (2011): S3–S16.

White, Ben. "Nucleus and Plasma: Contract Farming and the Exercise of Power in Upland West Java." In Li, *Transforming the Indonesian Uplands: Marginality, Power and Production*, 231–56.

White, Ben. "Remembering the Indonesian Peasants' Front and Plantation Workers' Union (1945–1966)." *Journal of Peasant Studies* 43, no. 1 (2016): 1–12.

White, Ben, Saturnino M. Borras Jr., Ruth Hall, Ian Scoones, and Wendy Wolford. "The New Enclosures: Critical Perspectives on Corporate Land Deals." *Journal of Peasant Studies* 39, no. 3–4 (2012): 619–47.

White, Benjamin. "Problems in the Empirical Analysis of Agrarian Differentiation." In *Agrarian Transformations: Local Processes and the State in Southeast Asia*, edited by Gillian Hart, Andrew Turton, and Benjamin White, 15–30. Berkeley: University of California Press, 1989.

White, Nicholas J. "Surviving Sukarno: British Business in Post-Colonial Indonesia, 1950–1967." *Modern Asian Studies* 46, no. 5 (2012): 1277–315.

Wie, Thee Kian. "The Impact of the Economic Crisis on Indonesia's Manufacturing Sector." *Developing Economies* 38, no. 4 (2000): 420–53.

Wijatnika Ika. "Menjaga Hutan Ala Masyarakat Sebadak Raya." *Wijatnika Ika* (blog). December 17, 2014. https://www.wijatnikaika.id/2014/12/belajar-hidup-dari-masyarakatsebadak.html.

Wilmar International. "No Deforestation, No Peat, No Exploitation Policy." December 5, 2013. https://www.wilmar-international.com/wp-content/uploads/2012/11/No-Deforestation-No-Peat-No-Exploitation-Policy.pdf.

Wolf, Eric. *Europe and the People without History*. Berkeley: University of California Press, 1982.

Wolf, Eric R., and Sidney W. Mintz. "Haciendas and Plantations in Middle America and the Antilles." *Social and Economic Studies* 6, no. 3 (1957): 380–412.

World Bank. *Indonesia Jobs Report: Towards Better Jobs and Security for All*. Jakarta: World Bank, 2010.

World Bank. *Indonesia's Rising Divide*. Jakarta: World Bank, 2016.

World Bank. *Towards Indonesian Land Reforms: Challenges and Opportunities—A Review of the Land Sector (Forest and Non-Forest) in Indonesia*. Jakarta: World Bank, 2015.

World Bank, and International Finance Corporation. *The World Bank Group Framework and IFC Strategy for Engagement with the Palm Oil Sector*. Washington, DC: IFC, 2011.

Wynter, Sylvia. "Novel and History, Plot and Plantation." *Savacou* 5 (1971): 95–102.

Yan, Wudan. "'I've Never Been Normal Again': Indonesian Women Risk Health to Supply Palm Oil to the West." *STAT*, April 18, 2017. https://www.statnews.com /2017/04/18/palm-oil-chemical-illness/.

Yurchak, Alexei. *Everything Was Forever, until It Was No More: The Last Soviet Generation*. Princeton, NJ: Princeton University Press, 2006.

Zen, Zahari, Colin Barlow, and Ria Gondowarsito. *Oil Palm in Indonesian Socio-Economic Improvement: A Review of Options*. Working Papers in Trade and Development. Canberra: Australian National University, 2005.

Zhuo, Xiaolin. "The Past, Present and Future of Pelampong. The Social Development of an All-Chinese Community in West Kalimantan, Indonesia." Undergraduate term paper, University of Toronto, 2010.

Index

abandonment: as corporate harm, 190–91; corporate justifications for, 153–55; as a form of life, 143–46; and the sovereign ban 6

advocacy: for environmental protection and human rights, 162–75

AMAN (Indigenous Peoples' Alliance), 165

army. See military

bankruptcy: of plantations, 33, 67, 86–87, 131, 180–83, 187

Bataks: as plantation managers, 30, 33, 39, 61, 80–81, 119, 134, 139

black campaign, 168, 177

blockades: major blockade at Natco, 38–39, 66, 140; major blockade at Priva, 118–20, 127, 181; as routine form of protest, 26, 47, 94, 96, 116, 118, 126, 186, 207n11

boycott (of palm oil), 167–68

capital: global, 3–4; 13, 23, 185, 212n17; for corporate investment, 13, 18, 20, 39, 96, 131, 137, 166–67, 181, 183, 204n83; for smallholder investment, 40, 47, 79, 96–98, 106–11

capitalism: corporate form, 5, 187; racial, 10

cattle, 25, 41, 68–69, 79

certification: challenges of implementation, 173–76, 182, 214n34; ISPO, 171–72, 178; NDPE, 172–73; RSPO, 168–72

Chinese Indonesians: and outmigration, 143, 148; as rubber traders, 30, 34, 53, 143

CIFOR (Centre for International Forest Research), 160–61, 166–67

citizenship: and Indonesia's "family state," 8; and racial rule, 10–11; and claims for equal treatment, 53–55; degraded by corporate occupation, 44, 57–58, 95–96, 123–31, 153–57, 186–91

class differentiation: among smallholders, 90–91, 105–13, 121, 178–80, 210n10

class struggle: suppression of, 84–87, 89, 130 208n4. See also unions (plantation worker)

climate change, 2, 166–67

coercion: and land acquisition, 12, 34, 42–45, 56, 58, 165, 173–75, 187, 207n23; in labor relations, 14, 72–73, 187. See also military; police

collaboration: with occupying force, 8–9, 29, 44–47, 57, 123–27, 155, 174, 186

collective action, 36–38, 41–42, 87, 116–20